PASS KEY
TO THE
PSAT
NMSQT

Preliminary SAT / National Merit Scholarship Qualifying Test

Samuel C. Brownstein
Former Chairperson, Science Department
George W. Wingate High School, Brooklyn, New York

Mitchel Weiner
Former Member, Department of English
James Madison High School, Brooklyn, New York

Sharon Weiner Green
Former Instructor in English
Merritt College, Oakland, California

Barron's Educational Series, Inc.

All inquiries should be addressed to:
Barron's Educational Series, Inc.
250 Wireless Boulevard
Hauppauge, New York 11788

Library of Congress Catalog Card No. 94-41848
International Standard Book No. 0-8120-9022-5

Library of Congress Cataloging-in-Publication Data
Brownstein, Samuel C.
    Barron's pass key to the PSAT/NMSQT : Preliminary SAT I/National merit scholarship qualifying test / Samuel C. Brownstein, Mitchel Weiner, Sharon Weiner Green.
        p.   cm.
    "Material in this book was adapted from Barron's basic tips on the PSAT/NMSQT and from Barron's How to prepare for the PSAT/NMSQT"—CIP t.p. verso.
    ISBN 0-8120-9022-5
    1. Preliminary Scholastic Aptitude Test—Study guides.   2. National merit scholarship qualifying test—Study guides.   I. Weiner, Mitchel, 1907–1986. II. Green, Sharon.   III. Brownstein, Samuel C.,   Basic tips on the PSAT/NMSQT.   IV. Brownstein, Samuel C.,   PSAT/NMSQT.   V. Title. VI. Title: Pass key to PSAT/NMSQT.
LB2353.56.B765   1995
378.1'664—dc20   94-41848
                                                            CIP

PRINTED IN THE UNITED STATES OF AMERICA

567   8800   987654321

Contents

Acknowledgments

SAT directions selected from *The New SAT I: Reasoning Test: A Preview of the Test Coming in 1994*, College Entrance Examination Board, 1993. Reprinted by permission of Educational Testing Service, the copyright owner of the test questions.

Permission to reprint SAT test directions does not constitute review or endorsement by Educational Testing Service or the College Board of this publication as a whole or of any other questions or testing information it may contain.

The authors gratefully acknowledge the following copyright holders for permission to reprint material used in the Critical Reading passages.

Pages 14–15: David Halberstam, *Summer of '49*.

Pages 15–16: A. Bartlett Giamatti, *Take Time for Paradise*, Summit Books, New York, 1989.

Pages 78–79: John Allen Paulos, "The Odds Are You're Innumerate," *The New York Times Book Review*, January 1, 1989.

Page 82: Michael Zelik, "The Birth of Massive Stars," *Scientific American*, April 1978.

Pages 156–158: Richard Shenkman, "*I Love Paul Revere, Whether He Rode Or Not*," Harper Perennial, New York, 1991.

Pages 159–161: Eudora Welty, *One Writer's Beginnings*, Harvard University Press, Cambridge, 1984.

Pages 173–174: Chet Raymo, *The Soul of the Night*, © 1985, Prentice Hall, Englewood Cliffs, NJ.

Pages 174–175: J. Madeleine Nash, "The Most Wanted Particle," *Time*, January 11, 1993.

Pages 213–214: M.F.K. Fisher, "The Captain's Dinner," from *As They Were*. Reprinted by permission of Alfred A. Knopf, Inc., New York

Pages 216–218: Eleanor Flexner, *Century of Struggle*, Harvard University Press, Cambridge.

Pages 231–237: Alistair MacLean, *Athabasca*, Copyright © 1980 by Alistair Maclean. Used by permission of Doubleday, a division of Bantam Doubleday Dell Publishing Group Inc.

Pages 233–235: Robert Claiborne, *Our Marvelous Native Tongue: The Life and Times of the English Language*, Times Books, New York, 1983.

Preface

Open the door to college with Barron's *Pass Key to the PSAT/NMSQT*. If you are thinking about taking the *new* PSAT, this packed but compact book will tell you what you need to know.

It introduces you to the new, non-multiple-choice questions in the mathematics section, teaching you shortcuts to solving problems and entering your own answers on a sample grid.

It briefs you on the new vocabulary-in-context and critical reading questions, giving you key tips on how to tackle these important verbal question types.

It takes you step by step through the new double reading passages, showing you how to work your way through a pair of reading passages without wasting effort or time.

It equips you with the *newly-revised* 320-word PSAT High-Frequency Word List—320 vital words that have been shown by computer analysis to occur and reoccur on actual published PSATs.

It gives you two full-length model tests identical to the new PSAT in length and difficulty, two crucial "dress rehearsals" for the day you walk into the examination room.

The new PSAT is your chance to get set for the tests ahead—the new SAT I and SAT II. It's also your chance to qualify for some of the nation's most prestigious college scholarships.

Take advantage of the size of your *Pass Key*. Carry it with you to use in study hall, as you wait for an appointment, or while riding in a bus or train. Each *Pass Key* session you fit in represents a step toward your ultimate goal of success on the PSAT/NMSQT. And if you find you need more practice, you can always move up to Barron's *How to Prepare for the PSAT/NMSQT*.

Timetable for the PSAT/NMSQT*

Total time: 2 hours

Section 1 **Verbal Reasoning** sentence completion critical reading	30 minutes	30 questions
Section 2 **Mathematical Reasoning** multiple choice	30 minutes	25 questions
BREAK		
Section 3 **Verbal Reasoning** analogies critical reading	30 minutes	30 questions
Section 4 **Mathematical Reasoning** quantitative comparison student-produced response	30 minutes	25 questions

*NOTE: Actual times will vary in accordance with the time the proctor completes the preliminary work and begins the actual test. Format and timing subject to change.

1 The Preliminary SAT/National Merit Scholarship Qualifying Test

Your plan to take the PSAT/NMSQT is perhaps your first concrete step toward planning a college career. PSAT/NMSQT, SAT I—what do they mean to you? When do you take them? Where? What sort of hurdle do you face? How do these tests differ from the tests you ordinarily face in school? In this chapter we answer these basic questions so that you will be able to move on to the following chapters and concentrate on preparing yourself for this test.

SOME BASIC QUESTIONS ANSWERED

What is the PSAT/NMSQT?

The PSAT/NMSQT is a standardized test designed to measure your ability to do college work. Students sometimes are able to take the test on a practice basis in junior high school. High school students get to take it "for real" early in their junior year.

The test consists of four sections: two testing verbal skills and two testing mathematical skills. One hour is allowed for answering the verbal questions; another hour for the mathematical questions.

Why is the test called the PSAT/NMSQT?

This preliminary SAT is also the qualifying test for the scholarship competitions conducted by the National Merit

Scholarship Corporation (NMSC). NMSC formerly offered a separate examination, but began cosponsoring this test in 1971.

What are Merit Scholarships?

Merit Scholarships are prestigious national awards that carry with them a chance for solid financial aid. Conducted by NMSC, an independent, nonprofit organization with offices at One America Plaza, Evanston, Illinois 60201, the Merit Program today is supported by grants from over 600 corporations, private foundations, colleges and universities, and other organizations. The top-scoring PSAT/NMSQT participants in every state are named Semifinalists. Those who advance to Finalist standing by meeting additional requirements compete for one-time National Merit $2000 Scholarships and renewable, four-year Merit Scholarships, which may be worth as much as $8000 a year for four years.

What is the National Achievement Scholarship Program for Outstanding Black Students?

This is a program aimed at honoring and assisting promising black high school students throughout the country. It is also administered by NMSC. Students who enter the Merit Program by taking the PSAT/NMSQT and who are also eligible to participate in the Achievement program mark a space on their test answer sheets asking to enter this competition as well. Top-scoring black students in each of the regions established for the competition compete for nonrenewable National Achievement $2000 Scholarships and for four-year Achievement Scholarships supported by over 1775 sponsor organizations. Note: To be considered for this program, you *must* mark the appropriate space on your answer sheet.

How can the PSAT/NMSQT help me?

If you are a high school junior, it will help you see just how able you are to do college work. It will give you some idea of which colleges you should apply to in your senior year. It will give you access to scholarship competitions. It will definitely give you practice in answering multiple-choice questions where timing is an important factor.

In addition, you may choose to take advantage of the College Board's Student Search Service. This service is free for students who fill out the biographical section of the PSAT/NMSQT. If you fill out this section, you will receive mail from colleges and search programs.

How do I apply for this test?

You apply through your school. Fees, when required, are collected by your school. The test is given in October. In December the results are sent to your school and to the scholarship program that you indicated on your answer sheet in the examination room.

What makes SAT-type tests different from other tests?

These tests are trying to measure your ability to reason using facts that are part of your general knowledge or facts that are included in your test booklet. You're not required to recall great chunks of history or literature or science. You're not even required to recall most math formulas—they're printed right in the test booklet.

SAT-type tests are essentially multiple-choice tests. Your score depends upon how many correct answers you get within a definite period of time. Speed is important. So is accuracy. You have to pace yourself so that you don't sacrifice speed to gain accuracy (or sacrifice accuracy to gain speed). However, on these tests, *you don't have to get every answer right to earn a solid score.*

How is the PSAT different from SAT I?

It's shorter by an hour. The PSAT consists of four 30-minute sections; SAT I consists of five 30-minute sections plus two

15-minute ones. You have to answer fewer questions; however, some of them are real stumpers. Some students feel that the PSAT is tougher than the SAT I they take in their junior or senior year.

How is the new PSAT different from the old PSAT?

It's trying to be more "user-friendly" and to focus more on real-life skills. The test-makers have divided the test into shorter sections. They've also allowed you more time in which to answer slightly fewer questions: you should feel a bit less time pressure when you take the test.

In the verbal sections, the test-makers have substituted generally appealing reading passages, the sort you might run across in good high school texts, for the old PSAT's dry, technical ones, and have provided short introductions to the passages to give you some context for what you read. They've also cut out the old antonym questions, replacing them with "vocabulary-in-context" questions that you may find easier to handle. In the math sections, they've decided to let you use a calculator if you wish, though they say they've set up the questions so that you don't actually *need* a calculator to work out the correct answers. They've also added some non-multiple-choice questions in which you can't just pick out an answer from a batch of choices. Instead, you have to come up with your own answer and mark it on a special grid. They hope to learn how good you are at working your way through problems, not just how good you are at playing multiple-choice games.

Is it smart to leave answers blank?

Probably not. But don't just make wild guesses. Wild guessing *will* lower your final score, since the test-makers subtract a fraction of your wrong answers from the number of your correct answers. Because wrong answers do count against you on the test, you may think that you should never guess if you aren't sure of the right answer to a question. But even if you guessed wrong four times for every time you guessed right, you would still come out even. A wrong answer costs you only 1/4 of a point (1/3 on the quantitative comparison questions). *On the multiple-choice questions*, the best advice is to guess if you can eliminate one or two of the answer choices. You have a better chance of hitting the right answer when you make this sort of "educated" guess.

As you go through this book, try this experiment to find out what kind of guesser you are. First, take part of any test that you have not taken before. You don't have to take an entire test section, but you should take at least 25 questions. Answer only those questions to which you *definitely* know the answers. See what your score is.

Next, take the same test section. Do not change any of your original answers, but whenever you can make an educated guess on one of the questions you originally skipped, do it. See what your score is now. Finally, retake the same test section, this time guessing blindly to answer all the remaining questions.

Compare your scores from the three different approaches to the test. For most people, the second score (the one with the educated guesses) will be the best one. But you may be different. Maybe you are such a poor guesser that you should never guess at all. Or maybe you are such a good guesser that you should try every question. The important thing is to know yourself.

What tactics can help me get ready for the PSAT?

1. Memorize the directions for each type of question. These are only slightly different from the exact words you'll find on the PSAT. The test time you would normally spend reading directions can be better spent answering questions.

2. Know the test. It has four sections; they will be organized into sub-sets as follows:

29-Question Verbal Section
16 sentence completion questions
13 critical reading questions

25-Question Mathematics Section
25 standard multiple-choice questions

29-Question Verbal Section
12 analogy questions
17 critical reading questions

25-Question Mathematics Section
15 quantitative comparison questions
10 student-produced responses ("grid") questions

3. Expect easy questions at the beginning of each set of the same question type. Within each set (except for the critical reading questions), the questions progress from easy to difficult. In other words, the first analogy question in a set will be easier than the last analogy in that set; the first quantitative comparison question will be easier than the last quantitative comparison question.

4. Take advantage of the easy questions to boost your score. Remember, each question is worth the same number of points. Whether it was easy or difficult, whether it took you ten seconds or two minutes to answer, you get the same number of points for each question you answer correctly. Your job is to answer as many questions as you possibly can without rushing ahead so fast that you make careless errors or lose points for failing to give some questions enough thought. Take enough time to get those easy questions right!

5. *First* answer all the easy questions; *then* tackle the hard ones if you have time. You know that the questions in each segment of the test get harder as you go along (except for the critical reading questions). But there's no rule that says you have to answer the questions in order. You're allowed to skip. So, if the last three analogy questions are driving you crazy, move

on to the reading passages right away. Likewise, don't let yourself get bogged down on a difficult quantitative comparison question when only three questions away the easy "grid" questions begin. Test-wise students know when it's time to move on.

6. Eliminate as many wrong answers as you can. Deciding between two choices is easier than deciding among five. Even if you have to guess, every answer you eliminate improves your chances of guessing correctly.

7. Change answers only if you have a reason for doing so. Don't give in to last-minute panic. It's usually better for you not to change your answers on a sudden hunch or whim.

8. Write in your test booklet: mark questions you want to take a second look at; circle ones you have to skip. Then if you have time at the end of the section, you will be able to locate them quickly. If you're using your calculator to do your math computations, jot down your results in the test booklet. There is absolutely no need for you to try to keep them in your head. And if it helps you to doodle while you think, then doodle away. The test booklet is yours. Use it.

9. Be careful not to make any stray marks on your answer sheet. This test is graded by a machine, and a machine cannot tell the difference between an accidental mark and a filled-in answer. When the machine sees two marks instead of one, it calls the answer wrong.

10. Check frequently to make sure you are answering the questions in the right spots. No machine is going to notice that you made a mistake early in the test, answered question 4 in the space for question 5, and all your following answers are in the wrong place. (One

way to avoid this problem is to mark your answers in your test booklet and transfer them to your answer sheet by blocks.)

11. Line up your test booklet with your answer sheet. Whether you choose to fill in the answers question by question or in blocks, you will do so most efficiently if you keep your test booklet and your answer sheet aligned.

12. Be particularly careful in marking the student-produced responses on the math grid. Before you fill in the appropriate blanks in the grid, write your answer at the top of the columns. Then go down each column, making sure you're marking only the spaces you want.

13. Don't get bogged down on any one question. By the time you get to the actual PSAT, you should have a fair idea of how much time to spend on each question. If a question is taking too long, leave it and go on to the next question. This is no time to try to show the world that you can stick to a job no matter how long it takes. All the machine that grades the test will notice is that after a certain point you didn't have any correct answers.

How can I prevent PSAT anxiety from setting in?

1. The best way to prepare for any test you ever take is to get a good night's sleep before the test so that you are well rested and alert.

2. Eat breakfast for once in your life. You have a full morning ahead of you. You should have a full stomach as well.

3. Allow plenty of time for getting to the test site. Taking a test is pressure enough. You don't need the extra

tension that comes from worrying about whether you will get there on time.

4. Recognize how long the test is going to take. There are four sections. Each one will take thirty minutes, with a five-minute break after the second section. Add to that half an hour for paper-pushing. If the test starts at 9:00 A.M., don't make a dentist appointment for 11:00 A.M. You can't possibly get there on time, and you'll just spend the last half-hour of the test worrying about it.

5. The College Board tells you to bring two sharpened number 2 pencils to the test. Bring four. They don't weigh much, and this might be the one day in the decade when two pencil points decide to break. And bring full-size pencils, not little stubs. They are easier to write with, and you might as well be comfortable.

6. Speaking of being comfortable, wear comfortable clothes. This is a test, not a fashion show. Aim for the layered look. Wear something light, but bring a sweater. The test room may be hot, or it may be cold. You can't change the room, but you can put on the sweater.

7. Bring an accurate watch. You need one. The room in which you take the test may not have a clock, and some proctors are not very good about posting the time on the blackboard. Don't depend on them. Each time you begin a test section, write down in your booklet the time according to *your* watch. That way you will always know how much time you have left.

8. Now that calculators are permitted in the test room, bring along a calculator you are comfortable using. No question on the test will *require* the use of a calculator, but if you are experienced using one, it

may be helpful for some questions. Almost any standard calculator will do: four-function, scientific, and graphing calculators all are allowed. However, printer-calculators, pocket organizers, palm-top minicomputers, and lap-tops are not.

9. Smuggle in some quick energy in your pocket—trail mix, raisins, a candy bar. Even if the proctors don't let you eat in the test room, you can still grab a bite en route to the rest rooms during the ten-minute break. Taking the test can leave you feeling drained and in need of a quick pickup—bring along your favorite comfort food.

10. There will be a break after the second thirty-minute section. Use this period to clear your thoughts. Take a few deep breaths. Stretch. Close your eyes and imagine yourself floating or sun-bathing. In addition to being under mental pressure, you're under physical pressure from sitting so long in an uncomfortable seat with a No. 2 pencil clutched in your hand. Anything you can do to loosen up and get the kinks out will ease your body and help the oxygen get to your brain.

SAMPLE PSAT QUESTIONS

The purpose of this section is to familiarize you with the kinds of questions that appear on the PSAT by presenting questions like those on recent PSATs. Knowing what to expect when you take the examination is an important step in preparing for the test and succeeding in it.

The directions that precede the various types of questions are similar to those on the PSAT. For all except the student-produced response questions, you are to choose the best answer and fill in the corresponding blank on the answer sheet.

Verbal Aptitude Sections

The verbal aptitude sections consist of 58 questions to be answered in 60 minutes. A typical test is made up of 16 sentence completion questions, 12 analogy questions, and 30 questions testing reading comprehension and vocabulary in context.

Sentence Completions

The sentence completion question tests your ability to use words in context and is in part a test of reading comprehension.

Each sentence below has one or two blanks, each blank indicating that something has been omitted. Beneath the sentence are five words or sets of words labeled A through E. Choose the best word or set of words that, when inserted in the sentence, best fits the meaning of the sentence as a whole.

Example:

Keats believed in the ---- power of great art, which would outlast its creators' brief lives.

(A) arbitrary   (B) temporary   (C) gradual
(D) popular   (E) enduring

---

1. Folk dancing is ---- senior citizens, and it is also economical; they need neither great physical agility nor special accoutrements to enjoy participating in the dance.

   (A) bewildering to   (B) costly for   (C) foreign to
   (D) appropriate for   (E) impracticable for

2. Fame is ----; today's rising star is all too soon tomorrow's washed-up has-been.

   (A) rewarding   (B) gradual   (C) essential   (D) spontaneous
   (E) transitory

3. The author contended that his insights were not ----, but had been made independently of others.

   (A) derivative   (B) esoteric   (C) fallacious   (D) hypothetical
   (E) concise

4. Suspicious of the ---- actions of others, the critic Edmund Wilson was in many ways a ---- man, unused to trusting anyone.

   (A) altruistic..cynical   (B) questionable..contrite
   (C) generous..candid   (D) hypocritical..cordial
   (E) benevolent..dauntless

5. Although Roman original contributions to government, jurisprudence, and engineering are commonly acknowledged, the artistic legacy of the Roman world continues to be judged widely as ---- the magnificent Greek traditions that preceded it.

   (A) an improvement on   (B) an echo of   (C) a resolution of
   (D) a precursor of   (E) a consummation of

6. ---- though she appeared, her journals reveal that her outward maidenly reserve concealed a passionate nature unsuspected by her family and friends.

   (A) Effusive   (B) Suspicious   (C) Tempestuous
   (D) Domineering   (E) Reticent

7. Crabeater seal, the common name of *Lobodon carcinophagus*, is ----, since the animal's staple diet is not crabs, but krill.

   (A) a pseudonym   (B) a misnomer   (C) an allusion
   (D) a digression   (E) a compromise

Analogies (Word Relationships)

The analogy question tests your ability to see relationships between words. These relationships may be degree of intensity, part to whole, class and member, synonyms, antonyms, or others. (Common analogy types are discussed fully in Chapter 3.)

Each question below consists of a related pair of words or phrases, followed by five pairs of words or phrases labeled A through E. Select the pair that best expresses a relationship similar to that expressed in the original pair.

Example:

DANDELION : WEED ::   (A) marigold : petal
  (B) plant : lawn   (C) corsage : flower
    (D) turnip : vegetable   (E) peanut : tree

Ⓐ Ⓑ Ⓒ ● Ⓔ

8. WOLF : PACK ::   (A) horse : saddle   (B) goose : flock
   (C) fox : lair   (D) pig : sow   (E) lion : cub
9. BRANCH : TREE ::   (A) lid : eye   (B) strap : sandal
   (C) sand : beach   (D) frame : picture   (E) wing : building
10. FOIL : SCHEME ::   (A) alter : decision   (B) conceal : weapon
   (C) sketch : blueprint   (D) block : passage
     (E) lose : competition
11. FLIMSY : PRETEXT ::   (A) frail : illness   (B) shaky : alibi
   (C) apprehensive : risk   (D) sorrowful : confession
     (E) final : judgment
12. EMBRACE : POSITION ::   (A) disentangle : knot
   (B) espouse : cause   (C) propose : ceremony
     (D) reverse : decision   (E) enforce : law
13. EAGER : OVERZEALOUS ::   (A) alluring : repulsive
   (B) finicky : fussy   (C) temperate : abstemious
     (D) guileless : ingenuous   (E) thrifty : parsimonious
14. QUACK : CHARLATANRY ::   (A) miser : extravagance
   (B) braggart : flattery   (C) insurgent : revelry
     (D) ascetic : misanthropy   (E) blackguard : knavery

Critical Reading

Your ability to read and understand the kind of material found in college texts and the more serious magazines is tested in the critical reading section of the PSAT/NMSQT. Passages generally range from 400–850 words in length. You may be asked to find the central thought of a passage, interpret just what the author means by a specific phrase or idea, determine the meaning of individual words from their use in the text, evaluate the special techniques the author uses to achieve his or her effects, or analyze the author's mood and motivation. You will also be asked to answer two or three questions that compare the viewpoints of two passages on the same subject. You can expect to spend about three-quarters of your verbal testing time reading the passages and answering the thirty critical reading questions.

> The passages below are followed by questions on their content; questions following a pair of related passages may also be based on the relationship between the paired passages. Answer the questions on the basis of what is <u>stated</u> or <u>implied</u> in the passages and in any introductory material that may be provided.

Questions 15–21 are based on the following passages.

The following passages are excerpted from books on America's national pastime, baseball.

Passage 1

DiMaggio had size, power, and speed. McCarthy, his longtime manager, liked to say that DiMaggio might have stolen 60 bases a season if he had given him the green light.
Line Stengel, his new manager, was equally impressed, and when
(5) DiMaggio was on base he would point to him as an example of the perfect base runner. "Look at him," Stengel would say as DiMaggio ran out a base hit, "he's always watching the ball. He isn't watching second base. He isn't watching third base. He knows they haven't been moved. He isn't watching
(10) the ground, because he knows they haven't built a canal or a

swimming pool since he was last there. He's watching the
ball and the outfielder, which is the one thing that is different
on every play."

DiMaggio complemented his natural athletic ability with
(15) astonishing physical grace. He played the outfield, he ran the
bases, and he batted not just effectively but with rare style.
He would glide rather than run, it seemed, always smooth, always ending up where he wanted to be just when he wanted
to be there. If he appeared to play effortlessly, his teammates
(20) knew otherwise. In his first season as a Yankee, Gene
Woodling, who played left field, was struck by the sound of
DiMaggio chasing a fly ball. He sounded like a giant truck
horse on the loose, Woodling thought, his feet thudding
down hard on the grass. The great, clear noises in the open
(25) space enabled Woodling to measure the distances between
them without looking.

He was the perfect Hemingway hero, for Hemingway in
his novels romanticized the man who exhibited grace under
pressure, who withheld any emotion lest it soil the purer
(30) statement of his deeds. DiMaggio was that kind of hero; his
grace and skill were always on display, his emotions always
concealed. This stoic grace was not achieved without a terri-
ble price: DiMaggio was a man wound tight. He suffered from
insomnia and ulcers. When he sat and watched the game he
(35) chain-smoked and drank endless cups of coffee. He was ever
conscious of his obligation to play well. Late in his career,
when his legs were bothering him and the Yankees had a
comfortable lead in a pennant race, columnist Jimmy Cannon
asked him why he played so hard—the games, after all, no
(40) longer meant so much. "Because there might be somebody
out there who's never seen me play before," he answered.

Passage 2

Athletes and actors—let actors stand for the set of performing artists—share much. They share the need to make

gesture as fluid and economical as possible, to make out of a
(45) welter of choices the single, precisely right one. They share
the need for thousands of hours of practice in order to train
the body to become the perfect, instinctive instrument to express. Both athlete and actor, out of that abundance of emotion, choice, strategy, knowledge of the terrain, mood of
(50) spectators, condition of others in the ensemble, secret
awareness of injury or weakness, and as nearly an absolute
concentration as possible so that all externalities are inte-
grated, all distraction absorbed to the self, must be able to
change the self so successfully that it changes us.

(55)   When either athlete or actor can bring all these skills to
bear and focus them, then he or she will achieve that state of
complete intensity and complete relaxation—complete coher-
ence or integrity between what the performer wants to do
and what the performer has to do. Then, the performer is
(60) free; for then, all that has been learned, by thousands of
hours of practice and discipline and by repetition of pattern,
becomes natural. Then intellect is upgraded to the level of an
instinct. The body follows commands that precede thinking.
      When athlete and artist achieve such self-knowledge
(65) that they transform the self so that we are re-created, it is finally an exercise in power. The individual's power to dominate, on stage or field invests the whole arena around the
locus of performance with his or her power. We draw from
the performer's energy, just as we scrutinize the performer's
(70) vulnerabilities, and we criticize as if we were equals (we are
not) what is displayed. This is why all performers dislike or
resent the audience as much as they need and enjoy it. Power
flows in a mysterious circuit from performer to spectator (I
assume a "live" performance) and back, and while cheers or
(75) applause are the hoped-for outcome of performing, silence or
gasps are the most desired, for then the moment has occurred—then domination is complete, and as the performer
triumphs, a unity rare and inspiring results.

15. In Passage 1, Stengel is most impressed by DiMaggio's

(A) indifference to potential dangers
(B) tendency to overlook the bases in his haste
(C) ability to focus on the variables
(D) proficiency at fielding fly balls
(E) overall swiftness and stamina

16. It can be inferred from the content and tone of Stengel's comment (lines 6–13) that he would regard a base runner who kept his eye on second base with

(A) trepidation
(B) approbation
(C) resignation
(D) exasperation
(E) tolerance

17. The phrase "a man wound tight" (line 33) means a man

(A) wrapped in confining bandages
(B) living in constricted quarters
(C) under intense emotional pressure
(D) who drank alcohol to excess
(E) who could throw with great force

18. Which best describes what the author is doing in the parenthetical comment "let actors stand for the set of performing artists" [lines 42–43]?

(A) Indicating that actors should rise out of respect for the arts
(B) Defining the way in which he is using a particular term
(C) Encouraging actors to show tolerance for thier fellow artists
(D) Emphasizing that actors are superior to other performing artists
(E) Correcting a misinterpretation of the role of actors

19. To the author of Passage 2, freedom for performers depends on

(A) their subjection of the audience
(B) their willingness to depart from tradition
(C) the internalization of all they have learned
(D) their ability to interpret material independently
(E) the absence of injuries or other weaknesses

20. The author's attitude toward the concept of the equality of spectators and performers (lines 70–71) is one of

(A) relative indifference
(B) mild skepticism
(C) explicit rejection
(D) strong embarrassment
(E) marked perplexity

21. The author of Passage 2 would most likely react to the characterization of DiMaggio presented in lines 38–41 by pointing out that DiMaggio probably

(A) felt some resentment of the spectator whose good opinion he supposedly sought
(B) never achieved the degree of self-knowledge that would have transformed him
(C) was unaware that his audience was surveying his weak points
(D) was a purely instinctive natural athlete
(E) was seldom criticized by his peers

Mathematical Reasoning Sections

There are two sections, each allowing 30 minutes. You will find some questions in the mathematical section require you to apply graphic, spatial, numerical, symbolic, and logical techniques to situations already familiar to you; these may be similar to exercises in your textbooks. In other questions you are presented with novel situations and are called upon to do original thinking and to solve problems. You will not be expected to use mathematical knowledge beyond elementary algebra and geometry.

Are All Questions of the Multiple-Choice Type?

Ten of the sixty mathematics questions require you to produce an answer that is entered on a grid, which is scored mechanically.

May Calculators Be Used in the Examination Room?

The College Board announced that in 1993, students taking the PSAT/NMSQT may use calculators for the math sections. In 1995, this practice will be evaluated. Students are permitted to use any four-function, scientific or graphing calculator in the exam room. The following will not be permitted: hand-held minicomputers, pocket organizers, lap-top computers, or calculators that use tape or printers. Hints:

1. Do not use the calculator on all math problems.
2. Use a simple, well-functioning calculator—one with which you are familiar.
3. Check the battery before the exam day.
4. If you forget the calculator or if it breaks down, don't panic. Go on without it. No solution depends upon the use of a calculator.

How Are the Answers Entered on the Grid?

The grid looks something like this:

These are the parts of the grid:

Write your
answer here →

			Fraction signs
	⊘	⊘	Fraction signs
⊙	⊙	⊙	⊙ Decimals
	⓪	⓪	⓪ Zeros
①	①	①	① Ones
②	②	②	② Twos
③	③	③	③ Threes
④	④	④	④ Fours
⑤	⑤	⑤	⑤ Fives
⑥	⑥	⑥	⑥ Sixes
⑦	⑦	⑦	⑦ Sevens
⑧	⑧	⑧	⑧ Eights
⑨	⑨	⑨	⑨ Nines

Observe the following grid entries:

Things to remember about the grid:

1. When you have arrived at an answer to a question of this type, enter that answer in the box above the various columns. Answers that are shorter than four characters may be entered beginning in any column:

| 3 | 7 | | | | | 3 | 7 | | | | | 3 | 7 |

2. You may not use more than one space in any column.

3. Don't be concerned about the form of your answer. If it is correct, you will receive credit whether you express it as a decimal or a fraction. For example, if your answer is one-half, the machine will accept .5 or 1/2:

4. The grid will not accept mixed numbers. For example an answer of $2\frac{1}{2}$ must be entered 5/2 or as 2.5.

5. None of the grid questions will have negative answers because the grid is not able to accommodate such entries. If you come up with a negative value for an answer, you know you have made a mistake.

Some formulas you may find useful in solving some questions

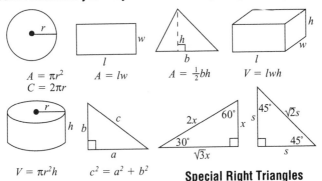

$A = \pi r^2$ $A = lw$ $A = \frac{1}{2}bh$ $V = lwh$
$C = 2\pi r$

$V = \pi r^2 h$ $c^2 = a^2 + b^2$ **Special Right Triangles**

Triangle: The sum of the measure in degrees of the angles of a triangle is 180.

If $\angle CDA$ is a right angle, then

(1) area of $\triangle ABC = \dfrac{AB \times CD}{2}$

(2) $AC^2 = AD^2 + DC^2$

The number of degrees of arc in a circle is 360.

The measure in degrees of a straight line is 180.

Definitions of symbols:

$\leq$	is less than or equal to	$\geq$	is greater than or equal to
$\parallel$	is parallel to	$\perp$	is perpendicular to
$=$	is equal to	$\neq$	is unequal to
$<$	is less than	$>$	is greater than

Notes: (1) The use of a calculator is permitted. All numbers used are real numbers. (2) Figures that accompany problems in this test are intended to provide information useful in solving the problems. They are drawn as accurately as possible EXCEPT when it is stated in a specific problem that the figure is not drawn to scale. All figures lie in a plane unless otherwise indicated.

In this section solve each problem, using any available space on the page for scratchwork. Then decide which is the best of the choices given and fill in the corresponding space on the answer sheet.

1. What is the exact quotient when 133,578 is divided by 543?

(A) 243   (B) 244   (C) 245   (D) 246   (E) 247

---

2. What part of an hour elapses from 11:55 A.M. to 12:15 P.M.?

(A) $\dfrac{1}{3}$ (B) $\dfrac{1}{4}$ (C) $\dfrac{1}{5}$ (D) $\dfrac{1}{6}$ (E) $\dfrac{2}{3}$

---

3. The enrollment at the North Shore Academy is b boys and g number of girls. What part of the academy student body is composed of girls?

(A) $\dfrac{b}{b + g}$ (B) $\dfrac{g}{b}$ (C) $\dfrac{b}{bg}$ (D) $\dfrac{b}{g + b}$ (E) b

---

4. In isosceles right triangle ABC, $AB = BC$ and $AC = 10$. What is the area of $\triangle ABC$?

(A) $5\sqrt{2}$

(B) $2\sqrt{5}$

(C) 5

(D) $\sqrt{25}$

(E) 25

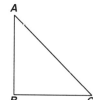

5. If the sum of the lengths of three sides of a square is r, then the perimeter of this square is

(A) $\dfrac{3}{r} + 1$ (B) $\dfrac{r}{3} + 4$ (C) $\dfrac{4r}{3}$

(D) $\dfrac{r}{3} + 1$ (E) $\dfrac{3}{r} + r$

6. When the rate for first-class postage was increased from 18¢ to 20¢, the percent of increase was

(A) 1.1%   (B) 2%   (C) 9%   (D) 10%   (E) 11.1%

7. If the angles of a triangle are in the ratio 3:4:5, then one of these angles must have a measure in degrees of

(A) 30   (B) 60   (C) 90   (D) 100   (E) 120

8. For which figure is the area equal to the product of two of its sides?

(A) right triangle   (B) isosceles triangle   (C) trapezoid
(D) rectangle   (E) parallelogram

9. What is the average measure of the angles of a triangle?

(A) 30°   (B) 45°   (C) 60°   (D) 90°
(E) cannot be determined from the information furnished

10. If $\dfrac{a + b}{c + 2b}$ equals 1, then b equals

(A) $\dfrac{a}{c + 2}$ (B) $a - c$ (C) $a + c$

(D) $\dfrac{a - c}{2}$ (E) $\dfrac{a + c}{3}$

11. If the perimeter of $\triangle ABC$ is 29 meters, then the length (in meters) of the shortest side is

(A) 3
(B) 5
(C) 7
(D) 10
(E) 12

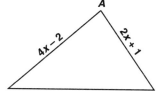

12. The length of a rectangle is 5 more than its width. If the width is represented by x, which expression represents the area of the rectangle?

(A) $x^2 + 5x$ (B) $x^2 + 5$ (C) $5x^2$ (D) $4x + 10$ (E) $6x^2$

13. $AB \perp BC$ and DBE is a line segment. In terms of x, $y =$

(A) x
(B) $x - 90$
(C) $90 - x$
(D) $180 - x$
(E) $x - 180$

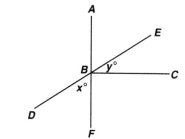

14. What is the value of z, if x = 100, y = 30, and AB is a line segment?

(A) 30
(B) 80
(C) 100
(D) 110
(E) 120

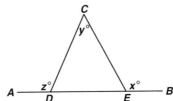

15. In rectangle DEBC, CA is drawn, forming △ABC. In terms of x, y, and z, what is the area of ACDE?

(A) $xy - yz$
(B) $yz - xy$
(C) $xy - z$
(D) $y(x - z)$
(E) $xy - \dfrac{yz}{2}$

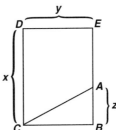

Quantitative Comparison

Another type of question you can expect to encounter is the type known as quantitative comparison. Questions 16–21 are examples. There are only four choices from which to select an answer. The following instructions are given for these questions.

Questions 16–21 each consist of two quantities in boxes, one in Column A and one in Column B. You are to compare the two quantities and on the answer sheet fill in
A if the quantity in Column A is greater;
B if the quantity in Column B is greater;
C if the two quantities are equal;

D if the relationship cannot be determined from the information given.

Notes: (1) In some questions, information is given about one or both of the quantities to be compared. In such cases, the given information is centered above the two columns and is not boxed. (2) In a given question, a symbol that appears in both columns represents the same thing in Column A as it does in Column B. (3) Letters such as x, n, and k stand for real numbers.

Examples

	Column A	Column B	Answers
E1.	2×6	$2 + 6$	● Ⓑ Ⓒ Ⓓ
E2.	$p - q$	$q + p$	Ⓐ Ⓑ Ⓒ ●
E3.	$180 - x$	y	Ⓐ Ⓑ ● Ⓓ

Column A   Column B

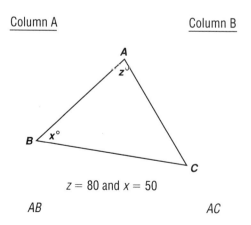

$z = 80$ and $x = 50$

16. AB AC

	Column A	Column B

$$xy = 16$$

| 17. | x | y |

| 18. | $\dfrac{k}{400}$ | $\dfrac{k}{4}\%$ |

| 19. | $\sqrt{14.4}$ | 0.12 |

$$a = 2$$
$$b = 3$$
$$c = 4$$

| 20. | $\dfrac{b^2 - a^2}{ab}$ | $\dfrac{a + b}{c}$ |

---

1 kilogram = 2.2 pounds

| 21. | 1 pound | 0.33 kilogram |

Questions 22 and 23: Write your answers to these two questions on the blank line that follows each. (In the model tests in this book and in the exam room, you will be entering your answers in the grids provided.)

22. Ten minutes after takeoff the plane is 40 miles from the airport. What is the average speed (in miles per hour) of this plane?

23. On a diagram of a camp site drawn to scale 1:120, the size of a building is $7\frac{1}{5}$ inches. What is the actual length (in feet) of this building?

Student-Produced Response

Each of the 5 questions following requires you to solve the problem and enter your answer by marking the spaces in the special grid.

Mixed numbers such as $2\frac{1}{2}$ must be gridded as 2.5 or $\frac{5}{2}$. (If $2\frac{1}{2}$ is gridded, it will be interpreted as $\frac{21}{2}$, not $2\frac{1}{2}$.)

Because the answer sheet will be machine-scored, *you will receive credit only if the spaces are filled in correctly.*

Although not required, it is suggested that you write your answer in the boxes at the top of the columns to help you fill in the spaces correctly.

Some problems may have more than one correct answer. In such cases, grid only one answer.

Decimal Accuracy: If you obtain a decimal answer, *enter the most accurate value that the grid will accommodate.* For example, if you obtain an answer such as 0.6666..., you should record the result as .666 or .667. *Less accurate values such as .66 or .67 are not acceptable.*

24. What is the minimum weight in ounces of 69 eggs taken from a crate containing a grade of eggs weighing 24 to 26 ounces per dozen?

24.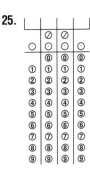

25. At the end of spring training a football coach discharged ⅕ of his squad and asked the remaining 32 boys to report on Labor Day. How many boys were on the squad during spring training?

25.

26. A stick 35 inches long is to be cut so that one piece is ¼ as long as the other. How many inches long must the shorter piece be?

26.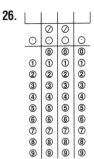

27. If $17xy = 22xy - 5$, what does x^2y^2 equal?

27.

28. If the area of a circle is twice the area of a triangle whose base is 4π and whose altitude is 4, what does the radius of the circle equal?

28.

29. In parallelogram $ABCD \angle B \overset{\circ}{=} 1\angle A + \angle C$. What is the measure, in degrees, of $\angle D$?

29.

Answer Key

Verbal

1. **D**	6. **E**	10. **D**	14. **E**	18. **B**
2. **E**	7. **B**	11. **B**	15. **C**	19. **C**
3. **A**	8. **B**	12. **B**	16. **D**	20. **C**
4. **A**	9. **E**	13. **D**	17. **C**	21. **A**
5. **B**				

Mathematical

1. **D**	6. **E**	11. **C**	16. **C**	21. **A**
2. **A**	7. **B**	12. **A**	17. **D**	22. **240**
3. **D**	8. **D**	13. **C**	18. **C**	23. **72**
4. **E**	9. **C**	14. **D**	19. **A**	
5. **C**	10. **B**	15. **E**	20. **B**	

(1)

24

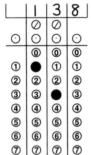

(3, 6)

25

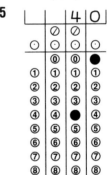

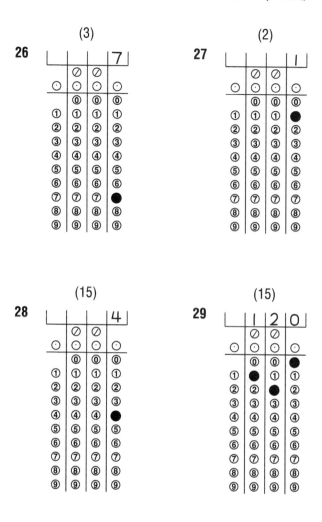

Answer Explanations

Verbal Aptitude Section

1. **(D)** *Because* senior citizens don't need great physical agility to enjoy folk dancing, it is an *appropriate* or suitable activity for them.

2. **(E)** If one's fame disappears as quickly as the second part of the sentence indicates, then fame must be brief or *transitory*.

3. **(A)** If the author got his insights independently, then he did not get or derive them from the insights of other people. In other words, his insights were not *derivative*.

4. **(A)** Someone given to distrusting the motives and actions of others is by definition *cynical*. Such a person would question even the *altruistic*, unselfish deeds of others, suspecting there to be ulterior motives for these charitable acts.

5. **(B)** The view of Rome's contributions to government, law, and engineering is wholly positive; these original additions to human knowledge are generally acknowledged or recognized. *In contrast*, Rome's original contributions to art are *not* recognized: they are seen as just an *echo* or imitation of the art of ancient Greece.
   Note that *Although* sets up the contrast here.

6. **(E)** Her outward appearance was one of "maidenly reserve" (self-restraint; avoidance of intimacy). Thus, she seemed to be *reticent* (reserved; disinclined to speak or act freely), even though she actually felt things passionately.

7. **(B)** Because these seals eat far more krill than crabs, it *misnames* them to call them crabeater seals. The term is thus a *misnomer*, a name that's wrongly applied to someone or something.
   Beware of eye-catchers. Choice A is incorrect. A *pseudonym* isn't a mistaken name; it's a false name that an author adopts.

8. **(B)** A *wolf* belongs to a *pack*. A *goose* belongs to a *flock*.
   (Group and Member)

9. **(E)** A *branch* is an offshoot from the main part of a *tree*. A *wing* is an extension from the main part of a *building*.

10. **(D)** To *foil* a *scheme* is to hinder or obstruct it. To *block* a *passage* is to close or obstruct it. (Function)

11. **(B)** A *flimsy pretext* (pretended reason) is by definition too weak to stand up to close examination. A *shaky alibi* (excuse to avoid blame) is likewise too weak to stand up to close examination. Beware of eye-catchers. Choice A is incorrect. While illness may make someone frail, an illness can't be described as being frail. (Defining Characteristic)

12. **(B)** To *embrace* a *position* is to choose a particular point of view; to *espouse* a *cause* is to support a particular movement.

(Function)

13. **(D)** Someone *overzealous* is excessively *eager*; someone *parsimonious* (stingy) is excessively *thrifty*.

(Degree of Intensity)

14. **(E)** A *quack* (impostor; fraud) is noted for *charlatanry* (making fraudulent claims). A *blackguard* (scoundrel; rogue) is noted for *knavery* (behaving villainously).   (Defining Characteristic)

15. **(C)** Stengel's concluding sentence indicates that DiMaggio watches "the one thing that is different on every play." In other words, DiMaggio *focuses on the variables*, the factors that change from play to play.

16. **(D)** The sarcastic tone of Stengel's comment suggests that he would be *exasperated* or irritated by a base runner who had his eye on second base when he should have been watching the ball and the outfielder.

17. **(C)** Look at the sentences following this phrase. They indicate that DiMaggio was a man *under intense emotional pressure*, one who felt so much stress that he developed ulcers and had problems getting to sleep.

18. **(C)** The author is taking a moment away from his argument to make sure the reader knows exactly who the subjects of his comparison are. He is not simply comparing athletes and actors. He is comparing athletes and *all* performing artists, "the set of performing artists," to use his words. Thus, in his side comment, he is *defining* how he intends to use the word *actors* throughout the discussion.

19. **(C)** Performers are free when all they have learned becomes so natural, so internalized, that it seems instinctive. In other words, freedom depends on the *internalization* of what they have learned.

20. (C) The author bluntly states that we spectators are not the performers' equals. Thus, his attitude toward the concept is one of
explicit rejection.

21. (A) Passage 1 indicates DiMaggio always played hard to live up to
his reputation and to perform well for anyone in the stands who
had never seen him play before. Clearly, he wanted the spectators to have a good opinion of him. Passage 2, however,
presents a more complex picture of the relationship between
the performer and his audience. On the one hand, the performer
needs the audience, needs its good opinion and its applause.
On the other hand, the performer also resents the audience,
resents the way spectators freely point out his weaknesses and
criticize his art. Thus, the author of Passage 2 might well point
out that DiMaggio *feet some resentment* of the audience whom
he hoped to impress with his skill.

Mathematical Reasoning Section

1. (D) This is not an arithmetic test. Also, time does not permit using
the standard method of long division. Observe that the dividend
ends with the digit 8 and the divisor ends with the digit 3. The
quotient must end with the digit 6.

$$\overset{\text{quotient}}{\text{divisor} \big) \text{dividend}}$$

2. (A) Time elapsed is 20 minutes.

$\dfrac{20}{60}$ is $\dfrac{1}{3}$ of an hour.

3. (D) The entire student body $= b + g$.

$\dfrac{g}{b + g}$ = part of entire student body composed of girls

4. (E) Let $x = BC = AB$.
Using the Pythagorean Theorem,
$(x)^2 + (x)^2 = (10)^2$
or $2x^2 = 100$, *or* $x^2 = 50$.

Area of $\triangle ABC = \dfrac{1}{2}(AB)(BC)$, or $\dfrac{1}{2}(x)(x)$, *or*

$\dfrac{1}{2}(x)^2$, *or* $\dfrac{1}{2}(50) = 25$

5. (C) If the sum of the lengths of 3 sides of a square $= r$, then each

side $= \dfrac{r}{3}$ and 4 sides $= \dfrac{4r}{3}$

6. (E) The increase was 2¢.

$$\dfrac{\text{increase}}{\text{original}} \times 100 = \text{percent increase}$$

$$\dfrac{2¢}{18¢} = \dfrac{1}{9} = 11.1\%$$

7. (B) $3x + 4x + 5x = 180°$
$12x = 180°$
$x = 15°$
∴ measure of angles $= 45°, 60°,$ and $75°$

8. (D) In a rectangle the length is perpendicular to the width. The area of the rectangle equals the product of the length (one of the sides) and the width (the other side).

9. (C) The sum of the measure of the angles of a triangle equals 180°. $180° \div 3 = 60°$.

10. (B) If the value of a fraction is 1, the numerator equals (has the same value as) the denominator.
$a + b = c + 2b$
$a - c = b$

11. (C) $4x - 2 + 2x + 1 + x + 9 = 29$
$7x + 8 = 29$
$7x = 21$
$x = 3$
Thus, side $4x - 2 = 10$
side $x + 9 = 12$
side $2x + 1 = 7$ (answer)

12. (A) $x = $ width (given)
∴ $x + 5 = $ length
$x(x + 5) = $ area, or area $= x^2 + 5x$

13. (C) $\angle ABE = \angle DBF$ (vertical angles)
$\angle DBF = x°$ (given)
$\therefore ABE = x°$
$\angle ABC = 90°$ ($AB \perp BC$)
$\therefore EBC = 90° - x°$
$y° = 90° - x°$
$y = 90 - x$

14. (D) $\angle CED = 80°$
$\angle CDE = 180° - (80° + 30°) \ or \ 70°$
$z = 180 - 70 \ or \ 110$

15. (E) The area of $ACDE$ = area of rectangle $BCDE$ − area of $\triangle ABC$.

Area of $BCDE = xy$

Area of $\triangle ABC = \dfrac{yz}{2}$

Area of $ACDE = xy - \dfrac{yz}{2}$

16. (C) $\angle ACB \triangleq 180 - (80 + 50) \ or \ 50$
$\therefore AB = AC$ (If 2 angles of a $\triangle$ are equal, the sides opposite those angles are equal.)

17. (D) x and/or y may have negative values.

18. (C) % means $\dfrac{}{100}$

$\dfrac{k}{4}\% = \left(\dfrac{k}{4}\right)\left(\dfrac{1}{100}\right) \ or \ \dfrac{k}{400}$

19. (A) $\sqrt{14.4} = 3+$
$3+ > 0.12$

20. (B) $\dfrac{9-4}{6} = \dfrac{5}{6}$ (Column A)

$\dfrac{2+3}{4} = \dfrac{5}{4}$ (Column B)

$\dfrac{5}{4} > \dfrac{5}{6}$

21. (A) 0.33 kilogram is about ⅓ of a kilogram or ⅓ of 2.2 pounds, which is 0.7 pound. Column A is 1 pound.

22. (240) Ten minutes is ⅙ of an hour. Because it covers 40 miles in ⅙ of an hour, it will cover, on the average, 240 miles per hour.

23. (72) (120) (7⅕ inches) = 864 inches or 72 feet.

24. (138) Minimum weight of 1 dozen eggs = 24 ounces
Minimum weight of 1 egg = 2 ounces
Minimum weight of 69 eggs = 138 ounces

25. (40) Let x = number of boys on the squad at the end of spring training.
$$\frac{4}{5}x = 32$$
$$x = 40$$

26. (7) Let x = length (inches) of shorter piece
Then $4x$ = length (inches) of longer piece.
$$4x + x = 35$$
$$5x = 35$$
$$x = 7$$

27. (1) $17xy = 22xy - 5$
$-5xy = -5$
$xy = 1$ [divide by -5]
$x^2y^2 = 1$ [square both sides of equation]

28. (4) Length of AOD = 8[11 $-$3]
$\therefore$ radius = 4
Area = $\pi(4)^2$
Area = 16π
Area of triangle = $\frac{1}{2}$ (altitude)(base) or $\frac{1}{2}$ (4)(4π) or 8π
Area of circle = $2(8\pi)$ [given]
Area of circle = 16π or πr^2
$$\pi r^2 = 16\pi$$
$$r^2 = 16$$
$$r = 4$$

29. (120) Because opposite angles of a parallelogram are equal,

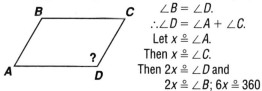

$\angle B = \angle D.$
$\therefore \angle D = \angle A + \angle C.$
Let $x \stackrel{\circ}{=} \angle A.$
Then $x \stackrel{\circ}{=} \angle C.$
Then $2x \stackrel{\circ}{=} \angle D$ and
$2x \stackrel{\circ}{=} \angle B;\ 6x \stackrel{\circ}{=} 360$

[sum of the angles of a quadrilateral $= 360°$].

$x \stackrel{\circ}{=} 60,\ \angle D$ or $2x \stackrel{\circ}{=} 120$

2 The Sentence Completion Question

Sentence completion questions are the first verbal questions you encounter as you take the PSAT. These questions test your ability to use your vocabulary and to recognize how the different parts of a sentence fit together to make sense.

The sentence completion questions ask you to choose the best way to complete a sentence from which one or two words have been omitted. You must be able to recognize the logic, style, and tone of the sentence, so that you will be able to choose the answer that makes sense in this context. You must also be able to recognize the different ways in which words are normally defined. At some time or another, you have probably had a vocabulary assignment in which you were asked to define a word and use it in a sentence. In these questions, you have to *fit* words into sentences. Once you understand the implications of the sentence, you should be able to choose the answer that will make the sentence clear, logical, and consistent in style and tone.

The subject matter of these sentences comes from a wide variety of fields—music, art, science, literature, history. However, this is not a test of your general knowledge. Though at times your knowledge of a particular fact may guide you in choosing the correct answer, you should be able to handle any of the sentences using your understanding of the English language.

Tips on Handling Sentence Completion Questions

1. **Before you look at the answer choices, think of a word that makes sense.** *Without looking at the answer choices*, your first step in answering a sentence completion question is to try to come up with a word

that fits in the blank. The word you think of may not be the exact word that appears in the answer choices, but it will probably be similar in meaning to the right answer. Then, when you turn to the answer choices, you'll have an idea of what you're looking for.

Try going through the sentence substituting the word *blank* for each missing word. Doing this will give you a feel for what the sentence means.

EXAMPLE 1

Unlike her gabby brother Bruce, Bea seldom *(blanks)* .

Just from looking at the sentence, you know the answer must be a synonym for *chatters* or *talks.*

At this point, look at the answer choices. If the word you thought of is one of your five choices, select it as your answer. If the word you thought of is *not* one of your five choices, look for a synonym of that word.

See how the process works in dealing with a more complex sentence.

EXAMPLE 2

The psychologist set up the experiment to test the rat's ----; he wished to see how well the rat adjusted to the changing conditions it had to face.

Even before you look at the answer choices, you can figure out what the answer *should* be.

Look at the sentence. A psychologist is trying to test some particular quality or characteristic of a rat. What quality? How do you get the answer?

Note how the part of the sentence following the semi-colon (the second clause, in technical terms) is being used to define or clarify what the psychologist is trying to test. He is trying to see how well the rat *adjusts.* What words does this suggest to you?

Flexibility, possibly, or *adaptability*. Either of these words could complete the sentence's thought.

Here are the five answer choices given.

(A) reflexes   (B) communicability   (C) stamina
(D) sociability   (E) adaptability

The answer clearly is *adaptability*, Choice (E).

Be sure to check out all five answer choices before you make your final choice. Don't leap at the first word that seems to fit. You are looking for the word that <u>best</u> fits the meaning of the sentence as a whole. In order to be sure you have not been hasty in making your decision, substitute each of the answer choices for the missing word. That way you can satisfy yourself that you have come up with the answer that best fits.

2. **Spot clues in the sentence: signal words.** Writers use transitions to link their ideas logically. These transitions or signal words are clues that can help you figure out what the sentence actually means.

Support Signals

Look for words that indicate that the omitted portion of the sentence continues a thought developed elsewhere in the sentence. Examples are *and, moreover, in addition*, and *furthermore*. In such cases, a synonym or near-synonym should provide the correct answer.

Here is an example of a sentence completion question in which a support signal provides a helpful clue.

EXAMPLE

He was habitually so docile and ---- that his friends could not understand his sudden outburst against his employer.

(A) submissive   (B) incorrigible   (C) contemptuous
(D) erratic   (E) hasty

The signal word *and* is your clue that the writer is trying to reinforce the notion of docility introduced in the sentence. Not only is this person docile, he is also __(*blank*)__ . Look through the answer choices for a synonym or near-synonym of *docile* or obedient. You find one immediately: Choice (A), **submissive**. Check through the other answer choices. Nothing else makes sense. The correct answer is Choice (A).

Contrast Signals

Look for words or phrases that indicate a contrast between one idea and another. Examples are *but, although, nevertheless, despite, however, even though*, and *on the other hand*. In such cases, an antonym or near-antonym for another word in the sentence should provide the correct answer.

Here is an example of a sentence completion question in which a contrast signal pinpoints the correct answer for you.

EXAMPLE

We expected her to be jubilant over her victory, but she was ---- instead.

(A) triumphant   (B) adult   (C) morose   (D) loquacious
(E) culpable

The signal word *but* suggests that the winner's expected reaction contrasts with her actual one. Instead of being "jubilant" (extremely joyful), she is sad. Look through the answer choices to find a word that is the *opposite* of jubilant. The correct answer is Choice (C), *morose* or gloomy.

Cause and Effect Signals

Look for words or phrases that indicate that one thing causes another, words like *because, since, therefore, consequently, accordingly, hence*, and *thus*.

Here is an example of a sentence completion question in which a cause and effect signal should prove helpful to you.

EXAMPLE

Because his delivery was ----, the effect of his speech on the voters was nonexistent.

(A) plausible   (B) moving   (C) audible   (D) halting
(E) respectable

What sort of delivery would make a speech have no effect? A *plausible* (superficially pleasing and persuasive) delivery would probably have some effect on the voters. A *moving* or eloquent delivery certainly would. An *audible* delivery, one the audience could hear, would be more likely to have an effect than an inaudible one would. A *respectable*, appropriate delivery probably would have some impact as well. Only a *halting* or stumbling delivery would mar the voters' appreciation of the speech and cause it to have little or no effect on them. Thus, the best answer is Choice (D).

3. **Notice negatives.** Watch out for negative words and words with negative prefixes: *No, not, none; non-, un-, in-*. These negative words and word parts are killers, especially in combination.

EXAMPLE

The damage to the car was insignificant.
  ("Don't worry about it—it's just a scratch.")
The damage to the car was not insignificant.
  ("Oh, no, Bart! We totaled Mom's car!")

In particular, watch out for *not*: it's easy to overlook, but it's a key word, as the following sentence clearly illustrates.

EXAMPLE

Madison was not ---- person and thus made few public addresses; but those he made were memorable, filled with noble phrases.

(A) a reticent   (B) a stately   (C) an inspiring
(D) an introspective   (E) a communicative

What would happen if you overlooked *not* in this question? Probably you'd wind up choosing Choice (A): Madison was a *reticent* (quiet; reserved) man. *For this reason* he made few public addresses.

Unfortunately, you'd have gotten things backward. The sentence isn't telling you what Madison was like. It's telling you what he was *not* like. And he was not a *communicative* person; he didn't express himself freely. However, when he did get around to expressing himself, he had some good things to say.

4. **Take one blank at a time.** Dealing with double-blank sentences can be tricky. Testing the first word of each answer pair helps you narrow things down.

Here's how to do it. Read through the entire sentence. Then insert the first word of each answer pair in the sentence's first blank. Ask yourself whether this particular word makes sense in this blank. If the initial word of an answer pair makes no sense in the sentence, you can eliminate the entire answer pair.

Next, check out the second word of each of the answer pairs that you haven't ruled out. Be careful. Remember, just as each word of the correct answer pair must make sense in its individual context, both words must make sense when used together.

Try this question to practice working with double-blank sentences.

EXAMPLE

The opossum is ---- the venom of snakes in the rattle-snake subfamily and thus views the reptiles not as ---- enemies but as a food source.

(A) vulnerable to..natural (B) indicative of..mortal
(C) impervious to..lethal (D) injurious to..deadly
(E) defenseless against..potential

Your first job is to eliminate any answer choices you can on the basis of their first word. Opossums might be *vulnerable* to snake poison. Keep Choice (A). Opossums are unlikely to be *indicative* or suggestive of snake poison. Cross out Choice (B). Opossums could be *impervious* to (unaffected by; immune to) snake poison. Keep Choice (C). Opossums couldn't be *injurious* or harmful to snake poison. Cross out Choice (D). Opossums could be *defenseless against* snake poison. Keep Choice (E).

Now examine the second half of the sentence. Opossums look on rattlesnakes as a food source. They can eat rattlers for a reason. Why? Is it because they are *vulnerable to* or *defenseless against* the poison? No. It's because they're *impervious* to the poison (that is, unharmed by it). That's the reason they can treat the rattlesnake as a *potential* source of food and not as a *lethal* or deadly enemy. The correct answer is Choice (C).

Note the cause-and-effect signal *thus*. The nature of the opossum's response to the venom explains *why* it can look on a dangerous snake as a possible prey.

5. **Break down unfamiliar words into recognizable parts.** If you're having vocabulary trouble, look for familiar parts—prefixes, suffixes, and roots—in unfamiliar words. They can provide you with clues to the meanings of unfamiliar words. For example, knowing that *mon-* usually means *warn* can help you deduce that an *admonition* is a warning, a *premonition* an advance warning, and so on.

EXAMPLE

Consider the tough sample sentence completion question from Chapter 1.

Crabeater seal, the common name of *Lobodon carcinophagus*, is ----, since the animal's staple diet is not crabs, but krill.

(A) a pseudonym   (B) a misnomer   (C) an allusion
(D) a digression   (E) a compromise

Knowing word parts definitely would have helped you answer this question.

> *Mis-* means bad or improper.
> *Nom-* or -*nym* means name.
> A *misnomer* is an improper or incorrectly given name.
> *Pseudo-* means false.
> A *pseudonym* is a false name (usually one assumed by an author to conceal his or her identity).

Thus, the name *Lobodon carcinophagus* is clearly a misnomer, not a pseudonym.

You'll find this tactic useful in dealing with unfamiliar words in analogy questions and reading passages as well.

Practice Exercises   **Answers given on page 53.**

Exercise A

Each of the following sentences has one or two blanks, each blank indicating that something has been omitted. Beneath the sentence are five lettered words or sets of words. Choose the word or set of words for each blank that <u>best</u> fits the meaning of the sentence as a whole.

1. Normally an individual thunderstorm lasts about 45 minutes, but under certain conditions the storm may ----, becoming ever more severe, for as long as four hours.

   (A) wane   (B) moderate   (C) persist   (D) vacillate
   (E) disperse

2. Ms. Sutcliffe's helpful notes on her latest wine discoveries and her no-nonsense warnings to consumers about ---- wines provide ---- guide to the numbing array of wines of Burgundy.

   (A) excellent..a useful   (B) overrated..an inadequate
   (C) overpriced..a trusty   (D) unsatisfactory..a spotty
   (E) vintage..an unreliable

3. If you are trying to make a strong impression on your audience, you cannot do so by being understated, tentative, or ----.

   (A) hyperbolic   (B) restrained   (C) argumentative
   (D) authoritative   (E) passionate

4. In one shocking instance of ---- research, one of the nation's most influential researchers in the field of genetics reported on experiments that were never carried out and published deliberately ---- scientific papers on his nonexistent work.

   (A) comprehensive..abstract   (B) theoretical..challenging
   (C) fraudulent..deceptive   (D) derivative..authoritative
   (E) erroneous..impartial

5. Measurement is, like any other human endeavor, a complex activity, subject to error, not always used ----, and frequently misinterpreted and ----.

   (A) mistakenly..derided   (B) erratically..analyzed
   (C) systematically..organized   (D) innovatively..refined
   (E) properly..misunderstood

6. Her novel published to universal acclaim, her literary gifts acknowledged by the chief figures of the Harlem Renaissance, her reputation as yet ---- by envious slights, Hurston clearly was at the ---- of her career.

   (A) undamaged..ebb   (B) untarnished..zenith
   (C) untainted..extremity   (D) blackened..mercy
   (E) unmarred..brink

7. Unlike other examples of ---- verse, Milton's *Lycidas* does more than merely mourn for the death of Edward King; it also denounces corruption in the Church in which King was ordained.

   (A) satiric   (B) elegiac   (C) free   (D) humorous
     (E) didactic

8. Few other plants can grow beneath the canopy of the sycamore tree, whose leaves and pods produce a natural herbicide that leaches into the surrounding soil, ---- other plants that might compete for water and nutrients.

   (A) inhibiting   (B) distinguishing   (C) nourishing
     (D) encouraging   (E) refreshing

9. Despite an affected ---- that convinced casual observers that he was indifferent about his painting and enjoyed only frivolity, Warhol cared deeply about his art and labored at it ----.

   (A) nonchalance..diligently   (B) empathy..methodically
     (C) fervor..secretly   (D) gloom..intermittently
       (E) hysteria..sporadically

10. Because she had a reputation for ----, we were surprised and pleased when she greeted us so ----.

    (A) insolence..irately   (B) hospitality..cordially
      (C) graciousness..amiably   (D) arrogance..disdainfully
        (E) querulousness..affably

11. The child was so spoiled by her indulgent parents that she pouted and became ---- when she did not receive all of their attention.

    (A) discreet   (B) suspicious   (C) elated   (D) sullen
      (E) tranquil

12. Just as disloyalty is the mark of the renegade, ---- is the mark of the ----.

    (A) timorousness..hero   (B) temerity..coward
      (C) avarice..philanthropist   (D) cowardice..craven
        (E) vanity..flatterer

13. The newest fiber-optic cables that carry telephone calls cross-country are made of glass so ---- that a piece 100 miles thick is clearer than a standard windowpane.

(A) fragile (B) immaculate (C) tangible (D) iridescent
(E) transparent

14. The reasoning in this editorial is so ---- that we cannot see how anyone can be deceived by it.

(A) coherent (B) astute (C) cogent (D) specious
(E) dispassionate

15. Because Inspector Morse could not contain his scorn for the police commissioner, he was imprudent enough to make ---- remarks about his superior officer.

(A) ambiguous (B) dispassionate (C) unfathomable
(D) interminable (E) scathing

Exercise B

Each sentence below has one or two blanks, each blank indicating that something has been omitted. Beneath the sentence are five lettered words or sets of words. Choose the word or set of words for each blank that <u>best</u> fits the meaning of the sentence as a whole.

1. Rebelling against ornateness, modern architecture has discarded the ---- trimming on buildings and has concentrated on an almost Greek simplicity of line.

(A) flamboyant (B) austere (C) inconspicuous
(D) aesthetic (E) derivative

2. Though he was theoretically a friend of labor, his voting record in Congress ---- that impression.

(A) implied (B) created (C) confirmed (D) belied
(E) maintained

3. The young researcher was quickly promoted when her employers saw how ---- she was in carrying out her duties.

(A) problematic (B) indifferent (C) assiduous
(D) lethargic (E) cursory

4. For Miro, art became a ---- ritual: paper and pencils were holy objects to him, and he worked as though he were performing a religious rite.

   (A) superficial (B) sacred (C) banal (D) cryptic
   (E) futile

5. In place of the more general debate about abstract principles of government that most delegates probably expected, the Constitutional Convention put ---- proposals on the table.

   (A) theoretical (B) vague (C) concrete (D) tentative
   (E) redundant

6. Japan's industrial success is ---- in part to its tradition of group effort and ----, as opposed to the emphasis on personal achievement that is a prominent aspect of other industrial nations.

   (A) responsive..independence (B) related..introspection
   (C) equivalent..solidarity (D) subordinate..individuality
   (E) attributed..cooperation

7. Her true feelings ---- themselves in her sarcastic asides; only then was her ---- revealed.

   (A) concealed..sweetness (B) manifested..bitterness
   (C) hid..sarcasm (D) developed..anxiety (E) grieved..charm

8. Critics of the movie *The Color Purple* ---- its saccharine, over-optimistic mood as out of keeping with the novel's more ---- tone.

   (A) applauded..somber (B) disparaged..hopeful
   (C) acclaimed..positive (D) denounced..sanguine
   (E) condemned..acerbic

9. The distinctive qualities of African music were not appreciated or even ---- by Westerners until fairly recently.

   (A) deplored (B) revered (C) ignored (D) neglected
   (E) perceived

10. Alec Guinness, who has few equals among English-speaking actors, reveals himself in his autobiography to be an uncommonly ---- prose stylist as well.

   (A) ambivalent (B) infamous (C) supercilious
   (D) felicitous (E) pedestrian

11. Unlike the gregarious Capote, who was never happier than when he was in the center of a crowd of celebrities, Faulkner, in later years, grew somewhat ---- and shunned company.

    (A) congenial   (B) decorous   (C) dispassionate
      (D) reclusive   (E) ambivalent

12. This island is a colony; however, in most matters, it is completely ----, receiving no orders from the mother country.

    (A) submissive   (B) amorphous   (C) distant
      (D) autonomous   (E) aloof

13. Studded starfish are well protected from most ---- and parasites by ---- surface whose studs are actually modified spines.

    (A) dangers..a vulnerable   (B) predators..an armored
     (C) threats..a fragile   (D) challenges..an obtuse
      (E) exigencies..a brittle

14. Although eighteenth-century English society as a whole did not encourage learning for its own sake in women, nonetheless it illogically ---- women's sad lack of education.

    (A) palliated   (B) postulated   (C) decried   (D) brooked
     (E) vaunted

15. The mind of a bigot is like the pupil of the eye: the more light you pour upon it, the more it will ----.

    (A) blur   (B) veer   (C) stare   (D) reflect   (E) contract

Answer Key

Exercise A

1. **C**	4. **C**	7. **B**	10. **E**	13. **E**
2. **C**	5. **E**	8. **A**	11. **D**	14. **D**
3. **B**	6. **B**	9. **A**	12. **D**	15. **E**

Exercise B

1. **A**	4. **B**	7. **B**	10. **D**	13. **B**
2. **D**	5. **C**	8. **E**	11. **D**	14. **C**
3. **C**	6. **E**	9. **E**	12. **D**	15. **E**

3 The Analogy Question

To most people, the analogy questions are the ones that stand out when they think about SAT I and the PSAT. Analogies may well be the most unfamiliar kind of question on the test, but they aren't impossible, and at least some of them will be fairly easy. If you're unfamiliar with this type of question, a sure way for you to boost your PSAT verbal score is for you to get acquainted with the form and content of some typical analogies.

Analogy questions ask you to look at relationships between words. You are given two words, linked by a colon. Think of how the dictionary defines these words. Ask yourself why these words belong together. What connects them? In what context have you seen them together? How are they generally used? Then look for a pair of words among the answer choices that are related in the same way.

Your correct answer choice has got to have the same characteristics as the original pair. The words must have a clear relationship. They must be related *by definition*. Be careful—remember that many words are defined in multiple ways. If you stay alert to the range of possibilities, you'll come up with correct answers, time after time.

Tips on Handling Analogy Questions

1. **Set up a test sentence that links the capitalized words.** Your first step in answering an analogy question is to make a test sentence that defines the two capitalized words and shows how they relate. You must think what each word means and then link them together. It's not that hard to do.

EXAMPLE

CHAPTER : BOOK ::   (A) title : story   (B) paper : page
(C) sentence : essay   (D) tune : melody   (E) act : play

In a short, clear sentence, state the relationship between the two words in capital letters. Then use that sentence to test the words in the answer choices.

> A CHAPTER is a major piece of a BOOK.
> A _(blank)_ is a major piece of a _(blank)_ .

Now substitute the words in each of the answer choices for the words in capital letters. You should wind up with one pair of words that makes good sense.

EXAMPLE

(A) A TITLE is a major piece of a STORY.
(B) A PAPER is a major piece of a PAGE.
(C) A SENTENCE is a major piece of an ESSAY.
(D) A TUNE is a major piece of a MELODY.
(E) An ACT is a major piece of a PLAY.

The correct answer is (E). Just as a BOOK is divided into CHAPTERS, a PLAY is divided into ACTS.

Note that Choice (C), while tempting, is incorrect. A sentence is defined as a grammatically self-contained group of words. While an essay is composed of sentences, a sentence is not _by definition_ a major piece of an essay.

2. **Fine-tune your test sentence.** Sometimes when you set up a test sentence it just doesn't work. More than one answer choice may fit your test sentence, leaving you looking for a way to narrow things down. _No_ answer choice may fit your test sentence, leaving you unsure what to try next. In such cases, you need

to fine-tune your test sentence, adjusting it until everything works.

When you fine-tune your test sentence, try different approaches. Look for other meanings of the individual words, other ways the words can relate. If more than one answer choice seems to fit, try making your sentence more specific. If *no* answer choice fits, try making your sentence more general.

EXAMPLE

MITTEN : HAND ::   (A) belt : leather   (B) ring : finger
(C) muffler : neck   (D) bracelet : clasp   (E) sandal : foot

You set up a test sentence:

You wear a MITTEN on your HAND.
You wear a _(blank)_ on your _(blank)_ .

Then you see that *several* answer choices could fit your test sentence. You wear a ring on your finger. You wear a muffler on your neck. You wear a sandal on your foot. Your test sentence is too general. It doesn't work.

Ask yourself *why* you wear a mitten on your hand. The answer is,

You wear a MITTEN to keep your HAND warm.

Similarly, you wear a *muffler* to keep your *neck* warm. The correct answer is (C).

3. **Words have many meanings—stay alert.** Watch out for those words that have more than one meaning. *Lie*, for example, can mean *recline*. It can also mean *fib*. Similarly, *minute* can mean sixty seconds. As an adjective, *minute* (my-NYOOT) can mean very, very small.

Be on the lookout for familiar-looking words defined in unfamiliar ways.

EXAMPLE

PAN : CAMERA :: (A) ban : book   (B) tune : radio
(C) charge : battery   (D) filter : lens   (E) rotate: periscope

Before you can answer this question, you have to know the definition of *pan*. You're not dealing with a frying pan or a gold miner's pan or a dishpan; *pan* here is a verb, not a noun. You can tell because the first word of each answer choice is also a verb. The verb ending *-ate* at the end of *rotate* gives that away.

The verb *pan*, however, has several meanings:

The miner panned for gold. (The miner washed gravel to separate out the gold.)

The chef panned the carrots. (The chef cooked the carrots in a pan with a small amount of fat or water.)

The critic panned the comedy. (The critic severely criticized the comedy.)

None of these is the meaning you want.

Think how *pan* relates to *camera*. When someone *pans* a camera, what happens? The cameraperson rotates the camera on its axis so that he or she can film a panoramic scene (or a moving person or object). Similarly, a submarine crewmember *rotates* or revolves a *periscope* on its axis so that he or she can make a panoramic observation. The correct answer is Choice (E).

4. **Watch out for answer choices that reverse the original relationship.** In an analogy you have two capitalized words that relate in a set way. In setting up the answer choices, the test-makers will often tempt you with pairs of words that relate in a grammatically opposite way. See how it works.

EXAMPLE

FUGITIVE : FLEE ::   (A) witness : summon
(B) captor : escape   (C) lawyer : retain
(D) bodyguard : protect   (E) runaway : trace

At first glance several of these answers may seem to work. "A fugitive is someone who flees." "A runaway is someone who is traced." The relationship looks promising, but it's not correct. Ask yourself *who is doing what to whom*? In the original pair, the fugitive is doing something: fleeing, or running away. In Choice (E), the runaway is *not* the person doing something. He is being traced; he doesn't get to trace or track down anyone. In other words, the runaway is the object of the verb *trace*, not the verb's subject. The original grammatical relationship is reversed. The same flaw eliminates Choices (A) and (C): a witness is someone who is summoned; a lawyer is someone who is retained (hired). Again, the original grammatical relationship is reversed.

The correct answer to this question is Choice (D). *By definition*, a fugitive is a person who flees. In the same way, *by definition*, a bodyguard is a person who protects.

5. Watch out for errors caused by eye-catchers. Sometimes the test-makers set out to tempt you into making a mistake. They come up with incorrect answer choices *designed* to catch your eye. These eye-catchers can distract your attention from the *real* answer— but not if you're aware of the test-makers' game.

In the previous example, when you looked at the answer choices, did Choice (B) seem to leap right off the page? If it did, watch out—you've run into an eye-catcher. Eye-catchers grab your attention because they somehow remind you of one (or both) of the capitalized words. In this case, *captor* immediately reminds you of *fugitive*. Similarly, *escape* reminds you of *flee*. The words feel as if they belong together, and your immediate impulse is to mark down Choice (B).

Choice (B), however, is wrong. A *captive* may try to escape; a *captor*, however, does not.

6. **Be guided by the parts of speech**. Grammatical information can help you recognize analogy types and spot the use of unfamiliar or secondary meanings of words. In PSAT analogy questions, the relationship between the parts of speech of the capitalized words and the parts of speech of the answer choices is consistent. If your capitalized words are a noun and a verb, each one of your answer pairs will be a noun and a verb. If they are an adjective and a noun, each one of your answer pairs will be an adjective and a noun. If you can recognize the parts of speech in a single answer pair, you know the parts of speech of every other answer pair, and of the original pair as well.

7. **Eliminate answer choices that don't express a specific relationship.** One of your basic PSAT strategies is to eliminate as many wrong answer choices as you can. One way to spot a wrong answer in an analogy question is to look for answer pairs whose terms are only vaguely linked.

In the capitalized pairs, the words are always clearly linked. They are linked *by definition*:

A FUGITIVE is *someone* who FLEES.
To PAN a CAMERA is to *rotate* it.

In the answer pairs, the relationship between the words may sometimes seem casual at best.

Compare the following word pairs:

CHAPTER : BOOK (clear dictionary relationship)
CHAPTER : PENCIL (no clear dictionary relationship)

As an analogy, CHAPTER : PENCIL just doesn't work.

8. **Know common analogy types.** Analogies tend to fall into certain basic patterns. You'll have an easier time recognizing weakly-linked answer pairs and coming up with good test sentences if you familiarize yourself with the most common analogy types.

One word of caution. Do not go overboard and try to memorize these analogy types. Just try to get a feel for them, so that you'll be able to recognize how each pair of words is linked.

COMMON ANALOGY TYPES

1. Definition
REFUGE : SHELTER
A *refuge* (place of asylum) by definition *shelters*.

2. Defining Characteristic
TIGER : CARNIVOROUS
A *tiger* is by definition *carnivorous* or meat-eating.

3. Class and Member
RODENT : SQUIRREL
A *squirrel* is a member of the *rodent* family.

4. Group and Member
WOLF : PACK
A *wolf* is a member of a *pack*.

5. Antonyms
WAX : WANE
Wax, to grow larger, and *wane* to dwindle, are opposites.

6. Antonym Variants
WILLFUL : OBEDIENCE
Willful means lacking in *obedience*.

7. Synonyms
NARRATE : TELL
Narrate and *tell* are synonyms; they have the same meaning.

8. Synonym Variants
VERBOSE : WORDINESS
Someone *verbose* is wordy; he or she exhibits *wordiness*.

9. Degree of Intensity
FLURRY : BLIZZARD
A *flurry* or shower of snow is less extreme than a *blizzard*.

10. Part to Whole
FINGER : HAND
The *finger* is part of the *hand*.

11. Function
BALLAST : STABILITY
Ballast provides *stability*.

12. Manner
STRUT : WALK
To *strut* is to *walk* in a proud manner.

13. Action and Its Significance
WINCE : PAIN
A *wince* is a sign that one feels *pain*.

14. Worker and Article Created
POET : SONNET
A *poet* creates a *sonnet*.

15. Worker and Tool
PAINTER : BRUSH
A *painter* uses a *brush* to paint.

---

16. Worker and Action
ACROBAT : CARTWHEEL
An *acrobat* performs a *cartwheel.*

---

17. Worker and Workplace
MINER : QUARRY
A *miner* works in a *quarry* or pit.

---

18. Tool and Its Action
CROWBAR : PRY
A *crowbar* is a tool used to *pry* things apart.

---

19. Cause and Effect
VIRUS : INFLUENZA
A *virus* causes *influenza.*

---

20. Sex
DOE : STAG
A *doe* is a female deer; a *stag*, a male deer.

---

21. Age
COLT : STALLION
A *colt* is a young *stallion.*

---

22. Time Sequence
CORONATION : REIGN
The *coronation* precedes the *reign.*

---

23. Spatial Location
CREST : WAVE
The *crest* is the highest point of the *wave.*

---

24. Symbol and Quality It Represents
DOVE : PEACE
A *dove* is the symbol of *peace.*

Practice Exercises   **Answers given on page 67.**

Each question below consists of a related pair of words or phrases, followed by five pairs of words or phrases labeled A through E. Select the pair that <u>best</u> expresses a relationship similar to that expressed in the original pair.

Exercise A

1. TELLER : BANK ::   (A) artist : museum   (B) cashier : check
   (C) waiter : restaurant   (D) borrower : loan
      (E) mourner : funeral

2. INNING : BASEBALL ::   (A) round : boxing   (B) puck : hockey
   (C) touchdown : football   (D) serve : tennis   (E) outing : hiking

3. DEGREE : TEMPERATURE ::   (A) ounce : weight
   (B) fathom : volume   (C) mass : energy   (D) time : length
      (E) light : heat

4. PICK : GUITAR ::   (A) peg : ukelele   (B) string : banjo
   (C) pipe : organ   (D) bow : violin   (E) head : tambourine

5. FRAGILE : BREAK ::   (A) fertile : smell   (B) hostile : invite
   (C) vivid : grow   (D) flexible : bend   (E) vital : destroy

6. SPOKE : WHEEL ::   (A) square : circle   (B) balance : lever
   (C) door : latch   (D) book : shelf   (E) rung : ladder

7. VESSEL : FLEET ::   (A) wolf : pack   (B) forest : clearing
   (C) vehicle : truck   (D) carriage : horse   (E) squadron : rank

8. PATRON : SUPPORT ::   (A) spouse : divorce
   (B) restaurant : management   (C) counselor : advice
      (D) host : hostility   (E) artist : imitation

9. CORPULENCE : STOUT ::   (A) baldness : hirsute
   (B) erudition : learned   (C) gauntness : beautiful
      (D) steadfastness : mercurial   (E) competence : strict

10. ASYLUM : SHELTER ::   (A) harbor : concealment
    (B) palisade : display   (C) stronghold : defense
       (D) hospice : exile   (E) cloister : storage

11. MOTION PICTURE : SCENARIO ::   (A) drama : setting
    (B) play : plot   (C) theater : program   (D) ballet : pirouette
       (E) recital: review

12. MILDEW : DANKNESS ::   (A) gangrene : infection
    (B) dew : sunshine   (C) dawn : darkness
       (D) canker : blossom   (E) rust : hardness

13. CALLOW : MATURITY ::   (A) fallow : productivity
  (B) crusty : incivility   (C) eager : anxiety
     (D) spoiled : common sense   (E) callous : growth

14. ENIGMA : PUZZLING ::   (A) dilemma : compelling
  (B) labyrinth : tortuous   (C) sphinx : massive
     (D) riddle : humorous   (E) maze : extensive

15. KERNEL : CORN ::   (A) neck : bottle   (B) eye : storm
  (C) grain : wheat   (D) stem : carrot   (E) nose : bouquet

16. SOLDIER : CARBINE ::   (A) author : book
  (B) chemist : test tube   (C) pilot : bombardier
     (D) trooper : platoon   (E) knight : lance

17. ARCHIPELAGO : ISLAND ::   (A) peninsula : strait
  (B) cluster : star   (C) border : nation   (D) nucleus : atom
     (E) skyscraper : building

18. HOBBLE : WALK ::   (A) gallop : run   (B) stammer : speak
  (C) stumble : fall   (D) sniff : smell   (E) amble : stroll

19. EXUBERANT : DOWNCAST ::   (A) exiled : overthrown
  (B) extravagant : lavish   (C) effusive : undemonstrative
     (D) parsimonious : eager   (E) formidable : dismal

20. MINISTER : SERMON ::   (A) politician : promises
  (B) heckler : interruptions   (C) doctor : diagnosis
     (D) lecturer : speech   (E) curator : museum

21. HOBNOB : COMPANIONS ::   (A) conspire : plotters
  (B) kowtow : servants   (C) blackmail : police
     (D) kidnap : victims   (E) quarrel : friends

22. GOURMET : DELICACY ::   (A) clairvoyant : seance
  (B) connoisseur : masterpiece   (C) socialite : seclusion
     (D) commoner : aristocracy   (E) chef : scullery

23. INADVERTENT : THOUGHT ::   (A) gauche : grace
  (B) clandestine : secrecy   (C) lugubrious : gloom
     (D) wealthy : money   (E) curious : opinion

24. GAGGLE : GEESE ::   (A) coop : chickens   (B) muzzle : dogs
  (C) gill : fish   (D) swarm : bees   (E) waddle : ducks

25. UNICORN : CHASTITY ::   (A) sea serpent : invulnerability
  (B) centaur : mortality   (C) sphinx : mystery
     (D) dragon : swiftness   (E) phoenix : loyalty

Exercise B

1. UNEMPLOYED : WORKER ::   (A) unknown : artist
  (B) fallow : field   (C) renovated : house
     (D) observant : spectator   (E) unconscious : sleeper

2. RUSE : DECEIVE ::   (A) policy : change
(B) argument : persuade   (C) subterfuge : revenge
(D) strategy : gamble   (E) denial : confuse

3. CATCALL : DERISION ::   (A) wolf whistle : admiration
(B) horselaugh : dismay   (C) snort : approval
(D) mutter : indifference   (E) sputter : sympathy

4. CRACK : CIPHER ::   (A) break : platter   (B) divide : number
(C) strike : hammer   (D) unriddle : mystery
(E) detonate : revolver

5. INTEREST : FASCINATE ::   (A) vex : enrage
(B) vindicate : condemn   (C) regret : rue   (D) appall : bother
(E) weary : fatigue

6. HAIR : SCALP ::   (A) dimple : cheek   (B) elbow : knee
(C) tooth : gum   (D) beard : moustache   (E) waist : torso

7. MANACLE : HANDS ::   (A) spectacle : eyes   (B) nostril : nose
(C) bracelet : wrist   (D) helmet : head   (E) hobble : legs

8. TOLERANCE : BIGOTRY ::   (A) prodigality : ribaldry
(B) magnanimity : parsimony   (C) exigency : urgency
(D) emulation : rivalry   (E) patience : conformity

9. BUNGLER : COMPETENCE ::   (A) beggar : influence
(B) jester : wit   (C) meddler : patience
(D) grumbler : satisfaction   (E) cobbler : leather

10. ABHOR : DISLIKE ::   (A) calcify : petrify
(B) torture : discomfort   (C) rebuke : ridicule
(D) admire : disdain   (E) magnify : enlarge

11. BULLY : BLUSTER ::   (A) coward : rant   (B) charlatan : snivel
(C) cutthroat : mutter   (D) stool pigeon : squeal
(E) blackguard : cringe

12. CARESS : AFFECTION ::   (A) curtsy : respect
(B) salute : admiration   (C) handshake : indifference
(D) wink : suspicion   (F) wave : agitation

13. FOOLHARDY : CAUTION ::   (A) hardhearted : fear
(B) careworn : anxiety   (C) high-strung : tension
(D) thick-skinned : sensitivity   (E) spendthrift : resource

14. VERTEX : CONE ::   (A) perimeter : rectangle
(B) whirlpool : pond   (C) pod : seed   (D) peak : mountain
(E) step : staircase

15. GEOLOGIST : FELDSPAR ::   (A) meteorologist : orbit
(B) botanist : zinnia   (C) architect : monolith
(D) cosmetologist : space   (E) philanthropist : stamp

16. FELON : PENITENTIARY ::   (A) perjurer : perjury
    (B) conniver : constabulary   (C) malefactor : sanctuary
      (D) juvenile delinquent : reformatory
        (E) hedonist : confessional

17. TRAVELER : ITINERARY ::   (A) tourist : vacation
    (B) lecturer : outline   (C) pedestrian : routine
      (D) explorer : safari   (E) soldier : furlough

18. AERIE : EAGLE ::   (A) hawk : falcon   (B) viper : reptile
    (C) venom : rattlesnake   (D) lair : wolf   (E) fang : adder

19. IMPROMPTU : REHEARSAL ::   (A) practiced : technique
    (B) makeshift : whim   (C) offhand : premeditation
      (D) glib : fluency   (E) numerical : calculation

20. EVANESCENT : VANISH ::   (A) volatile : vaporize
    (B) incandescent : flee   (C) ethereal : drift
      (D) celestial : disappear   (E) transient : gravitate

21. TIRADE : ABUSIVE ::   (A) diatribe : familial   (B) satire : pungent
    (C) panegyric : laudatory   (D) eulogy : regretful
      (E) elegy : religious

22. STICKLER : INSIST ::   (A) mumbler : enunciate
    (B) trickster : risk   (C) haggler : concede   (D) laggard : outlast
      (E) braggart : boast

23. PLUMAGE : BIRD ::   (A) foliage : horse   (B) fleece : sheep
    (C) forage : cattle   (D) hive : bee   (E) carnage : beast

24. TRUNCATE : PYRAMID ::   (A) excavate : ruin   (B) ignite : fire
    (C) consecrate : church   (D) erect : statue   (E) behead : man

25. ABOLITIONIST : SLAVERY ::   (A) capitalist : commerce
    (B) militarist : war   (C) pugilist : victory
      (D) conservationist : wildlife   (E) prohibitionist : liquor

Answer Key

Exercise A

1. C	6. E	11. B	16. E	21. A
2. A	7. A	12. A	17. B	22. B
3. A	8. C	13. A	18. B	23. A
4. D	9. B	14. B	19. C	24. D
5. D	10. C	15. C	20. D	25. C

Exercise B

1. B	6. C	11. D	16. D	21. C
2. B	7. E	12. A	17. B	22. E
3. A	8. B	13. D	18. D	23. B
4. D	9. D	14. D	19. C	24. E
5. A	10. B	15. B	20. A	25. E

4 Improving Critical Reading Skills

Now, more than ever, doing well on the critical reading questions can make the difference between success and failure on the PSAT. These last questions in each verbal section are also the most time-consuming and the ones most likely to bog you down. However, you *can* handle them, and this chapter will show you how.

Long-Range Strategy: *Read, Read, Read!*

Just do it. There is no substitute for extensive reading as a preparation for the PSAT and for college work. The only way to build up your proficiency in reading is by reading books of all kinds. As you read, you will develop speed, stamina, and the ability to comprehend the printed page. But if you want to turn yourself into the kind of reader the colleges are looking for, you must develop the habit of reading—closely and critically—every day.

Challenge yourself. Don't limit your reading to light fiction or popular biographies. Branch out a bit. Try to develop an interest in as many fields as you can. Sample some of the serious magazines: *The New Yorker, Smithsonian, Natural History, National Geographic, Newsweek, Time, The New York Review of Books, Scientific American, Harper's Magazine.* In these magazines you'll find articles on literature, music, science, philosophy, history, the arts—the whole range of fields touched on by the PSAT. If you take time to acquaint yourself with the contents of these magazines, you won't find the subject matter of the reading passages on the examination so strange.

Tips on Handling Critical Reading Questions

1. **Build on what you already know.** Tackle passages with familiar subjects before passages with unfamiliar ones. It is hard to concentrate when you read

about something wholly unfamiliar to you. Give yourself a break. In each section, first tackle the reading passage that interests you or deals with topics in which you are well grounded. Then move on to the other passage. You'll do better that way.

2. **Try *all* the questions about each passage.** If you are stumped by a tough reading question, do not skip the other questions on that passage. The critical reading questions following each passage are not arranged in order of difficulty. They tend to be arranged sequentially: questions on paragraph 1 come before questions on paragraph 2. So try all the questions on the passage. That tough question may be just one question away from one that's easy for you.

3. **First read the passage; then read the questions.** Reading the questions before you read the passage will not save you time. It will cost you time. If you read the questions first, when you turn to the passage you will have a number of question words and phrases dancing around in your head. You will be so involved in trying to spot the places they occur in the passage that you will not be able to concentrate on comprehending the passage as a whole.

4. **Don't rush—read.** Read as rapidly as you can with understanding, but do not force yourself. Do not worry about the time element. If you worry about not finishing the test, you will begin to take short cuts and in your haste, you will miss the correct answer.

5. **Be an active reader.** As you read the italicized introductory material preceding the passage and tackle the passage's opening sentences, try to anticipate what the passage will be about. Ask yourself who or what the author is talking about.

6. **Map out the passage as you read.** As you continue reading, try to identify what *kind* of writing this is, what *techniques* are being used, who the intended

audience may be, and what *feeling* (if any) the author has toward the subject. Try to retain names, dates, and places for quick reference later. In particular, try to remember where in the passage the author makes *major points.* Then, when you start looking for the phrase or sentence that will justify your choice of answer, you may be able to save time by going back to that section of the passage immediately without having to reread the entire selection.

7. **Always go back to the passage to check your answer choice.** When you tackle the questions, *go back to the passage* to verify your choice of answer. Do not rely on your memory alone, and, above all, do not ignore the passage and just answer questions on the basis of other things you've read. Remember, the questions are asking you about what *this* author has to say about the subject, not about what some other author you once read said about it in another book.

8. **Use the line numbers to find your way around the text.** Use the line references in the questions to be sure you've gone back to the correct spot in the passage. The reading passages on the new PSAT tend to be longer than those on the old PSAT. Fortunately, all the lines are numbered, and the questions often refer you to specific lines in the passage by number. It takes less time to locate a line number than to spot a word or phrase. Use the line numbers to orient yourself in the text.

9. **Tackle the double passages one at a time.** When dealing with the new double passages, tackle them one at a time. The questions are organized sequentially: questions about Passage 1 come before questions about Passage 2. So, do things in order. *First,* read Passage 1; then jump straight to the questions

and answer all those based on Passage 1. *Next*, read Passage 2; then answer all the questions based on Passage 2. *Finally*, tackle the two or three questions that refer to *both* passages. Go back to both passages as needed.

10. **Expect ideas to be worded in alternate ways.** When the questions ask about specific information in the passage, do not expect to find it stated in exactly the same words. If the question is:

> According to the passage, widgets are
> (A) good   (B) bad   (C) indifferent
> (D) pink   (E) purple

do not expect to find a sentence in the passage that says, "Widgets are bad." However, you may well find a sentence that says, "Widgets are wholly undesirable and have a strongly negative influence." That is close enough to tell you that the answer must be Choice (B).

11. **Spot key words in the passage: transitions.** When you read, watch for key words that indicate how a passage is being developed:

Equality or continuity of ideas (one idea is equal in importance to another, or continues a thought expressed earlier): *again, also, and, another, as well as, besides, first, furthermore, likewise, moreover, in addition.*

Contrast or change of topic: *although, despite, in spite of, instead of, notwithstanding, regardless, nevertheless, on the other hand, however.*

Conclusion: *accordingly, as a result, hence, in conclusion, in short, therefore, thus, consequently.*

12. **Don't overlook little words that mean a lot.** Be on the lookout for all-inclusive words, such as *always, at all times,* and *entirely,* and for negative or limiting words, such as *only, never, no, none, except,* and *but.*

Many of the following passages are shorter than the actual passages you will encounter on the PSAT. Use these short passages as your opportunity to tackle a wide range of the question types that appear on the test.

Exercise A

The passages below are followed by questions on their content. Answer the questions on the basis of what is <u>stated</u> or <u>implied</u> in the passages and in any introductory material that may be provided.

The chief characteristic of art today, if we are to judge by the reactions of the common man, is its obscurity. Everybody complains about obscurity in poetry, in painting, in music. I
Line do not suggest that in some cases the complaint is unjusti-
(5) fied. But we should remember that the really original work of art in any age seems obscure to the general public. From a certain point of view it would be true to say that no great work of art finds an appreciative public waiting for it. The work creates its own public, slowly and painfully. A work of
(10) art is born as an intellectual foundling. What is interesting to notice is that often the art specialists themselves are caught napping. It was André Gide, you remember, who first saw Proust's great novel while he was working as a reader for a firm of publishers. He turned it down without hesitation. Per-
(15) haps you remember Leigh Hunt's verdict on Blake as "an unfortunate madman whose mildness alone prevented him from being locked up." Wordsworth also thought Blake mad, and yet it was he who wrote: "Every great and original writer, in proportion as he is great and original, must himself create
(20) the taste by which he is judged."

1. The passage indicates that critics often

    (A) discover unknown geniuses
    (B) add to obscurity in art
    (C) create an audience for new works
    (D) misjudge a masterpiece
    (E) explain a work of art to the public

2. The phrase "are caught napping" (lines 11–12) is best taken to mean that the art specialists

    (A) are trapped in their profession
    (B) are off their guard
    (C) feel a need for rest
    (D) find their task captivating
    (E) would escape if they were able

3. The word "taste" in line 20 means

    (A) detectable flavor
    (B) small morsel
    (C) individual artwork
    (D) aesthetic attitude
    (E) slight experience

4. The last four sentences in the passage (lines 12–20) provide

    (A) a refutation of the contention made earlier
    (B) support for the immediately preceding assertion
    (C) examples of the inherent contradictions of an argument
    (D) a revision of a previously held position
    (E) a return to the author's original thesis

       Intuition is not a quality which everyone can understand. As the unimaginative are miserable about a work of fiction until they discover what flesh-and-blood individual served as
Line the model for the hero or heroine, so even many scientists
(5) doubt scientific intuition. They cannot believe that a blind person can see anything that they cannot see. They rely utterly on the celebrated inductive method of reasoning: the facts are to be exposed, and we are to conclude from them only what we must. This is a very sound rule—for mentalities that
(10) can do no better. But it is not certain that the really great

steps are made in this plodding fashion. Dreams are made of
quite other stuff, and if there are any left in the world who do
not know that dreams have remade the world, then there is
little that we can teach them.

5. The primary purpose of this passage is to

    (A) denounce the unimaginative snobbery of scientists
    (B) correct a misconception about the nature of dreams
    (C) argue against the use of inductive reasoning
    (D) explain the importance of intuition in science
    (E) show how challenging scientific research can be

6. The author's attitude toward those who rely solely on the inductive
    method of reasoning can best be described as

    (A) condescending
    (B) approving
    (C) indignant
    (D) ambivalent
    (E) hypocritical

7. The word "exposed" in line 8 means

    (A) bared to the elements
    (B) laid open to danger
    (C) held up to ridicule
    (D) unmasked
    (E) made known

8. The phrase "the really great steps" (lines 10–11) most likely refers to

    (A) extremely large paces
    (B) vast distances
    (C) grandiose fantasies
    (D) major scientific advances
    (E) broadly interpreted measures

      Too many parents force their children into group activi-
ties. They are concerned about the child who loves to do
things alone, who prefers a solitary walk with a camera to a
Line game of ball. They want their sons to be "good fellows" and
(5) their daughters "social mixers." In such foolish fears lie the
beginnings of the blighting of individuality, the thwarting of

personality, the stealing of the wealth of one's capital for living joyously and well in a confused world. What America
needs is a new army of defense, manned by young men and
(10) women who, through guidance and confidence, encourage-
ment and wisdom, have built up values for themselves and
away from crowds and companies.

9. According to the passage, too many parents push their children to be

   (A) unnecessarily gregarious
   (B) foolishly timorous
   (C) pointlessly extravagant
   (D) acutely individualistic
   (E) financially dependent

10. The primary point the author wishes to make is that

    (A) young people need times to themselves
    (B) group activities are harmful to children
    (C) parents knowingly thwart their children's personalities
    (D) independent thinking is of questionable value
    (E) America needs universal military training

11. The author puts quotation marks around the words "good fellows"
    and "social mixers" to indicate that he

    (A) is using vocabulary that is unfamiliar to the reader
    (B) intends to define these terms later in the course of the passage
    (C) can readily distinguish these terms from one another
    (D) prefers not to differentiate roles by secondary factors such as gender
    (E) refuses to accept the assumption that these are positive values

12. By "the wealth of one's capital for living joyously and well in a
    confused world" (lines 7–8), the author most likely means

    (A) the financial security that one attains from one's individual
        professional achievements
    (B) the riches that parents thrust upon children who would far
        prefer to be left alone to follow their own inclinations
    (C) the hours spent in solitary pursuits that enable one to develop
        into an independent, confident adult
    (D) the happy memories of childhood days spent in the company of
        true friends
    (E) the profitable financial and personal contacts young people
        make when they engage in group activities

"Sticks and stones can break my bones,
But names will never harm me."

No doubt you are familiar with this childhood rhyme;
Line perhaps, when you were younger, you frequently invoked
(5) whatever protection it could offer against unpleasant epithets. But like many popular slogans and verses, this one
will not bear too close scrutiny. For names will hurt you.
Sometimes you may be the victim, and find yourself an
object of scorn, humiliation, and hatred just because
(10) other people have called you certain names. At other
times you may not be the victim, but clever speakers and
writers may, through name calling, blind your judgment
so that you will follow them in a course of action wholly
opposed to your own interests or principles. Name calling
(15) can make you gullible to propaganda which you might
otherwise readily see through and reject.

13. The author's primary purpose in quoting the rhyme in lines 1–2 is to

(A) remind readers of their childhood vulnerabilities
(B) emphasize the importance of maintaining one's good name
(C) demonstrate his conviction that only physical attacks can
harm us
(D) affirm his faith in the rhyme's ability to shield one from
unpleasant epithets
(E) introduce the topic of speaking abusively about others

14. By "this one will not bear too close scrutiny" (lines 6–7), the author
means that

(A) the statement will no longer seem valid if you examine it too
closely
(B) the literary quality of the verse does not improve on closer
inspection
(C) people who indulge in name-calling are embarrassed when they
are in the spotlight
(D) the author cannot stand having his comments looked at critically
(E) a narrow line exists between analyzing a slogan and over-
analyzing it

15. According to the passage, name calling may make you more susceptible to

    (A) poetic language
    (B) biased arguments
    (C) physical abuse
    (D) risky confrontations
    (E) offensive epithets

16. The author evidently feels that slogans and verses frequently

    (A) appeal to our better nature
    (B) are disregarded by children
    (C) are scorned by unprincipled speakers
    (D) represent the popular mood
    (E) oversimplify a problem

       It takes no particular expert in foods, or even glut-
ton, to know that no meal on the table ever is as good
as the meal in the oven's roasting pan or the stove's cov-
Line ered kettle. There is something about the furtive lifting of
(5) the lid and the opening of the door that is better than all
sauces and gravies. Call it the surprise appetizer. Call it,
also, that one gesture which the proprietor of the kitchen
hates above all others, which brings forth the shortest,
most succinct sentences with the word "meddling" in
(10) them. Yet it is essentially a friendly gesture, one based
on good will, and not on its more general misconstruc-
tion, curiosity. It is quite proper, to state the case flatly,
to say that a little quiet investigation of what is cooking
is simply an attempt to share the good things of life. It
(15) is possible to state that, but it will take more than a
statement to convince the cook that it is not an act of
interference. The kitchen has special laws.

17. The author maintains that cooks

    (A) feel proprietary about their domain
    (B) readily share the good things they create
    (C) avoid making friendly gestures to strangers
    (D) exercise care in lifting hot pan lids
    (E) tend to be unusually laconic

18. We can infer that the tone of the short sentences to which the author refers (lines 8–9) is

    (A) admonitory
    (B) tentative
    (C) nonchalant
    (D) cordial
    (E) serious

19. The word "flatly" in line 12 means

    (A) evenly
    (B) horizontally
    (C) without animation
    (D) without qualification
    (E) lacking flavor

20. The author's tone in the concluding sentence can best be described as

    (A) bitterly resentful
    (B) mildly ironic
    (C) thoroughly respectful
    (D) openly bewildered
    (E) quietly curious

Exercise B

The passages below are followed by questions on their content. Answer the questions on the basis of what is <u>stated</u> or <u>implied</u> in the passages and in any introductory material that may be provided.

The following passage is taken from an article on mathematical and scientific illiteracy published in The New York Times *in January 1989, as Ronald and Nancy Reagan left the White House.*

    The abstractness of mathematics is a great obstacle for many intelligent people. Such people may readily understand narrative particulars, but strongly resist impersonal generali-
Line ties. Since numbers, science, and such generalities are
(5) intimately related, this resistance can lead to an almost willful

mathematical and scientific illiteracy. Numbers have appeal for many only if they're associated with them personally—hence part of the attraction of astrology, biorhythms, Tarot cards and the I Ching, all individually customized "sciences."

(10)   Mathematical illiteracy and the attitudes underlying it provide in fact a fertile soil for the growth of pseudoscience. In "Pseudoscience and Society in Nineteenth-Century America," Arthur Wrobel remarks that belief in phrenology, homeopathy, and hydropathy was not confined to the poor and the
(15) ignorant, but pervaded much of 19th-century literature. Such credulity is not as extensive in contemporary literature, but astrology is one pseudoscience that does seem to engage a big segment of the reading public. Literary allusions to it abound, appearing in everything from Shakespeare to Don
(20) DeLillo's "Libra." A 1986 Gallup poll showed that 52 percent of American teenagers subscribe to it, as does at least 50 percent of the nation's departing First Couple.

        Given these figures, it may not be entirely inappropriate to note here that no mechanism through which the alleged
(25) zodiacal influences exert themselves has ever been specified by astrologers. Gravity certainly cannot account for these natal influences, since even the gravitational pull of the attending obstetrician is orders of magnitude greater than that of the relevant planet or planets. Nor is there any empirical
(30) evidence; top astrologers (as determined by their peers) have failed repeatedly to associate personality profiles with astrological data at a rate higher than that of chance. Neither of these fatal objections to astrology, of course, is likely to carry much weight with literate but innumerate people who don't
(35) estimate magnitudes or probabilities, or who are overimpressed by vague coincidences yet unmoved by overwhelming statistical evidence.

1. The word "confined" in line 14 means

    (A) enclosed
    (B) jailed
    (C) isolated
    (D) restricted
    (E) preached

2. Which of the following best summarizes the reason given in lines 1–4 for the extent of mathematical and scientific illiteracy today?

    (A) Many intelligent people dislike the intimacy of the connection between numbers and science.
    (B) Many otherwise intelligent people have difficulty dealing with impersonal, abstract concepts.
    (C) Intelligent people prefer speaking in generalities to narrating particular incidents.
    (D) Few people are able to appreciate the benefits of an individually customized science.
    (E) People today no longer cherish their personal associations with numbers.

3. The author's primary purpose throughout the passage is to

    (A) contrast astrology and other contemporary pseudosciences with phrenology, homeopathy, and hydropathy
    (B) trace the development of the current belief in astrology to its nineteenth-century roots
    (C) apologize for the rise of mathematical and scientific illiteracy in the present day
    (D) relate mathematical illiteracy to the prevalence of invalid pseudoscientific beliefs today
    (E) disprove the difficulty of achieving universal mathematical and scientific literacy

4. The author most likely regards the lack of empirical evidence for astrology as

    (A) an oversight on the part of the astrologers
    (B) a key argument against its validity
    (C) a flaw that will be corrected in time
    (D) the unfortunate result of too small a sampling
    (E) a major reason to keep searching for fresh data

5. The author's point about the popularity of astrology is made through both

    (A) personal testimony and generalizations
    (B) assertions and case histories
    (C) comparisons and anecdotes
    (D) statistics and literary references
    (E) observation and analogy

       When there is no distance between people, the only way
that anyone can keep his or her distance is by a code of eti-
quette that has acceptance in a community. Manners are the
Line antidote to adjustment to the group. They make social inter-
(5) course possible without any forfeit of one's personal dignity.
They are armor against invasion of privacy; they are the advance patrols that report whether one should withdraw or advance into intimacy. They are the friendly but noncommittal
gestures of civilized people. The manners of crowded coun-
(10) tries are, I believe, always more formal than those of open
countries (as they are, for example, in Europe and Japan),
and it may be that we are seeing a rising concern about
American manners precisely because we encounter more
people in closer quarters than we ever have before. We feel
(15) the need to find ways in which to be part of the group without
selling out our privacy or our individuality for a mess of
adjustment.

6. The title that best expresses the idea of this passage is

    (A) The Function of Politeness
    (B) Invasions of Privacy
    (C) Reasons for Social Relationships
    (D) The Need for Complete Privacy
    (E) American Manners

7. According to the author, manners serve to

    (A) facilitate relationships among people
    (B) preserve certain ceremonies
    (C) help people to make friends quickly
    (D) reveal character traits
    (E) help one to please one's friends

8. By stating that manners "are armor against invasion of privacy" (line 6), the author wishes to convey that manners

(A) protect one from physical danger
(B) are a cold, hard barrier separating people
(C) allow us to vent our aggressions safely
(D) shield one from unwanted intrusions
(E) enable us to guard our possessions

9. The author suggests that in Europe good manners are

(A) informal
(B) excessive
(C) essential
(D) ignored
(E) individual

10. In the course of the passage, the author does all of the following EXCEPT

(A) state a possibility
(B) use a metaphor
(C) cite an example
(D) make a parenthetical remark
(E) pose a question

One simple physical concept lies behind the formation of the stars: gravitational instability. The concept is not new; Newton first perceived it late in the seventeenth century.

Line   Imagine a uniform, static cloud of gas in space. Imagine
(5) then that the gas is somehow disturbed so that one small spherical region becomes a little denser than the gas around it so that the small region's gravitational field becomes slightly stronger. It now attracts more matter to it and its gravity increases further, causing it to begin to contract. As it
(10) contracts its density increases, which increases its gravity even more, so that it picks up even more matter and contracts even further. The process continues until the small region of gas finally forms a gravitationally bound object.

11. The primary purpose of the passage is to

(A) demonstrate the evolution of the meaning of a term
(B) depict the successive stages of a phenomenon
(C) establish the pervasiveness of a process
(D) support a theory considered outmoded
(E) describe a static condition

12. The word "disturbed" in line 5 means

(A) hindered
(B) perplexed
(C) disarranged
(D) pestered
(E) thickened

13. It can be inferred from the passage that the author views the information contained within it as

(A) controversial but irrefutable
(B) speculative and unprofitable
(C) uncomplicated and traditional
(D) original but obscure
(E) sadly lacking in elaboration

14. The author provides information that answers which of the following questions?

I. How does the small region's increasing density affect its gravitational field?
II. What causes the disturbance that changes the cloud from its original static state?
III. What is the end result of the gradually increasing concentration of the small region of gas?
(A) I only
(B) II only
(C) I and II only
(D) I and III only
(E) I, II and III

15. Throughout the passage, the author's manner of presentation is

(A) argumentative
(B) convoluted
(C) discursive
(D) expository
(E) hyperbolic

Unlike the carefully weighed and planned compositions of Dante, Goethe's writings have always the sense of immediacy and enthusiasm. He was a constant experimenter with
Line life, with ideas, and with forms of writing. For the same rea-
(5) son, his works seldom have the qualities of finish or formal beauty which distinguish the masterpieces of Dante and Virgil. He came to love the beauties of classicism, but these were never an essential part of his make-up. Instead, the urgency of the moment, the spirit of the thing, guided his pen.
(10) As a result, nearly all his works have serious flaws of structure, of inconsistencies, of excesses and redundancies and extraneities.

In the large sense, Goethe represents the fullest development of the romanticist. It has been argued that he should
(15) not be so designated because he so clearly matured and outgrew the kind of romanticism exhibited by Wordsworth, Shelley, and Keats. Shelley and Keats died young; Wordsworth lived narrowly and abandoned his early attitudes. In contrast, Goethe lived abundantly and developed his faith in the spirit,
(20) his understanding of nature and human nature, and his reliance on feelings as man's essential motivating force. The result was an all-encompassing vision of reality and a philosophy of life broader and deeper than the partial visions and attitudes of other romanticists. Yet the spirit of youthfulness,
(25) the impatience with close reasoning or "logic-chopping," and the continued faith in nature remained his to the end, together with an occasional waywardness and impulsiveness and a disregard of artistic or logical propriety which savor strongly of romantic individualism. Since so many twentieth-
(30) century thoughts and attitudes are similarly based on the stimulus of the Romantic Movement, Goethe stands as particularly the poet of the modern man as Dante stood for medieval man and as Shakespeare for the man of the Renaissance.

16. The word "close" in line 25 means

    (A) nearby
    (B) intimate
    (C) fitting tightly
    (D) strictly logical
    (E) nearly even

17. A main concern of the passage is to

    (A) describe the history of Romanticism until its decline
    (B) suggest that romantic literature is similar to Shakespearean drama
    (C) argue that romantic writings are more fully developed than classical works
    (D) compare Goethe with twentieth-century writers and poets
    (E) explain the ways in which Goethe embodied the romantic spirit

18. A characteristic of romanticism NOT mentioned in this passage is its

    (A) elevation of nature
    (B) preference for spontaneity
    (C) modernity of ideas
    (D) unconcern for artistic decorum
    (E) simplicity of language

19. It can be inferred from the passage that classicism has which of the following characteristics?

    I. Sensitivity towards emotional promptings
    II. Emphasis on formal aesthetic standards
    III. Meticulous planning of artistic works
    (A) II only
    (B) III only
    (C) I and II
    (D) II and III
    (E) I, II, and III

20. The author's attitude towards Goethe's writings is best described as

    (A) unqualified endorsement
    (B) lofty indifference
    (C) reluctant tolerance
    (D) measured admiration
    (E) undisguised contempt

Answer Key

Exercise A

1. D	5. E	9. A	13. E	17. A
2. B	6. A	10. A	14. A	18. A
3. D	7. E	11. E	15. B	19. D
4. B	8. D	12. C	16. E	20. B

Exercise B

1. A	5. D	9. C	13. C	17. E
2. B	6. A	10. E	14. D	18. E
3. D	7. A	11. B	15. D	19. D
4. B	8. D	12. C	16. D	20. D

5 Building Your Vocabulary

Recognizing the meaning of words is essential to comprehending what you read. The more you stumble over unfamiliar words in a text, the more you have to take time out to look up words in your dictionary, and the more likely you are to wind up losing track of what the author has to say.

To succeed in college, you must develop a college-level vocabulary. The time you put in now learning vocabulary-building techniques for the PSAT will pay off later on, and not just on the PSAT.

In this chapter you will find a fundamental tool that will help you build your vocabulary: Barron's PSAT High-Frequency Word List. No matter how little time you have before you take the PSAT, you can familiarize yourself with the sort of vocabulary you will face on the test. First, look over the words you will find on the list: each of these 300 words, ranging from everyday words such as *abstract* and *versatile*, to less-commonly known ones such as *espouse* and *taciturn*, has appeared (as answer choices or as question words) four or more times on PSATs published in the 1980s and 1990s.

Not only will looking over the PSAT High-Frequency Word List reassure you that you *do* know some PSAT-type words, but also it may well help you on the actual day of the test. These words have turned up on recent tests: some of them may turn up on the test you take.

PSAT HIGH-FREQUENCY WORD LIST

absolve v. pardon (an offense); free from blame. The father confessor *absolved* him of his sins. absolution, N.

absorb v. involve fully; soak up. The researchers were completely *absorbed* in observing how much liquid the newly synthesized fabric could *absorb*.

abstract ADJ. theoretical; not concrete; nonrepresentational. To him, hunger was an *abstract* concept; he had never missed a meal.

accommodate v. oblige or help someone; adjust or bring into harmony; adapt. Mitch always did everything possible to *accommodate* his elderly relatives, from driving them to medical appointments to helping them with tax forms.

acknowledgment N. recognition; admission; expression of appreciation. Despite her *acknowledgment* of how hard it was to break into show business, Molly refused to quit trying.

acrimony N. harshness of speech or nature; bitterness. Still bitter a decade after the partnership broke up, Tim spoke of his ex-partner with an *acrimony* undimmed by time.

adapt v. alter; modify. Some species of animals have become extinct because they could not *adapt* to a changing environment.

adverse ADJ. unfavorable; negative; hostile. *Adverse* circumstances forced him to close his business. adversity, N.

aesthetic ADJ. artistic; dealing with or capable of appreciation of the beautiful. The beauty of Tiffany's stained glass appealed to Alice's *aesthetic* sense. aesthete, N.

aggressor N. attacker. Before you punish both boys for fighting, see whether you can determine which one was the *aggressor*.

alienate v. make hostile; separate. Her attempts to *alienate* the two friends failed because they had complete faith in one another.

alleviate v. relieve. This medicine should *alleviate* the pain; if it does not, we shall have to use stronger drugs.

altruistic ADJ. unselfishly generous; concerned for others. In an *altruistic* act that inspired other philanthropists, Eugene Lang provided tutorial help and college scholarships for hundreds of inner-city youths.

ambiguous ADJ. unclear or doubtful in meaning. His *ambiguous* instructions misled us; we did not know which road to take. ambiguity, N.

ambivalence N. the state of having contradictory or conflicting emotional attitudes. Torn between loving her parents one minute and hating them the next, she was confused by the *ambivalence* of her feelings.

amenable ADJ. willing to agree; readily managed. She was such an *amenable* person that I felt sure she would agree to take notes for me if I had to miss class.

ample ADJ. abundant. The burglar had *ample* opportunity to dispose of his loot before the police caught up with him.

antagonism N. hostility; opposition; active resistance. Tim showed his *antagonism* toward Tina's new boyfriend by sneering at Jim's Harvard accent and button-down shirts.

antiquated ADJ. old-fashioned; obsolete; out of date. Philip had grown so accustomed to typing his papers on word processors that he thought typewriters were too *antiquated* for him to use.

apathy N. lack of caring; indifference. A firm believer in democratic government, she could not understand the *apathy* of people who never bothered to vote.

apprentice N. novice learning a trade from a skilled worker. As a child, Pip had thought it would be wonderful to work as Joe's *apprentice*; now he hated his *apprenticeship* and scorned the blacksmith's trade.

appropriate ADJ. proper; fitting; suitable. Ben spent hours looking for a suit that would be *appropriate* to wear at a summer wedding.

aristocracy N. hereditary nobility; privileged class. In America we have mixed feelings about hereditary *aristocracy*: we say all men are created equal, but we describe particularly outstanding people as natural *aristocrats*.

arrogance N. pride; haughtiness. The members of the middle class resented the nobility for their *arrogance*.

assert V. state with confidence; insist on one's rights. Katya *asserted* that, if only Yoko *asserted* herself, people would not take advantage of her.

assumption N. something taken for granted; taking over or taking possession of. The young princess made the foolish *assumption* that the regent would not object to her *assumption* of power.

assurance N. promise or pledge; certainty; self-confidence. When Tyrone Guthrie gave Alec Guinness his *assurance* rehearsals were going well, he spoke with such *assurance* that Guinness felt relieved.

authentic ADJ. genuine. The art expert was able to distinguish the *authentic* van Gogh painting from the copy the forger had made. authenticate, V.

aversion N. firm dislike. Their mutual *aversion* was so great that they refused to speak to each other.

beneficial ADJ. helpful; useful. In later years, Scrooge saw to it that Tiny Tim received the best of medical care, which was *beneficial* to the child's health.

benevolent ADJ. generous; charitable. Scrooge was completely transformed from the grasping miser; indeed, his newly *benevolent* nature prevented him from refusing any beggar who approached him.

benign ADJ. kindly; favorable; not malignant. A gentle soul, the old man was well liked because of his *benign* attitude toward friend and stranger alike.

betray ADJ. be unfaithful; reveal (unconsciously or unwillingly). The spy *betrayed* his country by selling military secrets to the enemy. When he was taken in for questioning, the tightness of his lips *betrayed* his fear of being caught.

bias V. prejudice. Because the judge played golf regularly with the district attorney, we feared their friendship might *bias* him in the prosecution's favor.

boycott V. refrain from buying or using. In an effort to stop grape growers from using pesticides that harmed the farm workers' health, Cesar Chavez called for consumers to *boycott* grapes.

brittle ADJ. easily broken; difficult. My employer's *brittle* personality made it difficult for me to get along with her.

candor N. frankness. Absolute *candor* is not always the best policy: consider how you would feel if your roommates were totally frank about the way you look the first thing in the morning. candid, ADJ.

captivate V. charm; fascinate. Although he was predisposed to dislike Elizabeth, Darcy found himself *captivated* by her charm and wit.

censor N. overseer of morals; person who reads documents to eliminate inappropriate remarks. In times of war, *censors* read soldiers' letters to make sure the soldiers do not inadvertently reveal any military secrets. also V.

chronicle V. report; record (in chronological order). The gossip columnist was paid to *chronicle* the latest escapades of the socially prominent celebrities. also N.

circumspect ADJ. prudent; cautious. Someone who looks both ways before crossing the street is by definition *circumspect*.

cite V. quote; refer to; commend. Because Virginia could *cite* hundreds of biblical passages from memory, her pastor *cited* her for her studiousness. citation, N.

cliché N. phrase whose meaning is dulled by repetition. Good writers avoid standard descriptive *clichés* ("faster than a speeding bullet," "stubborn as a mule").

coalesce V. combine; fuse. The brooks *coalesce* to form one large river.

commend V. praise; cite approvingly; entrust. Her teacher *commended* Latifa for her efforts to improve her vocabulary.

comparable ADJ. similar. People whose jobs are *comparable* in difficulty should receive *comparable* pay.

compassion N. deep sympathy. Mother Hale manifested her *compassion* for suffering children by turning her home into a care center for children with AIDS.

compliance N. readiness to yield; conformity in fulfilling requirements. When I give an order, I expect *compliance*, not defiance. comply, V.

component N. element; ingredient. I wish all the *components* of my stereo system were working at the same time.

compromise V. adjust or settle by making mutual concessions; endanger the interests or reputation of. Sometimes the presence of a neutral third party can help adversaries *compromise* their differences. Unfortunately, your presence at the scene of the dispute *compromises* our claim to neutrality in this matter. also N.

compulsion N. coercion; state of being compelled; irresistible impulse. Unlike many of her contemporaries, Maria Montessori did not believe in a teacher's using physical *compulsion* to force a child to obey.

condemnation N. strong censure or disapproval; judicial sentencing. Hearing the tone of *condemnation* in his master's voice, the puppy knew he had been a bad dog.

confine V. shut in; restrict. The terrorists had *confined* their prisoner in a small room. However, they had not chained him to the wall or done anything else to *confine* his movements further. confinement, N.

confirm V. corroborate; verify; support. I have several witnesses who will *confirm* my account of what happened.

conformity N. harmony; agreement with established standards. In *conformity* with our rules and regulations, I am calling a meeting of our organization.

congenial ADJ. pleasant; friendly. My father loved to go out for a meal with *congenial* companions.

consistent ADJ. dependable; unchanging; compatible. Confused by the suddenness of the accident, the witnesses failed to come up with a *consistent* story of what had taken place.

console V. lessen sadness or disappointment; give comfort. When her father died, Marius did his best to *console* Cosette.

consolidation N. merger; combination. The *consolidation* of the two firms went smoothly; they merged without a hitch.

contagion N. infection. Fearing *contagion*, they took great steps to prevent the spread of the disease.

contemplative ADJ. thoughtful and observant; reflective. Gazing thoughtfully at her canvas, Jody clearly was in a *contemplative* mood, and we hesitated to disturb her.

contempt N. scorn; disdain. Brave, but unimaginative, the corporal felt only *contempt* for cowards. contemptuous, ADJ.

contentious ADJ. quarrelsome. Hearing loud and *contentious* noises in the children's room, Mauri hurried in to break up the fight.

convention N. social or moral custom; established practice. Flying in the face of *convention*, George Sand shocked society by taking lovers and wearing men's clothes.

conversion N. change (in character, function, attitude, etc.); physical transformation. The alchemist's goal was the *conversion* or transmutation of lead into gold.

curtail V. shorten; reduce. During the gasoline shortage, we were forced to *curtail* our use of the family car.

cynical ADJ. skeptical or distrustful of human motives. Deeply *cynical* at heart, he was suspicious when anyone claimed to act on a solely altruistic impulse. cynicism, N.

dawdle V. loiter; waste time. We have to meet a deadline; please don't *dawdle* over this job.

deception N. act of deceiving someone; fraud. The magicians Penn and Teller practice *deception* on a grand scale, misleading audiences with tricks and sleight of hand.

defiance N. refusal to yield; resistance. When I give an order, I don't expect to meet *defiance*. defy, V.

deficiency N. lack; inadequacy; weakness. If you are weak in math, you may want to take a special class to correct your *deficiency*.

degenerate V. become worse; deteriorate. As the fight dragged on, the champion's style *degenerated* until he could barely keep on his feet.

deliberate ADJ. done on purpose; calculated; studied. When Tina walked right past Tony as if he weren't there, it was a *deliberate* snub.

denounce V. condemn; criticize. The reform candidate *denounced* the corrupt city officers for having betrayed the public's trust. denunciation, N.

density N. solidity; compactness; dullness. When bones lose their *density* over the years, they tend to break more easily.

deny V. contradict; refuse. Do you *deny* his story, or do you support what he says? denial, N.

depict V. portray. Some newspaper accounts *depicted* the movie star as a reclusive prima donna; others portrayed her as a sensitive artist harassed by the media.

deplete V. reduce; exhaust. We must wait until we *deplete* our present inventory before we order new stock.

deplore V. regret; deeply disapprove of; mourn. Although I *deplore* the vulgarity of your language, I defend your right to express yourself freely. deplorable, ADJ.

derision N. ridicule. They greeted his proposal with *derision* and refused to consider it seriously. deride, V.

derivative ADJ. unoriginal; derived from another source. Although her early poetry was clearly *derivative* in nature, the critics felt she had promise and eventually would find her own voice.

detached ADJ. emotionally removed; calm and objective; indifferent. A psychoanalyst must maintain a *detached* point of view and stay uninvolved with her patients' personal lives. detachment, N. (secondary meaning)

determination N. resolve; measurement or calculation; decision. Nothing could shake his *determination* that his children would get the best education that money could buy. Thanks to my pocket calculator, my *determination* of the answer to the problem took only seconds of my time.

detour N. roundabout path. Instead of heading straight to Chicago, Philip took a *detour* that led him past the family cottage on Lake Michigan.

diagnosis N. art of identifying a disease; analysis of a condition. In medical school Margaret developed her skill at *diagnosis*, learning how to read volumes from a rapid pulse or a hacking cough. diagnose, V.; diagnostic, ADJ.

didactic ADJ. teaching; instructional. The *didactic* quality of his poetry overshadows its literary merit; the moral lesson he teaches is far more memorable than the verse he writes.

digression N. wandering away from the subject. Nobody minded when Professor Renoir wandered off the topic; his *digressions* were always more fascinating than the assignment of the day. digress, V.

dilute V. make less concentrated; reduce in strength. She preferred her coffee *diluted* with milk.

discernment N. acuteness of understanding; discrimination; perception. Because Martha said she admired his singing, Sol thought she was a woman of great musical *discernment*.

disclaimer N. disavowal; statement denying a claim. Tina said she renounced any claim she might have on Tony's property; Tony, however, refused to trust her *disclaimer*.

disclose V. reveal. Although competitors offered him bribes, he refused to *disclose* any information about his company's forthcoming product. disclosure, N.

discord N. lack of harmony; conflict. Watching Tweedledum battle Tweedledee, Alice wondered what had caused this pointless *discord*.

disinterested ADJ. unprejudiced. The only *disinterested* person in the room was the judge: everyone else had a stake in the outcome of the case.

dismay V. discourage; frighten. The huge amount of work she had left to do *dismayed* her. also N.

dismiss V. refuse to consider seriously; reject. Believing in John's love for her, Mary *dismissed* the notion that he might be unfaithful. (secondary meaning)

disparage V. belittle; speak slightingly of. Fearing his brothers would *disparage* his playing, at first Martin would practice piano only when no one else was at home.

disparate ADJ. basically different; unrelated. It is difficult, if not impossible, to organize these *disparate* elements into a coherent whole.

dispel V. scatter; drive away; cause to vanish. The bright sunlight eventually *dispelled* the morning mist.

disperse V. scatter. The police fired tear gas into the crowd to *disperse* the protesters.

dissent V. disagree. In the recent Supreme Court decision, Justice O'Connor *dissented* from the majority opinion. also N.

distinct ADJ. not identical; dissimilar; clear; notable. Though at first glance these cases appear identical, each illustrates an entirely *distinct* point of law. If the difference between them is not *distinct* to you, ask your tutor to point out how they differ.

distinction N. honor; contrast; discrimination. A holder of the Medal of Honor, George served with great *distinction* in World War II. He made a *distinction*, however, between World War II and Vietnam, which he considered an immoral conflict.

distort v. twist out of shape. It is difficult to believe the newspaper accounts of the riots because of the way some reporters *distort* and exaggerate the actual events. distortion, N.

diverse ADJ. differing in some characteristics; various. There are *diverse* ways of approaching this problem, each with its own advantages and disadvantages. diversity, N.

divulge v. reveal. No lover of gossip, Charlotte would never *divulge* anything that a friend told her in confidence.

docile ADJ. obedient; easily managed. As *docile* as he seems today, that old lion was once a ferocious, snarling beast.

dogmatic ADJ. positive; assertive; arbitrary. Don't be so *dogmatic* when you state your opinions; not everybody here shares your beliefs.

eclipse v. darken; extinguish; surpass. The new stock market high *eclipsed* the previous record set in 1985.

endorse v. approve; support. Everyone waited to see which one of the rival candidates for the city council the mayor would *endorse*. endorsement, N. (secondary meaning)

enhance v. advance; improve. Your chances for winning a National Merit Scholarship will *be enhanced* if you take some time to develop your vocabulary.

erratic ADJ. odd; unpredictable. Investors become anxious when the stock market appears *erratic*.

esoteric ADJ. hard to understand; known only to the chosen few. *New Yorker* short stories often include *esoteric* allusions to obscure people and events: the implication is, if you are in the in-crowd, you'll get the reference; if you come from Cleveland, you won't.

espouse v. adopt; support. She was always ready to *espouse* a worthy cause.

esteem v. respect; value; judge. Though I reject Ezra Pound's politics, I *esteem* him for his superb poetry and literary criticism. also N.

flippant ADJ. lacking proper seriousness. Some people make *flippant* comments at inappropriate times because they fear their friends will ridicule them if they appear to take things seriously. flippancy, N.

forthright ADJ. outspoken; frank. Never afraid to call a spade a spade, she was perhaps too *forthright* to be a successful party politician.

frail ADJ. weak. The sickly child seemed too *frail* to lift the heavy carton.

futile ADJ. ineffective; fruitless. Why waste your time on *futile* pursuits?

hamper V. obstruct. The minority party agreed not to *hamper* the efforts of the leaders to secure a lasting peace.

heed V. pay attention to; consider. We hope you shall *heed* our advice and get a good night's sleep before the PSAT. also N.

hindrance N. block; obstacle. Stalled cars along the highway are a *hindrance* to traffic that tow trucks should remove without delay. hinder, V.

hostility N. unfriendliness; hatred. Children often feel *hostility* toward the new baby in the family.

humble ADJ. modest; not proud. He spoke with great feeling of how much he loved his *humble* home, which he would not trade for a palace. humility, N.

hypocritical ADJ. pretending to be virtuous; deceiving. I resent his *hypocritical* posing as a friend, for I know he cares only for his own advancement. hypocrisy, N.

hypothetical ADJ. based on assumptions or hypotheses. Why do we have to consider *hypothetical* cases when we have actual case histories that we may examine? hypothesis, N.

immune ADJ. exempt. Because he fortunately was *immune* from the disease, he could take care of the sick.

impair V. injure; hurt. Drinking alcohol can *impair* your ability to drive safely; if you're going to drink, don't drive.

impartial ADJ. not biased; fair. As members of the jury, you must be *impartial*, showing no favoritism to either party but judging the case on its merits.

imperceptible ADJ. unnoticeable; undetectable. Fortunately, the stain on the blouse was *imperceptible* after the blouse had gone through the wash.

implication N. that which is hinted at or suggested. If I understand the *implications* of your remark, Holmes, you do not trust our captain. imply, V.

incongruity N. lack of harmony; absurdity. The *incongruity* of Tom's wearing sneakers with formal attire amused his more fashion-conscious friends.

indict V. charge. If the grand jury *indicts* the suspect, he will go to trial.

indifferent ADJ. unmoved; lacking concern. Because she felt no desire to marry, she was *indifferent* to his constant proposals.

induce V. persuade; bring about. After the quarrel, Tina said nothing could *induce* her to talk to Tony again. inducement, N.

inept ADJ. unsuited; absurd; incompetent. Incomparably *inept* as a carpenter, Ira was all thumbs.

inevitable ADJ. unavoidable. Death and taxes are both supposed to be *inevitable*; however, some people avoid taxes for years.

ingenious ADJ. clever. Always thinking of clever ways to recycle articles, she even came up with an *ingenious* use for styrofoam packing balls. ingenuity, N.

innovative ADJ. novel; introducing a change. The establishment of our PSAT computer data base has enabled us to come up with some *innovative* tactics for doing well on the PSAT.

intricacy N. complexity; knottiness. Philip spent many hours designing mazes of such great *intricacy* that none of his classmates could solve them. intricate, ADJ.

intuition N. power of knowing without reasoning. When asked how she knew so much about people, she smiled and said, "Woman's *intuition.*" intuitive, ADJ.

irrelevant ADJ. not applicable; unrelated. Once out of college, you will find that your SAT scores are *irrelevant* to how well you do in life.

justification N. good or just reason; defense; excuse. The jury found him guilty of the more serious charge because they could see no possible *justification* for his actions.

laud V. praise. The president *lauded* the heroic efforts of the rescue workers during the midwestern floods.

loathe V. detest. Everyone in the audience *loathed* the wicked villain, Darth Vader.

meek ADJ. quiet and obedient; spiritless. Can Lois Lane see through Superman's disguise and spot the superhero masquerading as the *meek*, timorous Clark Kent?

momentous ADJ. very important. We must treat this *momentous* occasion with the appropriate solemnity.

monotony N. sameness leading to boredom. He took a clerical job, but soon grew to hate the *monotony* of his daily routine. monotonous, ADJ.

mutable ADJ. changing in form; fickle. His opinions were *mutable*, easily influenced by anyone with the slightest powers of persuasion.

naivete N. quality of being unsophisticated. I cannot believe that her *naivete* is genuine; she seems too old to be so lacking in worldliness. naive, ADJ.

novelty N. something new; newness. The computer is no longer a *novelty* around the office. novel, ADJ.

obscure ADJ. dark; vague; unclear. Even after I read the poem a fourth time, its meaning was still *obscure*. obscurity, N.

obscure V. darken; make unclear. At times he seemed purposely to *obscure* his meaning, preferring mystery to clarity.

obsessive ADJ. related to thinking about something constantly; preoccupying. Ballet, which had been a hobby, began to dominate his life; his love of dancing became *obsessive*.

opaque ADJ. dark; not transparent. The *opaque* window kept the sun out of the room. opacity, N.

optimist N. person who looks on the good side. The pessimist says the glass is half-empty; the *optimist* says it is half-full.

paradox N. statement that looks false but is actually correct; a contradictory statement. Wordsworth's "The child is father to the man" is an example of *paradox*.

passive ADJ. not active; acted upon. Mahatma Gandhi urged his followers to pursue a program of *passive* resistance because he felt non-violence was more effective than riots and acts of terrorism.

perjury N. false testimony while under oath. When several witnesses appeared to challenge his story, he was indicted for *perjury*.

pervasive ADJ. spread throughout; permeating. The *pervasive* odor of mothballs clung to the clothes and did not fade away until they had been thoroughly aired.

pessimism N. belief that life is basically bad or evil; gloominess. The good news that we have been hearing lately suggests that there is little reason for your *pessimism*.

petulant ADJ. touchy; peevish. The feverish patient was *petulant* and restless.

philanthropist N. lover of mankind; doer of good. In her later years, Mrs. Astor became famous as a *philanthropist* and benefactor of civic organizations.

precedent N. something preceding in time that may be used as an authority or guide for future action. This decision sets a *precedent* for future cases of a similar nature.

pretentious ADJ. ostentatious; self-important; pompous; overly ambitious. Unwilling to seem *pretentious* about his academic achievements, John refused to wear his Phi Beta Kappa key to work. pretention, N.

prologue N. introduction (to a poem or play). In the *prologue* to *Romeo and Juliet*, Shakespeare introduces the audience to the feud between the Montagues and the Capulets.

prophetic ADJ. foretelling the future. I have no magical *prophetic* powers; when I predict what will happen, I base my predictions on common sense. prophesy, V.

provoke V. annoy; anger; incite to action; produce a reaction. The bully kicked sand in the little boy's face to *provoke* him into a fight. provocation, N.

recluse N. hermit. The *recluse* lived alone in a hut in the forest. reclusive, ADJ.

refute V. disprove. The defense called several respectable witnesses whose testimony *refuted* the false statements made by the prosecution's only witness.

reproachful ADJ. expressing disapproval. He never could do anything wrong without imagining the *reproachful* look in his mother's eye.

repudiate V. disown; disavow. On separating from Tony, Tina announced that she would *repudiate* all debts incurred by her soon-to-be ex-husband.

resentment N. indignation; displeasure. The Danish court was aware of Prince Hamlet's *resentment* of his mother's hasty remarriage.

resolution N. determination. Nothing could shake his *resolution* to succeed despite all difficulties. resolute, ADJ.

restraint N. controlling force. She dreamt of living an independent life, free of all *restraints*.

reticent ADJ. reserved; uncommunicative; inclined to silence. Howard Hughes preferred *reticent* employees to loquacious ones, noting that the formers' dislike of idle chatter might ensure their discretion about his private affairs. reticence, N.

reverence N. respect. His attitude of *reverence* was appropriate in a house of worship.

sarcasm N. scornful remarks; stinging rebuke. Bob's feelings were hurt by the *sarcasm* of his supposed friends.

satirize V. mock. Cartoonist Gary Trudeau often *satirizes* contemporary politicians; through the comments of the *Doonesbury* characters, Trudeau ridicules political corruption and folly.

scrutinize V. examine closely and critically. Searching for flaws, the sergeant *scrutinized* every detail of the private's uniform.

serenity N. calmness; placidity. The *serenity* of the sleepy town was shattered by a tremendous explosion.

sever V. cut; separate. Wanting to begin a new life, the released prisoner hoped to *sever* his connections with his criminal past.

shrewd ADJ. clever; astute. A *shrewd* investor, he took clever advantage of the fluctuations of the stock market to amass a fortune.

skeptical ADJ. doubting; suspending judgment until having examined the evidence supporting a point of view. I am *skeptical* about this proposed project; I want some proof that it can work. skepticism, N.

stagnation N. inactivity; lack of progress or development; staleness. Under Lee Iaccoca's leadership, Chrysler became revitalized after a long period of *stagnation*. stagnate, V.

subdued ADJ. less intense; quieter. In the hospital people spoke in a *subdued* tone of voice.

substantial ADJ. ample; solid; in essentials. A National Merit scholarship represents a *substantial* sum of money.

suppress V. crush; subdue; inhibit. After the armed troops had *suppressed* the rebellion, the city was placed under martial law.

surpass V. exceed. Her PSAT scores *surpassed* our expectations.

symmetry N. arrangement of parts so that balance is obtained; congruity. The addition of a second tower will give this structure the *symmetry* that it now lacks.

taciturn ADJ. habitually silent; talking little. New Englanders are reputedly *taciturn* people who dislike idle chatter.

termination N. end. Because of the unexpected *termination* of his contract, Jim desperately needed a new job.

transparent ADJ. permitting light to pass through freely; easily detected. Your excuse is so *transparent* that only a fool couldn't see through it.

uniformity N. sameness; monotony. After a while, the *uniformity* of TV situation comedies becomes boring. uniform, ADJ.

vacillate V. waver; fluctuate. Uncertain which suitor she ought to marry, the princess *vacillated*, saying now one, now the other. vacillation, N.

versatile ADJ. having many talents; capable of working in many fields. Kim was a *versatile* athlete; at college she earned varsity letters in basketball, softball, and track.

vigor N. active strength. Although he was over seventy years old, Jack had the *vigor* of a man in his prime. vigorous, ADJ.

vivacious ADJ. animated; lively. People were immediately drawn to Lise because of her *vivacious* and sparkling manner.

volatile ADJ. changeable; explosive; evaporating rapidly. The political climate today is extremely *volatile*: no one can predict what the electorate will do next. Ethyl chloride is an extremely *volatile* liquid: it evaporates instantly.

vulnerable ADJ. susceptible to wounds. Achilles was *vulnerable* only in his heel.

withhold V. refuse to give; hold back. The NCAA may *withhold* permission for academically-underprepared athletes to participate in intercollegiate sports as freshmen.

6 Reviewing Mathematics

1. **Read each question carefully to understand what the question is asking.** In the multiple-choice questions, look at the answer choices to direct your attention to the purpose of the question. You may find that some of the answer choices are contrary to fact. As you eliminate those that are obviously wrong, you have fewer items from which to choose. Also, sometimes it is quicker to work back from the answers, but try the easiest choices first. Very often the test makers reward ingenuity.

2. **Avoid lengthy computation.** Bear in mind that the test is constructed so that the 50 math questions can be completed in 60 minutes. Should you find yourself involved in lengthy computation, you may be misreading the question or missing a shortcut. If you are dealing with a right triangle of the 3-4-5, 5-12-13, or 8-15-17 type, avoid lengthy computations involving the Pythagorean Theorem. Use your time wisely.

3. If you are answering a question that requires you to apply a formula not given to you (for example, the area or circumference of a circle or the sides of a 30°-60°-90° or 45°-45°-90° triangle), **write the formula on the question paper** to be sure you substitute it correctly.

4. In the multiple-choice questions, **estimate your answer.** Make sure you have chosen a reasonable answer. Give your answer the common-sense test.

5. **Don't panic if you encounter a new type of question.** It may be nothing more than a combination of familiar topics. If unusual symbols are used, replace them with the definitions that accompany them.

6. **Don't expect to be able to answer all questions.** Very few students do. Work carefully and accurately on the questions you can answer, and don't waste time worrying about the others.

7. If you skip a question, make sure to **skip the corresponding number** on the answer sheet.

8. **Express your answer in the units required.** In solving word problems, convert measurements to the same units. If the problem involves hours, minutes, and seconds and you observe that all the answer choices are in minutes, confine your calculations to minutes.

9. If you find that none of the answer choices resemble the answer you get, **the equivalent of your answer may be there.** For example,

$$\frac{a + b}{b} = \frac{a}{b} + 1.$$

10. **If a geometry problem does not provide a figure, draw one.** However, don't waste time making a work of art. No one looks at your scratchwork. If a diagram is furnished, mark it up to help you solve the problem. Also, look for diagrams marked NOT DRAWN TO SCALE. Don't make unwarranted assumptions.

11. All but the student-produced response questions will ask you to choose the one right answer from five choices. In such questions, if you have spotted a choice you are sure is correct, **do not waste time**

examining the other choices. However, a special type of question sometimes occurs in which several possibilities are presented within the question itself; these possibilities are always identified with Roman numerals I, II, and III. You are then asked to state whether I only is true, II only is true, I and II only are true, and so forth. In this type of question, you must examine *all* the possibilities since several of them (and maybe even all of them) may be correct.

12. Most questions present five possible choices, only one of which fits the requirements stated in the question. However, sometimes a special question is asked in which all *except* one of the choices fit the requirements stated in the question and you are asked to choose the one that is the exception. The examiners warn you of this reverse emphasis by printing the word EXCEPT in bold capital letters. In answering such a question, it is helpful to **try to spot some common property that all but one choice share;** for example, all but one may be even numbers, or all but one may be positive numbers.

13. Because most of the regular mathematics questions provide five choices, a random guess is likely to be correct only $\frac{1}{5}$ of the time. But $\frac{1}{4}$ of a point is deducted for each wrong answer in the scoring. Therefore, **it is unwise to make a random guess.** However, if you can definitely rule out one choice, it is not foolhardy to make a guess from the remaining four choices since your odds for picking the right choice now equal the deduction cost for a wrong answer. If you can rule out more than one choice, it is definitely advisable to guess from among the remaining ones because the odds for picking the correct choice are greater than the deduction cost for a wrong answer.

BASIC MATHEMATICS

Symbols

$=$	equals	$\therefore$	therefore
$\neq$	not equal to	$\triangle$	triangle
$>$	more than	$\frown$	arc of circle
$<$	less than	$°$	degree
$\geq$	greater than or equal to	$\angle$	angle
$\leq$	less than or equal to	m $\angle$	measure of the angle
$\cong$	congruent		(degrees)
$\sim$	similar	$\perp$	perpendicular
$\stackrel{\circ}{=}$	equals in degrees	$\parallel$	parallel

Whole Numbers

Integers The numbers 0, 1, 2, 3, 4, 5,...are called POSI-TIVE INTEGERS; 7½ is *not* an integer. WHOLE NUMBERS are 1, 2, 3, 4, 5, ...

Divisibility The number 12 divides by 4 evenly. We therefore say that 12 is divisible by 4 or that 4 is a FACTOR of 12. Besides 4, other factors of 12 are: 1, 2, 3, 6, and 12. Any whole number is divisible by itself and 1.

Prime Numbers A whole number greater than 1 which is divisible only by itself and 1 is a PRIME NUMBER; 2, 3, 5, 7, 11, and 13 are all prime. 14 is not prime since it is divisible by 2 and 7.

Odd and Even Numbers A whole number which is divisible by 2 is called an EVEN NUMBER. Other numbers are ODD NUM-BERS.

Addition: Even + even = even; odd + odd = even; even + odd = odd.

Subtraction: Even − even = even; odd − odd = even; even − odd or odd − even = odd.

Multiplication: Even × even = even; odd × odd = odd; even × odd = even.

Division (assuming the quotient is an integer): odd ÷ odd = odd; even ÷ odd = even; even ÷ even can be even or odd [if the dividend has more factors of 2 than the divisor, the quotient is even; if the dividend has the same number of factors of 2 as the divisor, the quotient is odd: $36 ÷ 6 = (9 × 2 × 2) ÷ (3 × 2) = 6$, but $36 ÷ 12 = (9 × 2 × 2) ÷ (3 × 2 × 2) = 3$].

If an odd number is divided by an even number, the quotient can never be a whole number.

Consecutive Numbers A collection of numbers is CONSECUTIVE if each number is the successor of the number which precedes it. For example, 7, 8, 9, 10 are consecutive, but 7, 8, 10, 13 are not. The following are examples of consecutive even numbers: 4, 6, 8, 10. The following are examples of consecutive primes: 7, 11, 13, 17. However, 7, 13, 19, 23 are not consecutive primes since 11 is a prime between 7 and 13.

Least Common Multiple (L.C.M.) The LEAST COMMON MULTIPLE of two numbers is the smallest number which is a common multiple of both numbers.

Real Numbers

The REAL NUMBERS, also called SIGNED NUMBERS, are *positive numbers, negative numbers*, or *zero*. Zero is neither positive nor negative. The following are real numbers: $+3$, -5, $+6.3$, -0.2, and $+2/3$. If no sign precedes a number, it may be assumed to be positive. Thus 3 may be considered $+3$.

Real numbers can be represented on a line. On a horizontal line a point is selected as a starting point (called the *origin*) and is designated by zero. A unit length is selected, and units marked off to the right of the origin are $+1$, $+2$, $+3$, $+4$, etc.; if this length is marked off to the left of the origin, we obtain points -1, -2, -3, -4, etc. Note the location of $+1\frac{1}{2}$ and $-2\frac{1}{2}$.

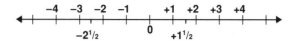

Absolute Value The absolute value of a signed number is the distance of that number from the origin (zero). Thus the value of any nonzero number is *positive*. The absolute value of −3 is 3; the absolute value of +3 is also 3.

Fundamental Operations

Addition To add numbers with the *same sign*, add their absolute values and write the result with the common sign.

$$14 + 12 = 26$$
$$-8 + (-9) = -17$$

To add numbers with *opposite signs*, find their absolute values, subtract the lesser absolute value from the greater, and then write the result with the same sign as that of the number with the greater absolute value. For example, to add −36 and +14, subtract 14 from 36 to get 22 and write the result as −22 since the −36 had the greater absolute value.

$$+36 + (-14) = 22$$
$$-50 + 33 = -17$$
$$50 + (-33) = 17$$
$$16 + (-16) = 0$$

To add *three or more numbers with different signs* you can, of course, combine them in the order given but it is simpler to add all the positives and all the negatives, and then combine the results. Thus, to add −22 +37 +64 −18 −46 +13 −85, we add 37 + 64 + 13 = 114 and −22 −18 −46 −85 = −171. Then we combine the results:

$$-171 + 114 = -57$$

Subtraction Subtraction is based on the following property: $a - b = a + (-b)$

This means that subtracting a number is the same as adding its opposite. The number being subtracted is called the *subtrahend*, so to subtract signed numbers, simply change the sign of the subtrahend and add.

$$
\begin{aligned}
27 - (-18) &= 27 + 18 &&= 45 \\
-37 - (-29) &= -37 + 29 &&= -8 \\
-26 - 14 &= -26 + (-14) &&= -40 \\
42 - (-42) &= 84 \\
-18 - 15 &= -33
\end{aligned}
$$

Multiplication Multiply signed numbers by multiplying their absolute values. If the numbers have the same sign, write your answer with a positive sign. If their signs are opposite, write the answer with a negative sign.

$$
\begin{aligned}
(-4)(-3) &= 12 \\
(12)(10) &= 120 \\
(+8)(-7) &= -56 \\
(-7)(16) &= -112
\end{aligned}
$$

Division Division follows the same rule: divide absolute values and choose a positive sign for your answer if the original signs were the same, or use a negative sign if they were opposite:

$$
\begin{aligned}
35 \div 7 &= 5 \\
-36 \div (-9) &= 4 \\
16 \div (-4) &= -4 \\
-27 \div 3 &= -9
\end{aligned}
$$

Multiplication and Division Involving Fractions

Questions on the PSAT sometimes require knowing the consequences of multiplying or dividing by fractions. If two positive numbers greater than 1 (they may be whole numbers or fractions such as $\frac{3}{2}$) are multiplied together, the product is greater than either of them. For example: $2 \times 3 = 6$

If two positive numbers are multiplied together, and one is greater than 1 and the other is a fraction less than 1, the product is greater than one number and less than the other. For example:

$$4 \times \frac{1}{2} = 2$$

If two positive fractions, both less than 1, are multiplied together, the product is less than either of them. For example:

$$\frac{1}{2} \times \frac{1}{3} = \frac{1}{6}$$

If a positive number greater than 1 is divided by a positive fraction less than 1, the quotient is greater than either of them. For example:

$$4 \div \frac{1}{2} = 4 \times \frac{2}{1} = 8$$

If a positive fraction less than 1 is raised to a power, it becomes smaller; the higher the power, the smaller it becomes. For example:

$$\left(\frac{1}{2}\right)^2 = \frac{1}{4} \text{ and } \left(\frac{1}{2}\right)^3 = \frac{1}{8}$$

ALGEBRA

Some Important Facts

1. In algebra we use letters to represent numbers or sets of numbers. Such letters are called *variables*. When two variables, or a numeral and a variable, are written with no sign of operation between them, we mean that the numbers they represent are to be multiplied. Thus $4abc$ means $4 \times a \times b \times c$.

2. The *factors* of a product are two or more numbers or letters which when multiplied yield the product. For example, the factors of 12 are 4 and 3, and the factors of $2xy$ are 2, x, and y. The factors of $x^2 - y^2$ are $(x + y)$ and $(x - y)$.

3. The *coefficient* is any factor of a term. Ordinarily the numerical value that is multiplied by the other terms is called the coefficient. In the term $5xy$, the coefficient is 5.

4. The *exponent*, written as a small number or letter above and to the right of another number or letter, indicates how many times the number or letter is multiplied by itself: $b^4 = b \times b \times b \times b$.

5. An *equation* is an expression of equality between two quantities. Thus $5x = 20$ is an equation because $5x$ is equal to 20 only when $x = 4$.

6. A *root* of an equation is a number that satisfies an equation. In the preceding example, 4 is a root.

7. A *monomial* is an expression consisting of one term, such as $14ab$, $6x$, or xy.

8. A *binomial* is the sum or difference of two monomials, such as $2x + 4y$.

9. A *trinomial* has three terms, such as $9x^2 + 9xy - 4$.

Fundamental Operations

Addition and Subtraction Most algebraic additions and subtractions are carried out with the aid of a simple pattern known as the *distributive law:*

$$ab + ac = a(b + c)$$

or its corollary:

$$ab - ac = a(b - c).$$

When adding polynomials (more than 2 terms), arrange the like terms in vertical columns. For example, to add $3x^2 + 9x - 4$ and $-7x^2 - 4x + 8$, arrange your work as follows:

$$
\begin{array}{r}
3x^2 + 9x - 4 \\
-7x^2 - 4x + 8 \\
\hline
-4x^2 - 5x + 4
\end{array}
$$

When two polynomials are to be subtracted, arrange them in vertical columns according to like terms and change the sign of every term in the subtrahend. For example, to subtract $9x^2 - 3x - 5$ from $2x^2 + 3x - 8$, change the signs of the first polynomial to $-9x^2 + 3x + 5$, and then add:

$$
\begin{aligned}
2x^2 + 3x - 8 \\
- 9x^2 + 3x + 5 \\
\hline
- 7x^2 + 6x - 3
\end{aligned}
$$

Multiplication To multiply monomials, multiply the coefficients and add the exponents of variables with the same base. For example:

$$(6x^2)(5x^4) = (6 \cdot 5)(x^2 \cdot x^4) = 30x^6$$

To multiply a polynomial by a monomial, multiply each term of the polynomial by the monomial. For example:

$$3x^2(5x^3 + 2x - 3y) = 15x^5 + 6x^3 - 9x^2y$$

To multiply a polynomial by a polynomial, multiply each term of one polynomial by each term of the other, and combine like terms.

A special case of multiplying polynomials is worth studying separately because of its use in factoring. To multiply a binomial by a binomial, note first how the pairs of terms are named:

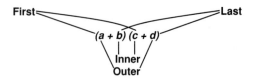

Multiply the binomials term by term in the order F, O, I, L. Frequently, the O and I terms combine to make the product a trinomial or a binomial. For example, to find the product of $3x^2 - 2x - 7$ and $2x - 4$:

$$3x^2 - 2x - 7$$
$$2x - 4$$
$$\overline{6x^2 - 4x^2 - 14x}$$

(Partial product when the multiplier is $2x$)

$$-12x^2 - 8x + 28$$

(Partial product when the multiplier is -4)

$$\overline{6x^2 - 16x^2 - 6x + 28}$$

Removing Parentheses Parentheses are used as grouping symbols and as indicators of multiplication. Often it is necessary to remove the parentheses to simplify expressions that have grouped terms. If the parentheses are preceded by a positive sign they may be removed with no further alteration necessary.

$$(x + y) - (3x + 2y) = x + y + 3x - 2y$$
$$= x + 3x + y - 2y = 4x - y$$

If the parentheses are preceded by a negative sign, then they may be removed only if the signs of each term inside the parentheses are changed to the opposite sign.

$$(x + y) - (3x - 2y) = x + y - 3x + 2y$$
$$= x - 3x + y + 2y = -2x + 3y$$

$$(3x^2 + 2x) - (4x^2 - 3x + 5) = 3x^2 + 2x - 4x^2 + 3x - 5$$
$$= -x^2 + 5x - 5$$

If the parentheses are preceded by a multiplier, carry out the multiplication first and then use one of the rules just mentioned.

$$(x + y) - 5(x + y) = (x + y) - (5x + 5y)$$
$$= x + y - 5x - 5y = -4x - 4y$$

$$4(3x^2 + 2x) - 8(x^2 + 3x - 2)$$
$$= (12x^2 + 8x) - (8x^2 + 24x - 16)$$
$$= 12x^2 + 8x - 8x^2 - 24x + 16$$
$$= 4x^2 - 16x + 16$$

When additional grouping symbols are needed, we use brackets, [ ], and braces, { }. If grouping symbols appear within other sets, remove one set at a time starting with the innermost.

$$4x - \{2x - 3[(x + 2) - (3 - x)]\} =$$
$$4x - \{2x - 3[x + 2 - 3 - x]\} =$$
$$4x - \{2x - 3[2x - 1]\} =$$
$$4x - \{2x - 6x + 3\} = 4x - \{-4x + 3\}$$
$$= 4x + 4x - 3 = 8x - 3$$

Division To divide a monomial by a monomial, divide the coefficients algebraically and subtract exponents of factors that have the same base.

$$x^6 \div x^2 = x^{6-2} = x^4$$
$$-15x^6y^3 \div 3x^2y = \tfrac{-15}{3}\, x^{6-2}y^{3-1} + - 5x^4y^2$$
$$-18x^3yz^2 \div (-6xyz) = \tfrac{-18}{-6}\, x^{3-1}y^{1-1}z^{2-1} = 3x^2z$$

(Note that $y^\circ = 1$ as long as y is any number except 0.) To divide a polynomial by a monomial, divide each term of the dividend by the divisor.

$$(-18x^4 - 6x^3 + 2x^2) \div 2x^2 =$$
$$\frac{-18x^4 - 6x^3 + 2x^2}{2x^2} = \frac{-18x^4}{2x^2} + \frac{-6x^3}{2x^2} + \frac{2x^2}{2x^2}$$
$$= -9x^2 - 3x + 1$$

Factoring

To factor an expression is to find two or more expressions whose product is the given expression. An expression or a number is *prime* if it does not have any factors except itself and one.

Type 1. To factor a polynomial that has a common monomial factor, find the largest monomial which will divide into each term of the polynomial. This is one factor. Divide the polynomial by this factor to obtain the other factor.

Factor: $4x^3y^3 - 22xy^2$
$$2xy^2(2x^2y - 11)$$

Type 2. To factor an expression that is the difference of two perfect squares, find the square root of each term. The sum of the two square roots is one factor and the difference of the two square roots is the other factor.

Factor: $x^2 - 64$
$(x + 8)(x - 8)$

Type 3. Trinomials of the form: $ax^2 + bx + c$

The factors are two binomials where (a) the product of the first terms of both binomials equals the first term of the trinomial; (b) the product of the last terms of both binomials equals the last term of the trinomial; and (c) the algebraic sum of the cross products of these terms equals the middle term of the trinomial.

Factor: $x^2 + 8x + 12$
$(x + 6)(x + 2)$

(a)	(b)	(c)
$x + 6$	$x + 6$	$x + 6$
$x + 2$	$x + 2$	$x + 2$
x^2	$+ 12$	$+ 6x$
		$+ 2x$
		$+ 8x$

Factor: $x^2 + 6x + 8$
$(x - 4)(x - 2)$

(a)	(b)	(c)
$x - 4$	$x - 4$	$x - 4$
$x - 2$	$x - 2$	$x - 2$
x^2	$+ 8$	$- 4x$
		$- 2x$
		$- 6x$

Factor: $x^2 - 3x - 10$
$(x - 5)(x + 2)$

(a)	(b)	(c)
$x - 5$	$x - 5$	$x - 5$
$x + 2$	$x + 2$	$x + 2$
x^2	$- 10$	$- 5x$
		$+ 2x$
		$- 3x$

Roots of Numbers

Some Important Facts

1. The *square root* of a number is one of its two equal factors. The square root of 100 is $+10$, since $(+10)(+10) = 100$. Also -10 is the square root of 100, since $(-10)(-10) = 100$. Thus every number has two square roots.

2. The *principal square root* is its positive square root. It is indicated by writing a radical sign in front of the number. Thus $\sqrt{100} = +10$.

3. A *negative square root* is indicated by a minus sign in front of the radical. Thus $-\sqrt{100}$ means the negative square root of 100.

4. A *radical* is an indicated root of a number or expression. The index of the root is written as a small number above the radical sign. Thus $\sqrt[3]{8}$ where the index is 3, means the cube root of 8, which is 2 since $(2)(2)(2) = 8$. Where no index is written, as in $\sqrt{100}$, the number 2 is understood. Thus $\sqrt{100}$ means $\sqrt[2]{100}$.

5. A *rational* number is a number that can be expressed as the ratio of two integers. Thus, $2\frac{1}{3}$ is a rational number since $2\frac{1}{3} = \frac{7}{3}$.

6. An *irrational* number is a number that cannot be expressed as the ratio of two integers. Thus, $\sqrt{5}$ is an irrational number.

7. To add or subtract, like radicals are combined. To add or subtract unlike radicals, change them to like radicals. To simplify a radical, separate into two factors, one of which is a perfect square. Thus, to simplify $\sqrt{98}$, write it as $\sqrt{49}\ \sqrt{2}$, which equals $7\sqrt{2}$.

REVIEWING MATHEMATICS   117

EXAMPLES:

$$2\sqrt{5} + 5\sqrt{5} = 7\sqrt{5}$$
$$6\sqrt{3} - 3\sqrt{3} = 3\sqrt{3}$$

$\sqrt{50} + \sqrt{2}$ can be written as $\sqrt{25}\sqrt{2} + \sqrt{2}$, *or*
   $5\sqrt{2} + \sqrt{2}$ *or* $6\sqrt{2}$

$3\sqrt{27} + \sqrt{108}$ can be written as $3\sqrt{9}\sqrt{3} + \sqrt{36}\sqrt{3}$ *or*
   $(3)(3)\sqrt{3} + 6\sqrt{3}$ *or* $9\sqrt{3} + 6\sqrt{3}$ *or* $15\sqrt{3}$

$4\sqrt{32} - 6\sqrt{8}$ can be written as $4\sqrt{16}\sqrt{2} - 6\sqrt{4}\sqrt{2}$ *or*
   $(4)(4)\sqrt{2} - (6)(2)\sqrt{2}$ *or* $16\sqrt{2} - 12\sqrt{2}$ *or* $4\sqrt{2}$

8. To multiply radicals, the product of the square roots of two expressions is equal to the square root of the product of the two expressions. Thus
$$(\sqrt{2})(\sqrt{8}) = \sqrt{16} = 4.$$

EXAMPLES:

$$(\sqrt{18})(\sqrt{2}) = \sqrt{36} = 6$$
$$(2\sqrt{8})(3\sqrt{18}) = 6\sqrt{144} = (6)(12) = 72$$
$$\left(\tfrac{2}{3}\sqrt{3}\right)(9\sqrt{27}) = \left(\tfrac{2}{3}\right)\left(\tfrac{9}{1}\right)(\sqrt{81}) = \left(\tfrac{2}{3}\right)\left(\tfrac{9}{1}\right)\left(\tfrac{9}{1}\right) = 54$$
$$\left(\tfrac{1}{3}\sqrt{8}\right)(3\sqrt{2}) = \left(\tfrac{1}{3}\right)\left(\tfrac{3}{1}\right)(\sqrt{16}) = \left(\tfrac{1}{3}\right)\left(\tfrac{3}{1}\right)\left(\tfrac{4}{1}\right) = 4$$
$$\left(\tfrac{1}{25}\sqrt{5}\right)(5\sqrt{5} = \left(\tfrac{1}{25}\right)\left(\tfrac{5}{1}\right)(\sqrt{25}) = \left(\tfrac{1}{25}\right)\left(\tfrac{5}{1}\right)\left(\tfrac{5}{1}\right) = 1$$

9. To divide radicals, the quotient of the square roots of two expressions is equal to the square root of the quotient of the two expressions. Thus
$$\sqrt{32} \div \sqrt{2} = \sqrt{16} = 4.$$

EXAMPLES:

$$\sqrt{75} \div \sqrt{3} = \sqrt{25} = 5$$
$$21\sqrt{162} \div 7\sqrt{2} = 3\sqrt{81} = (3)(9) = 27$$
$$\frac{25\sqrt{32}}{5\sqrt{2}} = 5\sqrt{16} = (5)(4) = 20$$
$$24\sqrt{10} \div 3\sqrt{10} = (8)(1) = 8$$
$$\tfrac{1}{3}\sqrt{27} \div \tfrac{1}{3}\sqrt{3} = \left(\tfrac{1}{3}\right)\left(\tfrac{3}{1}\right)(\sqrt{9}) = 3$$

Solving Equations

Some Important Facts

1. An *equation* is an expression of equality between two quantities. Thus $4x = 20$ is an equation because $4x$ is equal to 20 only when $x = 5$.
2. A *root* of an equation is a number that satisfies an equation. In the equation $4x = 20$, the root is 5.
3. Some equations have more than one root. In the equation, $x^2 - 7x + 12 = 0$, the roots are 4 and 3.
4. An equation is not put out of balance if an arithmetic process done to one-half of the equation is also done to the other half of the equation. We may
   add a quantity
   subtract a quantity
   multiply by a quantity
   divide by a quantity
   raise to a higher power
   extract square root, cube root, etc.,

   provided the process is applied to both sides of the equation.

EXAMPLES:

Solve for x.
$x - 4 = 12$
Add 4 to both sides of the equation:
$x = 16$

Solve for x.
$4x - 5 = 3x + 2$
Add 5 to both sides of the equation:
$4x = 3x + 7$
Subtract $3x$ from both sides of the equation:
$x = 7$

Solve for x.
$$\frac{x}{4} = 12$$
Multiply both sides of the equation by 4:
$x = 48$

Solve for x.
$4x = 12$
Divide both sides of the equation by 4:
$x = 3$

Solve for x.
$3\sqrt{x + 2} - 3 = 4$
Add 3 to both sides of the equation:
$3\sqrt{x + 2} - 7$
Square both sides of the equation:
$9(x + 2) = 49$
Remove the parentheses:
$9x + 18 = 49$
Subtract 18 from both sides of the equation:
$9x = 31$
Divide both sides of the equation by 9:
$$x = \frac{31}{30} = 3\frac{4}{9}$$

Solve for x.

$x + 4 = 12$

Subtract 4 from both sides of the equation:

$x = 8$

Solve for x.

$\sqrt{x^2 - 4} = 4 - x$

Square both sides of the equation:

$(\sqrt{x^2 - 4})^2 = (4 - x)^2$ or

$x^2 - 4 = 16 - 8x + x^2$

Subtract x^2 from both sides of the equation:

$-4 = 16 - 8x$

Add $8x$ to both sides of the equation:

$8x - 4 = 16$

Add 4 to both sides of the equation:

$8x = 20$

Divide both sides of the equation by 8:

$x = \dfrac{20}{8}$ or $2\dfrac{1}{2}$

Solve for x.

$(\sqrt{3x - 1}) = 2$

Square both sides of the equation:

$(\sqrt{3x - 1})^2 = (2)^2$

$3x - 1 = 4$

Add 1 to both sides of the equation:

$3x = 5$

Divide both sides of the equation by 3:

$x = \dfrac{5}{3}$ or $1\dfrac{2}{3}$

Solve for x.

$\sqrt{\dfrac{x}{b}} = a^2$

Square both sides of the equation:

$$\left(\sqrt{\frac{x}{b}}\,\right)^2 = (a^2)^2$$

$$\frac{x}{b}\,a^4$$

Multiply both sides of the equation by b:

$x = a^4 b$

GEOMETRY

A SUMMARY OF IMPORTANT RELATIONSHIPS

Right Triangles

In a right triangle, (leg)² + (leg)² = (hypotenuse)², or $a^2 + b^2 = c^2$ (Pythagorean Theorem).

Special right triangles have sides in the ratio 3-4-5, or 5-12-13, or 8-15-17, with the longest side in each case representing the hypotenuse.

In a 30°-60°-90° triangle:

the length of the leg opposite the 30° angle equals one-half the length of the hypotenuse;

the length of the leg opposite the 60° angle equals $\frac{1}{2}$ the length of the hypotenuse times $\sqrt{3}$.

the ratio of the shorter leg to the hypotenuse is 1:2.

The relationships can be learned and applied by memorizing the diagram:

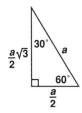

In a 45°-45°-90° triangle:

the length of the hypotenuse equals the length of a leg times $\sqrt{2}$;

the length of the leg equals $\frac{1}{2}$ the length of the hypotenuse

times $\sqrt{2}$.

The relationships can be learned and
applied by memorizing the diagram:

Equilateral Triangles

Each angle of an equilateral triangle has a
measure of 60°. Each altitude of an
equilateral triangle coincides with
a median and an angle bisector,

and its length equals $\frac{1}{2}$ the

side times $\sqrt{3}$.

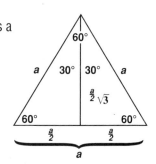

Areas of Polygons

Area of a rectangle = bh.

Area of a square = s^2.

Area of a parallelogram = bh.

Area of a triangle = $\frac{1}{2} bh$.

Area of a right triangle = $\frac{1}{2}$ leg × leg.

Area of a trapezoid = $\frac{1}{2} h(b_1 + b_2)$, where h is the altitude and b_1
and b_2 are the lengths of the bases.

Area of a rhombus = $\frac{1}{2} d_1 d_2$, where d_1 and d_2 are the lengths of
the diagonals.

Circles

The circumference of a circle $= \pi D$ or $2\pi r$.

Length of an arc $= \dfrac{n}{360} \times 2\pi r$.

Area of a circle $= \pi r^2$.

Coordinate Geometry

Distance between two points $= \sqrt{(x_1 - x_2)^2 + (y_1 - y_2)^2}$

Coordinates of midpoint of line $= \dfrac{1}{2}(x_1 - x_2), \dfrac{1}{2}(y_1 - y_2)$

Slope of a line $= \dfrac{y_2 - y_1}{x_2 - x_1}$

Practice Exercises   **Answers given on page 128.**

Fractions

Questions 1–5 are multiple choice. Determine which is the best answer. In the practice tests in this book and in the actual test, you will fill in spaces on the answer sheet. For these questions, circle or highlight the letter of your answer, or write it in the margin.

1. Ann, who owns $\dfrac{5}{6}$ of a parcel of property, sells $\dfrac{4}{5}$ of her share for $48,000. At that value the entire property is worth

(A) $64,800   (B) $69,200   (C) $72,000   (D) $73,600
(E) $84,000

2. A group consists of 22 girls and 18 boys. What part of the group is composed of boys?

(A) $\dfrac{9}{11}$ (B) $\dfrac{9}{22}$ (C) $\dfrac{19}{28}$ (D) $\dfrac{9}{15}$ (E) $\dfrac{9}{20}$

3. In a recent civil service examination, $\frac{1}{8}$ of the candidates failed the first part of the test. Of those eligible to take the second part of the competitive examination, $\frac{2}{7}$ successfully passed. What part of the original candidates were successful in the examination?

(A) $\frac{1}{28}$ (B) $\frac{9}{56}$ (C) $\frac{1}{5}$ (D) $\frac{1}{4}$ (E) $\frac{3}{4}$

4. Jonathan has $\frac{1}{3}$ as many green marbles as he has red marbles and $\frac{1}{6}$ as many red marbles as he has yellow marbles. What part of his collection is made up of yellow marbles?

(A) $\frac{9}{11}$ (B) $\frac{1}{6}$ (C) $\frac{2}{11}$ (D) $\frac{3}{22}$ (E) $\frac{1}{22}$

5. If a 15-gallon gasoline tank is $\frac{3}{8}$ full, how many gallons must be added to completely fill the tank?

(A) 5   (B) $5\frac{5}{8}$ (C) 9   (D) $9\frac{3}{8}$ (E) 10

Questions 6–10 are not multiple choice. They are designed to give practice for the questions on the test with student-produced responses. In the practice tests in this book, and in the actual test, you will be asked to enter your answers in a special grid. For the following questions, write your answer in the blank provided.

6. When 10 gallons are removed from a tank that is $\frac{5}{8}$ full, the tank is completely emptied. How many gallons are now needed to fill this tank?

_____

7. The number which when increased by $\frac{1}{3}$ of itself equals 96 is

_____

8. Joan is three years younger than Martin. How old will Joan be when she is $\frac{4}{5}$ his age?

_____

9. A gasoline gauge registers $\frac{1}{8}$ full. After purchasing 12 gallons of gasoline it registers $\frac{7}{8}$ full. What is the capacity of the tank (in gallons)?

_____

10. After 75 gallons of oil are removed from a cylindrical tank, its level is lowered from $\frac{1}{6}$ to $\frac{1}{7}$ of its capacity. How many gallons should now be added to the tank to fill it?

_____

Percent

Questions 1–5 are multiple choice. Determine which is the best answer. In the practice tests in this book and in the actual test, you will fill in spaces on the answer sheet. For these questions, circle or highlight the letter of your answer, or write it in the margin.

1. In a class composed of x girls and y boys what percent of the class is composed of girls?

(A) $100xy$ (B) $\dfrac{x}{x + y}$ (C) $\dfrac{100x}{x + y}$

(D) $\dfrac{y}{x + y}$ (E) $\dfrac{100y}{x + y}$

2. Seven percent of what number is 14?

(A) 50   (B) 98   (C) 100   (D) 200   (E) 400

3. A baseball team won W games and lost L games. What percent of its games did it win?

(A) $\dfrac{100W}{L}$ (B) $\dfrac{100W}{L + W}$ (C) $\dfrac{W}{L}$

(D) $\dfrac{W}{L + W}$ (E) $\dfrac{100W}{100L + W}$

4. The enrollment in an art class was 300 when the studio opened. The present enrollment is 1200. What is the percentage in increase?

(A) 25%   (B) 40%   (C) 75%   (D) 300%   (E) 400%

5. If a merchant makes a profit of 20% based on the selling price of an article, what percent profit does he make on the cost?

(A) 20%   (B) 25%   (C) 30%   (D) 40%   (E) 80%

Questions 6–10 are not multiple choice. They are designed to give practice for the questions on the test with student-produced responses. In the practice tests in this book, and in the actual test, you will be asked to enter your answers in a special grid. For the following questions, write your answer in the blank provided.

6. What percent of 12 is 3?   _____

7. $66\frac{2}{3}$ % of 30 is 20% of   _____

8. On the average, 8% of the motorists make a right turn at a particular intersection. At that rate, out of 250 motorists, how many will most probably make this turn?

_____

9. Thirty prizes were distributed to 5% of the original entrants in a contest. The number of entrants in this contest was

_____

10. In June a baseball team that played 60 games had won 30% of its games played. After a phenomenal winning streak this team raised its average to 50%. How many games must the team have won in a row to attain this average?

_____

Averages

Questions 1–5 are multiple choice. Determine which is the best answer. In the practice tests in this book and in the actual test, you will fill in spaces on the answer sheet. For these questions, circle or highlight the letter of your answer, or write it in the margin.

---

1. The average of A and another number is B. The other number is

(A) $\dfrac{AB}{2}$ (B) $2B - A$ (C) $2A - B$

(D) $A - B$ (E) $\dfrac{A + B}{2}$

---

2. The average of two numbers is XY. If one number is equal to X the other number is equal to

(A) Y (B) $2Y$ (C) $XY - X$ (D) $2XY - X$ (E) $XY - 2X$

---

3. If b boys each have m marbles, and g girls each have n marbles, what is the average number of marbles per child?

(A) $m + n$ (B) $\dfrac{m + n}{2}$ (C) $\dfrac{m + n}{b + g}$

(D) $\dfrac{bm + gn}{m + n}$ (E) $\dfrac{bm + gn}{b + g}$

---

4. During a closeout sale, 30 pairs of pants are sold at $60 each. The price is then reduced to $50 and 20 pairs of pants are sold. At what price must the remaining 10 pairs be sold in order to attain an average of $55 for the entire 60 pairs of pants?

(A) $50   (B) $52.50   (C) $55   (D) $57.50   (E) $60

---

5. The average of *n* numbers is *a*. If *x* is subtracted from each number, the average will be

(A) $\dfrac{ax}{n}$ (B) $\dfrac{an}{x}$ (C) $an - x$

(D) $n - x$ (E) $a - x$

Questions 6–10 are not multiple choice. They are designed to give practice for the questions on the test with student-produced responses. In the practice tests in this book and in the actual test, you will be asked to enter your answers in a special grid. For the following questions, write your answer in the blank provided.

---

6. What number must be added to 8, 18, and 26 to attain an average of exactly 18?

_____

---

7. A student who strives to attain an average of 80% has the following grades in a certain subject: 70, 74, 81, and 85. What grade must he get in the next test to achieve his goal?

_____

---

8. What was the grade a student received on the fourth test in the Latin class if this student received grades of 80%, 90%, and 95% on the first tests, and then had an average of 75% for all four examinations?

_____

9. If the average of the ages of three men is 44 and no one of them is younger than 42, what is the maximum age (years) of any one man?

_____

10. The average closing price of the five most active stocks was $42. The average closing price of the first four stocks on the most active list was $37. The closing price of the stock that was fifth on the most active list was

_____

Motion

Questions 1–5 are multiple choice. Determine which is the best answer. In the practice tests in this book and in the actual test, you will fill in spaces on the answer sheet. For these questions, circle or highlight the letter of your answer, or write it in the margin.

1. How many seconds will it take an automobile to cover one mile if it is traveling at 45 miles per hour?

(A) 27   (B) 45   (C) 60   (D) 80   (E) 90

2. How many feet will an automobile cover in one second when it travels at 45 miles per hour? (1 mile = 5280 feet)

(A) 66   (B) 660   (C) 2138   (D) 3960   (E) 6600

3. A boy rides his bicycle ten miles at an average rate of twelve miles an hour and twelve miles at an average rate of ten miles an hour. What is the average rate for the entire trip?

(A) 10.8   (B) 11   (C) 12   (D) 20.3   (E) 22

4. A man covers *d* miles in *t* hours. At that rate how long (in hours) will it take him to cover *m* miles?

(A) *dmt*   (B) $\dfrac{md}{t}$ (C) $\dfrac{mt}{d}$ (D) $\dfrac{dt}{m}$ (E) $\dfrac{d}{t}$

5. A motorist travels for 2 hours at 30 miles per hour and then covers the same distance in 3 hours. What was his average rate (in miles per hour) for the entire trip?

(A) 24   (B) 25   (C) 26   (D) 27   (E) none of these

Questions 6–10 are not multiple choice. They are designed to give practice for the questions on the test with student-produced responses. In the practice tests in this book, and in the actual test, you will be asked to enter your answers in a special grid. For the following questions, write your answer in the blank provided.

6. At 40 miles per hour the number of minutes it will take to drive 18 miles is

_____

---

7. How far (in miles) can a car traveling at 30 miles per hour go in an hour and twenty minutes?

_____

---

8. How far (in miles) does a car travel when its average rate is 35 miles per hour and it travels for 3 hours and 24 minutes?

_____

---

9. An automobile party leaves at 7:55 A.M., and arrives at its destination 15 miles away at 8:15 A.M. What was the average rate on this trip (in M.P.H.)?

_____

---

10. Twenty minutes after a plane leaves the airport, it is reported to be 160 miles away. What is the average speed of the plane in miles per hour?

Ratio and Proportion

Questions 1–5 are multiple choice. Determine which is the best answer. In the practice tests in this book and in the actual test, you will fill in spaces on the answer sheet. For these questions, circle or highlight the letter of your answer, or write it in the margin.

1. If p pencils cost c cents, n pencils at the same rate will cost

(A) $\dfrac{pc}{n}$ cents   (B) npc cents   (C) $\dfrac{cn}{p}$ cents

(D) $\dfrac{np}{c}$ cents   (E) $\dfrac{1}{npc}$ cents

2. A formula for infant feeding requires 13 oz. of evaporated milk and 18 oz. of water. If only 10 oz. of milk are available, how much water, to the nearest ounce, should be used?

(A) 7 oz.   (B) 14 oz.   (C) 15 oz.   (D) 16 oz.   (E) 21 oz.

3. Joan can wire x radios in $\dfrac{3}{4}$ minute. At this rate, how many radios can she wire in $\dfrac{3}{4}$ of an hour?

(A) $\dfrac{x}{60}$ (B) $\dfrac{60}{x}$ (C) $60x$ (D) 60 (E) $x + 60$

4. There are 27 students in a chemistry class and 22 students in a physics class. Seven of these students take physics and chemistry. What is the ratio of the number of students taking only physics to those taking only chemistry?

(A) 4:3   (B) 34:29   (C) 7:6   (D) 3:4   (E) 22:27

5. The cost of 7 dozen rulers at $15.60 per gross is

(A) $.91   (B) $1.09   (C) $1.30   (D) $2.23   (E) $9.10

Questions 6–10 are not multiple choice. They are designed to give practice for the questions on the test with student-produced responses. In the practice tests in this book, and in the actual test, you will be asked to enter your answers in a special grid. For the following questions, write your answer in the blank provided.

---

6. The scale of a certain map is $\frac{3}{4}$ inch = 12 miles. Find in square miles the actual area of a part represented on the map by a square whose side is $\frac{5}{8}$ inch.

_____

---

7. If a light flashes every 6 seconds, how many times will it flash in $\frac{3}{4}$ of an hour?

_____

---

8. How many miles are there in 9.66 kilometers if there are 7 miles in 11.27 kilometers?

_____

---

9. If 15 cans of food are needed for 7 campers for 2 days, the number of cans needed for 4 campers for 7 days is

_____

10. A diagram of a plane is drawn to the scale of 0.5 inches equals 80 feet. If the length of the diagram is 4.5 inches, the actual length in feet of the plane is

---

Algebra
Fundamental Operations

Questions 1–5 are multiple choice. Determine which is the best answer. In the practice tests in this book and in the actual test, you will fill in spaces on the answer sheet. For these questions, circle or highlight the letter of your answer, or write it in the margin.

1. If $a = \dfrac{1}{2}$, $b = \dfrac{2}{3}$ and $c = \dfrac{3}{4}$, what is the value of $\dfrac{2a + 3b}{c}$?

(A) $\dfrac{1}{4}$ (B) $1\dfrac{1}{2}$ (C) $2\dfrac{1}{4}$ (D) 3   (E) 4

---

2. Which of the following is the equivalent of $\dfrac{4(O - P) - 8P}{6P - 20}$?

(A) -3 (B) -2 (C) 0   (D) 1   (E) 2

---

3. One-half a number is 17 more than one-third of that number. What is the number?

(A) 52   (B) 84   (C) 102   (D) 112   (E) 204

4. In which, if any, of the following can the 2's be cancelled out without changing the value of the expression?

(A) $2x - 2m$ (B) $\dfrac{\dfrac{x}{2}}{\dfrac{2}{m}}$ (C) $\dfrac{2x - m}{2}$

(D) $\dfrac{x^2}{m^2}$ (E) none of these

5. $-\dfrac{1}{7}$ and 0 are the roots of which of the following equations?

(A) $7x^2 - 3x = 0$ (B) $7x^2 + 3 = 0$ (C) $7x^2 - 3 = 0$
(D) $7x^2 + x = 0$ (E) $7x + 3 = 0$

Questions 6–10 are not multiple choice. They are designed to give practice for the questions on the test with student-produced responses. In the practice tests in this book, and in the actual test, you will be asked to enter your answers in a special grid. For the following questions, write your answer in the blank provided.

6. $\dfrac{1}{y} = \sqrt{.16}$; $y =$ _____

7. If $x^2 = 5$, then $6x^6$ equals _____

8. If $17x + 7 = 19xy$, $4xy =$ _____

9. $3x + 10 = 9x - 20$

$(x + 5)^2 =$ _____

10. $3r - 2s = 0;\ \dfrac{9r^2}{s^2} =$ _____

Solving Problems by Equations

Questions 1–10 are multiple choice. Determine which is the best answer. In the practice tests in this book and in the actual test, you will fill in spaces on the answer sheet. For these questions, circle or highlight the letter of your answer, or write it in the margin.

1. How many cents are there in $2x - 1$ dimes?

(A) $10x$ (B) $20x - 10$ (C) $19x$

(D) $\dfrac{2x - 1}{10}$ (E) $\dfrac{x}{5} - 1$

2. How many nickels are there in c cents and q quarters?

(A) $\dfrac{c}{5} + 5q$ (B) $5(c + q)$ (C) $5c + \dfrac{q}{5}$

(D) $\dfrac{c + q}{5}$ (E) $c + 25q$

3. How many days are there in w weeks and w days?

(A) $7w^2$ (B) 7 (C) $8w$ (D) $14w$ (E) $7w$

4. How many pupils can be seated in a room with s single seats and d double seats?

(A) sd (B) $2sd$ (C) $2(s + d)$ (D) $2d + s$ (E) $2s + d$

5. A classroom has r rows of desks with d desks in each row. On a particular day when all pupils are present 3 seats are left vacant. The number of pupils in this class is

(A) $dr - 3$ (B) $d + r + 3$ (C) $dr + 3$

(D) $\dfrac{r}{d} + 3$ (E) $\dfrac{d}{r} + 3$

6. A storekeeper had n loaves of bread. By noon he had s loaves left. How many loaves did he sell?

(A) $s - n$ (B) $n - s$ (C) $n + s$

(D) $sn - s$ (E) $\dfrac{n}{s}$

7. A man has d dollars and spends s cents. How many dollars has he left?

(A) $d - s$ (B) $s - d$ (C) $100d - s$

(D) $\dfrac{100d - s}{100}$ (E) $\dfrac{d - s}{100}$

8. How much change (in cents) would a woman receive if she purchases p pounds of sugar at c cents per pound after she gives the clerk a one-dollar bill?

(A) $100 - p - c$ (B) $pc - 100$ (C) $100 - pc$
(D) $100 - p + c$ (E) $pc + 100$

9. Sylvia is two years younger than Mary. If Mary is m years old, how old was Sylvia two years ago?

(A) $m + 2$ (B) $m - 2$ (C) $m - 4$ (D) $m + 4$
(E) $2m - 2$

10. A storekeeper sold n articles at $\$D$ each and thereby made a profit of r dollars. The cost to the storekeeper for each article was

(A) $Dn - r$ (B) $D(n - r)$ (C) $\dfrac{Dn - r}{n}$

(D) $\dfrac{D(n - r)}{n}$ (E) $\dfrac{Dn + r}{n}$

Inequalities

Questions 1–10 are multiple choice. Determine which is the best answer. In the practice tests in this book and in the actual test, you will fill in spaces on the answer sheet. For these questions, circle or highlight the letter of your answer, or write it in the margin.

1. If $x = y$ and $a < b$, then

(A) $a + x = b + y$ (B) $a + x < b + y$ (C) $a + x > b + y$
(D) $a + x = b$ (E) $a + x = y$

2. If $a < b$ and $c < d$, then

(A) $ac = bd$ (B) $a = d$ (C) $b = c$ (D) $a + c > b + d$
(E) $a + c < b + d$

3. If $k < m$ and $x = y$, then

(A) $k - x > m - y$ (B) $k + x = m + y$ (C) $k - x < m - y$
(D) $k + y = m + x$ (E) $kx = my$

4. If $a = b$ and $x > y$, then

(A) $a - x = b - y$ (B) $a - x > b - y$ (C) $a - x < b - y$
(D) $a + x = b + y$ (E) $a + y = b + x$

5. If $x < y$, $z = \dfrac{x}{2}$, and $a = \dfrac{y}{2}$, then

(A) $z < a$ (B) $a > z$ (C) $a = z$ (D) $2a > y$ (E) $2x > 2z$

6. If $2y > 5$, then

(A) $y > 2.5$ (B) $y < 2.5$ (C) $y = 2.5$ (D) $y = 10$
(E) $y = 5$

7. In △ABC, K is a point on AB and L is a point on AC, such that KB = LC and AC > AB. Which of the following is true?

(A) $KL = \dfrac{1}{2}BC$

(B) AK > AB

(C) AL < AK

(D) AL > AK

(E) AC < AL

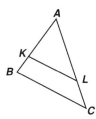

8. If C is the midpoint of AB, and F is the midpoint of DE, and AC > FE, then

(A) AC < DF

(B) DF > CB

(C) AC = FE

(D) AB < DE

(E) AC + CB > DF + FE

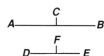

9. Which of the following is true for △ABC? (diagram not drawn to scale)

(A) AC < AB

(B) BC = AC

(C) AC > BC

(D) BC > AC

(E) AB + BC < AC

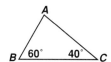

10. *LM* of $\triangle KLM$ is extended to *N*. All of the following are true except

(A) $x = 120$
(B) $y + z = 120$
(C) $x = y + z$
(D) $x < y$
(E) $x > z$

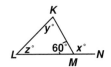

Geometry

Questions 1–5 are multiple choice. Determine which is the best answer. In the practice tests in this book and in the actual test, you will fill in spaces on the answer sheet. For these questions, circle or highlight the letter of your answer, or write it in the margin.

1. A rectangular lot 50 feet by 100 feet is surrounded on all sides by a concrete walk 5 feet wide. Find the number of square feet in the surface of the walk.

(A) 775   (B) 1500   (C) 1600   (D) 5000   (E) 6600

2. A cord 200 inches long can go around a square block 10 times. The area of one side of this square is

(A) 20 square inches   (B) 25 square inches
(C) 100 square inches   (D) 400 square inches
(E) 500 square inches

3. *JK* is perpendicular to *KL* and *MN* is perpendicular to *JL*. If *JM* is 6, *JN* is 4, and *JL* is 18, what is *JK*?

(A) 4
(B) 12
(C) 18
(D) 27
(E) none of these

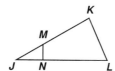

4. Straight line *SROV* is a diameter of circle *O*. *QRT* is a 12-inch chord perpendicular to *SROV*, and *RS* is 3 inches. How many inches is a radius of circle *O*?

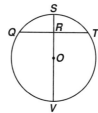

(A) 4.5
(B) 6
(C) 7.5
(D) 9
(E) 12

5. If the length of a rectangle is $3u + 2v$ and its perimeter is $10u + 6v$, the width is

(A) $2u + v$ (B) $7u + 4v$ (C) $4u + 2v$ (D) $3.5u + 2v$
(E) $2v + u$

Questions 6–10 are not multiple choice. They are designed to give practice for the questions on the test with student-produced responses. In the practice tests in this book, and in the actual test, you will be asked to enter your answers in a special grid. For the following questions, write your answer in the blank provided.

6. Straight line *AD* intersects circle *O* at *B* and *C*. *BC* equals radius *OD*. The measure of the angle formed by drawing radii *OB* and *OC* is

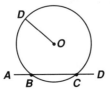

_____

7. Rectangle *ABCD* is formed by joining the centers of equal circles, each having an area of 4π. The perimeter of *ABCD* is

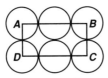

_____

8. The distance between a point with coordinates (5, 9) and another point with coordinates (2, 5) is

_____

9. The center of square *ABCD* is located at point (3, 3) and its sides are along the *x* and *y* axes. The area of *ABCD* is

_____

10. The vertices of rectangle *ABCD* are the points *A* (0, 0), *B* (8, 0), *C* (8, *k*) and D (0, 5): *k* equals

_____

Quantitative Comparison Questions

Questions 1–10 consist of two quantities, one in Column A and one in Column B. Information concerning both quantities appears centered above both quantities. Diagrams need not be assumed to be drawn to scale. Letters used represent real numbers. After comparing the two quantities, choose

(A) if the quantity in Column A is greater;
(B) if the quantity in Column B is greater;
(C) if the two quantities are equal;
(D) if the relationship between the two quantities cannot be determined from the information given.

Column A	Column B

$$a:b = c:d$$

1. bc ad

---

2. $\sqrt{\dfrac{1}{25}}$ 20%

---

3. $\sqrt{1440}$ 120

---

4. The average of 90%, $\dfrac{3}{5}$, and 1.5   3

	Column A	Column B
5.	$\dfrac{a}{4}$ % of 400	a
6.	$\dfrac{a-b}{-c}$	$\dfrac{b-a}{c}$

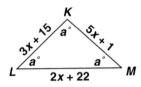

7.	x	7

$$b \neq -c$$
$$\frac{a}{-b-c} = \frac{-5}{c+b}$$

8.	5	a
9.	2 hours, 40 minutes	The elapsed time from 8:55 P.M. to 10:15 the same evening

The distance from Mark's house to the Waban school is 3 miles, while the distance from Sara's house to this school is 4 miles.

10.	The distance from Mark's house to Sara's house	5 miles

Answer Key

Fractions

1. C	3. D	5. D	7. 72	9. 16
2. E	4. A	6. 16	8. 12	10. 2700

Percent

1. C	3. B	5. B	7. 100	9. 600
2. D	4. D	6. 25	8. 20	10. 24

Averages

1. B	3. E	5. E	7. 90	9. 48
2. D	4. A	6. 20	8. 35	10. 62

Motion

1. D	3. A	5. A	7. 40	9. 45
2. A	4. C	6. 27	8. 119	10. 480

Ratio and Proportion

1. C	3. C	5. E	7. 450	9. 30
2. B	4. D	6. 100	8. 6	10. 720

Algebra

1. E	3. C	5. D	7. 750	9. 100
2. B	4. E	6. 2.5	8. 14	10. 4

Solving Problems by Equations

1. B	3. C	5. A	7. D	9. C
2. A	4. D	6. B	8. C	10. C

Inequalities

1. B	3. C	5. B	7. D	9. D
2. E	4. C	6. A	8. E	10. D

Geometry

1. **C**	3. **B**	5. **A**	7. **24**	9. **36**
2. **B**	4. **C**	6. **60**	8. **5**	10. **4**

Quantitative Comparison Questions

1. **C**	3. **B**	5. **C**	7. **C**	9. **A**
2. **A**	4. **B**	6. **C**	8. **C**	10. **D**

7 Practice PSAT Exams

Many students, after taking the PSAT/NMSQT, report that they found the experience very exhausting. Two hours on difficult test material may prove to be very grueling.

To alleviate this situation, the authors wish to offer two suggestions:

1. Become acquainted with the time situation before taking the actual test. Taking the practice exams in this chapter under time conditions will make you familiar with the situation before you take the actual exam. This familiarity should enable you to find the actual exam less rigorous.

2. If you recognize that the exam may be physically tiring, you should recognize that you need to be physically fit. The best advice we can offer is that you stop preparation for the exam several days before the scheduled date. Rest and relaxation will enable you to avoid the fatigue of a long examination and will prove to be more profitable than last-minute "cramming."

ANSWER SHEET—Test 1

Section 1

1. Ⓐ Ⓑ Ⓒ Ⓓ Ⓔ
2. Ⓐ Ⓑ Ⓒ Ⓓ Ⓔ
3. Ⓐ Ⓑ Ⓒ Ⓓ Ⓔ
4. Ⓐ Ⓑ Ⓒ Ⓓ Ⓔ
5. Ⓐ Ⓑ Ⓒ Ⓓ Ⓔ
6. Ⓐ Ⓑ Ⓒ Ⓓ Ⓔ
7. Ⓐ Ⓑ Ⓒ Ⓓ Ⓔ
8. Ⓐ Ⓑ Ⓒ Ⓓ Ⓔ
9. Ⓐ Ⓑ Ⓒ Ⓓ Ⓔ
10. Ⓐ Ⓑ Ⓒ Ⓓ Ⓔ
11. Ⓐ Ⓑ Ⓒ Ⓓ Ⓔ
12. Ⓐ Ⓑ Ⓒ Ⓓ Ⓔ
13. Ⓐ Ⓑ Ⓒ Ⓓ Ⓔ
14. Ⓐ Ⓑ Ⓒ Ⓓ Ⓔ
15. Ⓐ Ⓑ Ⓒ Ⓓ Ⓔ
16. Ⓐ Ⓑ Ⓒ Ⓓ Ⓔ
17. Ⓐ Ⓑ Ⓒ Ⓓ Ⓔ
18. Ⓐ Ⓑ Ⓒ Ⓓ Ⓔ
19. Ⓐ Ⓑ Ⓒ Ⓓ Ⓔ
20. Ⓐ Ⓑ Ⓒ Ⓓ Ⓔ
21. Ⓐ Ⓑ Ⓒ Ⓓ Ⓔ
22. Ⓐ Ⓑ Ⓒ Ⓓ Ⓔ
23. Ⓐ Ⓑ Ⓒ Ⓓ Ⓔ
24. Ⓐ Ⓑ Ⓒ Ⓓ Ⓔ
25. Ⓐ Ⓑ Ⓒ Ⓓ Ⓔ
26. Ⓐ Ⓑ Ⓒ Ⓓ Ⓔ
27. Ⓐ Ⓑ Ⓒ Ⓓ Ⓔ
28. Ⓐ Ⓑ Ⓒ Ⓓ Ⓔ
29. Ⓐ Ⓑ Ⓒ Ⓓ Ⓔ

Section 2

1. Ⓐ Ⓑ Ⓒ Ⓓ Ⓔ
2. Ⓐ Ⓑ Ⓒ Ⓓ Ⓔ
3. Ⓐ Ⓑ Ⓒ Ⓓ Ⓔ
4. Ⓐ Ⓑ Ⓒ Ⓓ Ⓔ
5. Ⓐ Ⓑ Ⓒ Ⓓ Ⓔ
6. Ⓐ Ⓑ Ⓒ Ⓓ Ⓔ
7. Ⓐ Ⓑ Ⓒ Ⓓ Ⓔ
8. Ⓐ Ⓑ Ⓒ Ⓓ Ⓔ
9. Ⓐ Ⓑ Ⓒ Ⓓ Ⓔ
10. Ⓐ Ⓑ Ⓒ Ⓓ Ⓔ
11. Ⓐ Ⓑ Ⓒ Ⓓ Ⓔ
12. Ⓐ Ⓑ Ⓒ Ⓓ Ⓔ
13. Ⓐ Ⓑ Ⓒ Ⓓ Ⓔ
14. Ⓐ Ⓑ Ⓒ Ⓓ Ⓔ
15. Ⓐ Ⓑ Ⓒ Ⓓ Ⓔ
16. Ⓐ Ⓑ Ⓒ Ⓓ Ⓔ
17. Ⓐ Ⓑ Ⓒ Ⓓ Ⓔ
18. Ⓐ Ⓑ Ⓒ Ⓓ Ⓔ
19. Ⓐ Ⓑ Ⓒ Ⓓ Ⓔ
20. Ⓐ Ⓑ Ⓒ Ⓓ Ⓔ
21. Ⓐ Ⓑ Ⓒ Ⓓ Ⓔ
22. Ⓐ Ⓑ Ⓒ Ⓓ Ⓔ
23. Ⓐ Ⓑ Ⓒ Ⓓ Ⓔ
24. Ⓐ Ⓑ Ⓒ Ⓓ Ⓔ
25. Ⓐ Ⓑ Ⓒ Ⓓ Ⓔ

ANSWER SHEET

Section 3

30 Ⓐ Ⓑ Ⓒ Ⓓ Ⓔ
31 Ⓐ Ⓑ Ⓒ Ⓓ Ⓔ
32 Ⓐ Ⓑ Ⓒ Ⓓ Ⓔ
33 Ⓐ Ⓑ Ⓒ Ⓓ Ⓔ
34 Ⓐ Ⓑ Ⓒ Ⓓ Ⓔ
35 Ⓐ Ⓑ Ⓒ Ⓓ Ⓔ
36 Ⓐ Ⓑ Ⓒ Ⓓ Ⓔ
37 Ⓐ Ⓑ Ⓒ Ⓓ Ⓔ
38 Ⓐ Ⓑ Ⓒ Ⓓ Ⓔ
39 Ⓐ Ⓑ Ⓒ Ⓓ Ⓔ
40 Ⓐ Ⓑ Ⓒ Ⓓ Ⓔ
41 Ⓐ Ⓑ Ⓒ Ⓓ Ⓔ
42 Ⓐ Ⓑ Ⓒ Ⓓ Ⓔ
43 Ⓐ Ⓑ Ⓒ Ⓓ Ⓔ
44 Ⓐ Ⓑ Ⓒ Ⓓ Ⓔ
45 Ⓐ Ⓑ Ⓒ Ⓓ Ⓔ
46 Ⓐ Ⓑ Ⓒ Ⓓ Ⓔ
47 Ⓐ Ⓑ Ⓒ Ⓓ Ⓔ
48 Ⓐ Ⓑ Ⓒ Ⓓ Ⓔ
49 Ⓐ Ⓑ Ⓒ Ⓓ Ⓔ
50 Ⓐ Ⓑ Ⓒ Ⓓ Ⓔ
51 Ⓐ Ⓑ Ⓒ Ⓓ Ⓔ
52 Ⓐ Ⓑ Ⓒ Ⓓ Ⓔ
53 Ⓐ Ⓑ Ⓒ Ⓓ Ⓔ
54 Ⓐ Ⓑ Ⓒ Ⓓ Ⓔ
55 Ⓐ Ⓑ Ⓒ Ⓓ Ⓔ
56 Ⓐ Ⓑ Ⓒ Ⓓ Ⓔ
57 Ⓐ Ⓑ Ⓒ Ⓓ Ⓔ
58 Ⓐ Ⓑ Ⓒ Ⓓ Ⓔ

Section 4

26 Ⓐ Ⓑ Ⓒ Ⓓ
27 Ⓐ Ⓑ Ⓒ Ⓓ
28 Ⓐ Ⓑ Ⓒ Ⓓ
29 Ⓐ Ⓑ Ⓒ Ⓓ
30 Ⓐ Ⓑ Ⓒ Ⓓ
31 Ⓐ Ⓑ Ⓒ Ⓓ
32 Ⓐ Ⓑ Ⓒ Ⓓ
33 Ⓐ Ⓑ Ⓒ Ⓓ
34 Ⓐ Ⓑ Ⓒ Ⓓ
35 Ⓐ Ⓑ Ⓒ Ⓓ
36 Ⓐ Ⓑ Ⓒ Ⓓ
37 Ⓐ Ⓑ Ⓒ Ⓓ
38 Ⓐ Ⓑ Ⓒ Ⓓ
39 Ⓐ Ⓑ Ⓒ Ⓓ
40 Ⓐ Ⓑ Ⓒ Ⓓ

ANSWER SHEET

Section 4 (continued)

Only the filled-in spaces in the grids will be scored. Credit will not be given for answers written above the grids.

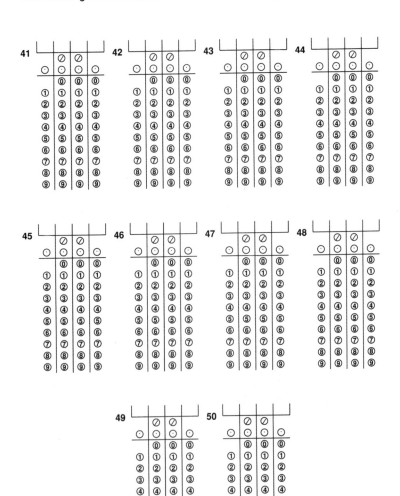

PRACTICE PSAT TEST 1
SECTION 1

29 Questions—30 minutes

For each question in this section, select the best answer from among the choices given and fill in the corresponding space on the answer sheet.

Each sentence below has one or two blanks, each blank indicating that something has been omitted. Beneath the sentence are five words or sets of words labeled A through E. Choose the word or set of words that, when inserted in the sentence, best fits the meaning of the sentence as a whole.

Example:

Medieval kingdoms did not become constitutional republics overnight; on the contrary, the change was ----.

(A) unpopular   (B) unexpected   (C) advantageous
(D) sufficient   (E) gradual

1. Grown weary of constant crowds of reporters pursuing her, the candidate sought ---- at a family hideaway in Vermont.

   (A) company   (B) publicity   (C) seclusion   (D) fulfillment
   (E) diversion

2. Because his helping of food had been far too ----, Oliver Twist beseeched the cook to give him more.

   (A) abundant   (B) savory   (C) generous   (D) balanced
   (E) meager

3. Many educators believe that, far from being a temporary stopgap, useful only as a transitional measure, bilingual education has proved to have definite ---- education in any one tongue.

   (A) correlations with   (B) advantages over
      (C) connotations for   (D) limitations on   (E) influence on

4. Despite all the advertisements singing the ---- of the new product, she remained ---- its merits, wanting to see what *Consumer Reports* had to say about its claims.

   (A) virtues...an optimist about   (B) praises...a skeptic about
      (C) joys...a convert to   (D) defects...a cynic about
       (E) advantages...a believer in

5. Although the coach was a tyrant who ---- his athletes regularly, the players were ---- as long as they won their games.

   (A) pampered...outspoken   (B) bullied...dissatisfied
      (C) browbeat...untroubled   (D) oppressed...rebellious
       (E) neglected...intimidated

6. Though the assault victim had regained consciousness, he was not yet completely ----, and so the police delayed questioning him until he seemed better able to tell a coherent tale.

   (A) listless   (B) impaired   (C) lucid   (D) verbose
      (E) inarticulate

7. In a time of general architectural simplicity and minimalism, the ornate new civic center was ---- for its flamboyance.

   (A) representative   (B) contemptible   (C) conspicuous
      (D) definitive   (E) conventional

8. In the course of learning to deal with the world of ideas, the adolescent gradually becomes able to express him or herself in ---- such as courage and philosophy.

   (A) abstractions   (B) hypotheses   (C) proverbs
      (D) epigrams   (E) alliterations

9. The columnist was very gentle when she mentioned her friends, but she was bitter and even ---- when she discussed people who ---- her.

(A) laconic...infuriated   (B) acerbic...irritated
(C) remorseful...encouraged   (D) militant...distressed
(E) stoical...alienated

10. Gertrude Stein, the novelist and biographer, was the archetypal ---- American: dissatisfied with life in Oakland, she fled abroad, living in France until her death at the age of 72.

(A) parochial   (B) conventional   (C) expatriate
(D) territorial   (E) domestic

11. Since the propensity to migrate has persisted in every epoch, its explanation requires a theory ---- any particular period of time.

(A) tailored to   (B) unconscious of   (C) inapplicable to
(D) independent of   (E) anomalous in

12. Idealistic by nature, James disapproved of the ---- materialism of his classmates who boorishly considered only money and possessions worthy of respect.

(A) crass   (B) altruistic   (C) ethical   (D) cumbersome
(E) credulous

13. Relatively few politicians willingly forsake center stage, although a touch of ---- on their parts now and again might well increase their popularity with the voting public.

(A) garrulity   (B) misanthropy   (C) self-effacement
(D) self-dramatization   (E) self-righteousness

14. In observing the ceremonies and rituals of worship, we must not make a show of our faith: the challenge of religion is to be ---- without becoming ----.

(A) reverent...relevant   (B) irreverent...blasphemous
(C) heretical...caught   (D) pious...sanctimonious
(E) indulgent...obvious

15. The term "rare earths" is in fact a ----, for, paradoxically, the rare-earth elements are in actuality ----, being present in low concentration in virtually all minerals.

   (A) truism...essential   (B) misnomer...ubiquitous
     (C) disclaimer...ephemeral   (D) metaphor...figurative
      (E) mnemonic...unmemorable

16. The term *baroque*, originally applied to the lavishly ornamented style of architecture that succeeded the Renaissance, is used generally in literary criticism to describe excessive or grandiloquent works that lack ---- of style.

   (A) diversity   (B) economy   (C) prolixity   (D) adornment
     (E) comprehension

Each passage below is followed by questions based on its content. Answer the questions following each passage on the basis of what is <u>stated</u> or <u>implied</u> in that passage and in any introductory material that may be provided.

Questions 17–21 are based on the following passage.

The following passage is taken from a book of popular history written in 1991.

     The advantage of associating the birth of democracy with the Mayflower Compact is that it is easy to do so. The public loves a simple explanation, and none is simpler than
Line the belief that on November 11, 1620—the day the compact
(5) was approved—a cornerstone of American democracy was laid. Certainly it makes it easier on schoolchildren. Marking the start of democracy in 1620 relieves students of the responsibility of knowing what happened in the hundred some years before, from the arrival of the *Santa Maria* to the land-
(10) ing of the *Mayflower*.

The compact, to be sure, demonstrated the Englishman's striking capacity for self-government. And in affirming
the principle of majority rule, the Pilgrims showed how far
they had come from the days when the king's whim was law
(15) and nobody dared say otherwise.

But the emphasis on the compact is misplaced. Scholarly research in the last half century indicates that the compact had nothing to do with the development of self-government in America. In truth, the Mayflower Compact was no
(20) more a cornerstone of American democracy than the Pilgrim
hut was the foundation of American architecture. As Samuel
Eliot Morison so emphatically put it, American democracy
"was not born in the cabin of the *Mayflower.*"

The Pilgrims indeed are miscast as the heroes of Ameri-
(25) can democracy. They spurned democracy and would have
been shocked to see themselves held up as its defenders.
George Willison, regarded as one of the most careful students of the Pilgrims, states that "the merest glance at the
history of Plymouth" shows that they were not democrats.

(30) The mythmakers would have us believe that even if the
Pilgrims themselves weren't democratic, the Mayflower Compact itself was. But in fact the compact was expressly designed to curb freedom, not promote it. The Pilgrim governor
and historian, William Bradford, from whom we have gotten
(35) nearly all of the information there is about the Pilgrims,
frankly conceded as much. Bradford wrote that the purpose
of the compact was to control renegades aboard the
Mayflower who were threatening to go their own way when
the ship reached land. Because the Pilgrims had decided to
(40) settle in an area outside the jurisdiction of their royal patent,
some aboard the *Mayflower* had hinted that upon landing
they would "use their owne libertie, for none had power to
command them." Under the terms of the compact, they
couldn't; the compact required all who lived in the colony to
(45) "promise all due submission and obedience" to it.

Furthermore, despite the compact's mention of majority rule, the Pilgrim fathers had no intention of turning over the colony's government to the people. Plymouth was to be ruled by the elite. And the elite wasn't bashful in the least about ad-
(50) vancing its claims to superiority. When the Mayflower Compact was signed, the elite signed first. The second rank consisted of the "goodmen." At the bottom of the list came four servants' names. No women or children signed.

Whether the compact was or was not actually hostile to
(55) the democratic spirit, it was deemed sufficiently hostile that during the Revolution the Tories put it to use as "propaganda for the crown." The monarchists made much of the fact that the Pilgrims had chosen to establish an English-style government that placed power in the hands of a governor, not a
(60) cleric, and a governor who owed his allegiance not to the people or to a church but to "our dread Sovereign Lord King James." No one thought it significant that the Tories had adopted the principle of majority rule. Tory historian George Chalmers, in a work published in 1780, claimed the central
(65) meaning of the compact was the Pilgrims' recognition of the necessity of royal authority. This may have been not only a convenient argument but a true one. It is at least as plausible as the belief that the compact stood for democracy.

17. The author's attitude toward the general public (lines 2–3) can best be described as

(A) egalitarian
(B) grateful
(C) sympathetic
(D) envious
(E) superior

18. The phrase "held up" in line 26 means

(A) delayed
(B) cited
(C) accommodated
(D) carried
(E) waylaid

19. According to the passage (lines 36–39), the compact's primary purpose was to

(A) establish legal authority within the colony
(B) outlaw non-Pilgrims among the settlers
(C) preach against heretical thinking
(D) protect each individual's civil rights
(E) countermand the original royal patent

20. The author of the passage can best be described as

(A) an iconoclast
(B) an atheist
(C) a mythmaker
(D) an elitist
(E) an authoritarian

21. In lines 50–53, the details about the signers of the Mayflower Compact are used to emphasize

(A) the Pilgrims' respect for the social hierarchy
(B) the inclusion of servants among those signing
(C) their importance to American history
(D) the variety of social classes aboard
(E) the lack of any provision for minority rule

Questions 22–29 are based on the following passage.

In this excerpt from her autobiography, One Writer's Beginnings, *the short-story writer Eudora Welty introduces her parents.*

My father loved all instruments that would instruct and
fascinate. His place to keep things was the drawer in the "library table" where lying on top of his folded maps was a tele-
Line scope with brass extensions, to find the moon and the Big
(5) Dipper after supper in our front yard, and to keep appointments with eclipses. In the back of the drawer you could find
a magnifying glass, a kaleidoscope, and a gyroscope kept in a
black buckram box, which he would set dancing for us on a
string pulled tight. He had also supplied himself with an as-
(10) sortment of puzzles composed of metal rings and intersect-
ing links and keys chained together, impossible for the rest of

us, however patiently shown, to take apart; he had an almost childlike love of the ingenious.

In time, a barometer was added to our diningroom wall,
(15) but we didn't really need it. My father had the country boy's accurate knowledge of the weather and its skies. He went out and stood on our front steps first thing in the morning and took a good look at it and a sniff. He was a pretty good weather prophet.

(20)   "Well, I'm *not*," my mother would say, with enormous self-satisfaction.

He told us children what to do if we were lost in a strange country. "Look for where the sky is brightest along the horizon," he said. "That reflects the nearest river. Strike
(25) out for a river and you will find habitation." Eventualities were much on his mind. In his care for us children he cautioned us to take measures against such things as being struck by lightning. He drew us all away from the windows during the severe electrical storms that are common where we live. My
(30) mother stood apart, scoffing at caution as a character failing. "Why, I always loved a storm! High winds never bothered me in West Virginia! Just listen at that! I wasn't a bit afraid of a little lightning and thunder! I'd go out on the mountain and spread my arms wide and *run* in a good big storm!"

(35)   So I developed a strong meteorological sensibility. In years ahead when I wrote stories, atmosphere took its influential role from the start. Commotion in the weather and the inner feelings aroused by such a hovering disturbance emerged connected in dramatic form. (I tried a tornado first,
(40) in a story called "The Winds.")

From our earliest Christmas times, Santa Claus brought us toys that instruct boys and girls (separately) how to build things—stone blocks cut to the castle-building style, Tinker Toys, and Erector sets. Daddy made for us himself elaborate
(45) kites that needed to be taken miles out of town to a pasture long enough (and my father was not afraid of horses and cows watching) for him to run with and get up on a long cord

to which my mother held the spindle, and then we children
were given it to hold, tugging like something alive at our
(50) hands. They were beautiful, sound, shapely box kites,
smelling delicately of office glue for their entire short lives.
And of course, as soon as the boys attained anywhere near
the right age, there was an electric train, the engine with its
pea-sized working headlight, its line of cars, tracks equipped
(55) with switches, semaphores, its station, its bridges, and its
tunnel, which blocked off all other traffic in the upstairs hall.
Even from downstairs, and through the cries of excited children, the elegant rush and click of the train could be heard
through the ceiling, running around and around its figure
(60) eight.

All of this, but especially the train, represents my father's fondest beliefs—in progress, in the future. With these
gifts, he was preparing his children.

And so was my mother with her different gifts.

(65) I learned from the age of two or three that any room in
our house, at any time of day, was there to read in, or be read
to. My mother read to me. She'd read to me in the big bed-
room in the mornings, when we were in her rocker together,
which ticked in rhythm as we rocked, as though we had a
(70) cricket accompanying the story. She'd read to me in the diningroom on winter afternoons in front of the coal fire, with
our cuckoo clock ending the story with "Cuckoo," and at
night when I'd got in my own bed. I must have given her no
peace. Sometimes she read to me in the kitchen while she sat
(75) churning, and the churning sobbed along with *any* story. It
was my ambition to have her read to me while *I* churned;
once she granted my wish, but she read off my story before I
brought her butter. She was an expressive reader. When she
was reading "Puss in Boots," for instance, it was impossible
(80) not to know that she distrusted *all* cats.

22. In saying that her father used the telescope to "keep appointments with eclipses" (lines 5–6), Welty means that

(A) the regularity of eclipses helped him avoid missing engagements
(B) his attempts at astronomical observation met with failure
(C) he made a point of observing major astronomical phenomena
(D) he tried to instruct his children in the importance of keeping appointments
(E) he invented ingenious new ways to use the telescope

23. We can infer from lines 16–18 that Welty's father stood on the front steps and sniffed first thing in the morning

(A) because he disapproved of the day's weather
(B) because he suffered from nasal congestion
(C) to enjoy the fragrance of the flowers
(D) to detect signs of changes in the weather
(E) in an instinctive response to fresh air

24. The word "measures" in line 27 means

(A) legislative actions
(B) preventative steps
(C) yardsticks
(D) food rations
(E) warnings

25. When Welty's mother exclaims "Just listen at that!" (line 32), she wants everyone to pay attention to

(A) her husband's advice
(B) her memories of West Virginia
(C) the sounds of the storm
(D) her reasons for being unafraid
(E) the noise the children are making

26. Compared to Welty's father, her mother can best be described as

(A) more literate and more progressive
(B) proud of her knowledge of the weather, but imprudent about storms
(C) unafraid of ordinary storms, but deeply disturbed by tornados
(D) more protective of her children, but less patient with them
(E) less apt to foresee problems, but more apt to enjoy the moment

27. The word "fondest" in line 62 means

    (A) most affectionate
    (B) most foolish
    (C) most radical
    (D) most cherished
    (E) most credulous

28. By the phrase "brought her butter" (line 78), Welty means that she

    (A) manufactured butter
    (B) fetched butter
    (C) spread butter
    (D) purchased butter
    (E) melted butter

29. Why does Welty recount these anecdotes about her parents?

    (A) She wishes to prove that theirs was an unhappy marriage of opposites.
    (B) The anecdotes are vivid illustrations of truths that she holds dear.
    (C) She seeks to provide advice for travelers lost in the wilderness.
    (D) She envisions her parents chiefly as humorous subjects for ironic characterization.
    (E) She wishes to provide background on early influences on her as a writer.

IF YOU FINISH BEFORE TIME IS CALLED, YOU MAY CHECK YOUR WORK ON THIS SECTION ONLY. DO NOT TURN TO ANY OTHER SECTION IN THE TEST.

S T O P

SECTION 2

25 Questions—30 minutes

Some formulas you may find useful in solving some questions

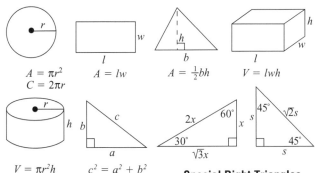

$A = \pi r^2$
$C = 2\pi r$

$A = lw$

$A = \frac{1}{2}bh$

$V = lwh$

$V = \pi r^2 h$

$c^2 = a^2 + b^2$

Special Right Triangles

Triangle: The sum of the measure in degrees of the angles of a triangle is 180.

If $\angle CDA$ is a right angle, then

(1) area of $\triangle ABC = \dfrac{AB \times CD}{2}$

(2) $AC^2 = AD^2 + DC^2$

The number of degrees of arc in a circle is 360.

The measure in degrees of a straight line is 180.

Definitions of symbols:

$\leq$ is less than or equal to	$\geq$ is greater than or equal to
$\parallel$ is parallel to	$\perp$ is perpendicular to
$=$ is equal to	$\neq$ is unequal to
$<$ is less than	$>$ is greater than

<u>Notes</u>: (1) The use of a calculator is permitted. All numbers used are real numbers. (2) Figures that accompany problems in this test are intended to provide information useful in solving the problems. They are drawn as accurately as possible EXCEPT when it is stated in a specific problem that the figure is not drawn to scale. All figures lie in a plane unless otherwise indicated.

In this section solve each problem, using any available space on the page for scratchwork. Then decide which is the best of the choices given and fill in the corresponding space on the answer sheet.

1. If $x > 1$, which of the following expressions decrease(s) in value as x increases?

   I. $x + \dfrac{1}{x}$

   II. $x^2 - 10x$

   III. $\dfrac{1}{x + 1}$

   (A) I only   (B) II only   (C) III only   (D) I and II only
   (E) I, II, and III

2. Which of the following has the largest numerical value?

   (A) $\dfrac{1}{5}$ (B) $\left(\dfrac{1}{5}\right)^2$ (C) 0.3   (D) $\sqrt{0.16}$ (E) 0.01π

3. Which of the following is greater than $\frac{1}{4}$?

   (A) $(0.25)^2$ (B) $\sqrt{\dfrac{1}{4}}$ (C) $\left(\dfrac{1}{4}\right)^4$ (D) 0.04   (E) $\dfrac{1}{250}$

4. The equation $x + 3y = 9$ and the equation $2x + 6y = 18$ are plotted on the same graph chart. All of the following points will lie on both graphs EXCEPT

(A) (9,0)   (B) (0,3)   (C) (6,1)   (D) (12,−1)   (E) (3,4)

---

5. If $ab^2c^3 > 0$ which of the following products is always positive?

(A) ab^2 (B) bc (C) b^2c^2 (D) abc (E) ac

---

6. What is the thickness (in inches) of a pipe that has an inner diameter of 1.25 inches and an outer diameter of 1.55 inches?

(A) 0.15   (B) 0.2   (C) 0.4   (D) 1.65   (E) 0.3

---

7. If $x + x + x + x = y + y + y$, then $4x − 3y =$

(A) 0   (B) 1   (C) x (D) y (E) $x − y$

---

8. The price of a shirt is $8 more than $\frac{8}{10}$ of its price. What is the price of this shirt?

(A) $4   (B) $20   (C) $40   (D) $60   (E) $80

9. If $(x + \frac{1}{2}) + (x - \frac{1}{2}) = 5$, then $2x =$

(A) $\frac{2}{5}$ (B) $\frac{5}{2}$ (C) $2\frac{1}{5}$ (D) 5   (E) 10

---

10. If two parts of molasses are mixed with three parts of sugar, what part of the mixture is molasses?

(A) $\frac{1}{3}$ (B) $\frac{2}{5}$ (C) $\frac{3}{5}$ (D) $\frac{2}{3}$ (E) $\frac{3}{2}$

---

11. What percent of 2 is 20% of 20?

(A) 2%   (B) 4%   (C) 20%   (D) 50%   (E) 200%

---

12. In a school election where 3 candidates sought election the winning candidate received $\frac{3}{5}$ of the votes. One losing candidate received $\frac{1}{4}$ of the remaining votes. What part of the total votes did the candidate with the least number of votes receive?

(A) $\frac{1}{10}$ (B) $\frac{1}{5}$ (C) $\frac{3}{10}$ (D) $\frac{2}{5}$ (E) $\frac{9}{20}$

---

13. If the complete contents of a fish tank $18 \times 6 \times 8$ inches is poured into a tank with a base of 36×18 inches, the height of the water (in inches) will be

(A) $\frac{1}{6}$ (B) $\frac{1}{3}$ (C) $\frac{3}{4}$ (D) $1\frac{1}{3}$ (E) $1\frac{2}{3}$

14. $r = \dfrac{rs}{1-s}$

$s^2 + 2s + 1 =$

(A) $\dfrac{1}{2}$ (B) $1\dfrac{1}{2}$ (C) $2\dfrac{1}{4}$ (D) 3   (E) $3\dfrac{1}{4}$

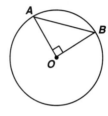

15. In circle O, $AO \perp OB$. The area of $\triangle AOB$ is $\dfrac{7}{\pi}$ The area of circle O is

(A) 7   (B) 14   (C) 7π (D) 14π (E) 49π

---

16. If the diagonal of a table with a square top is 6 feet, what is the area of the table top (in square feet)?

(A) $\sqrt{18}$ (B) 9π (C) 18   (D) $18\sqrt{2}$ (E) 36

---

17. In $\triangle ABC$ the measures of the three angles are represented by $2(x)°$, $(3x - 10)°$, and $(3x + 30)°$. What kind of triangle is ABC?

(A) acute   (B) isosceles   (C) oblique   (D) obtuse
(E) right

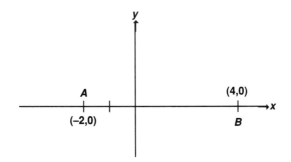

18. In the accompanying figure, points A and B are vertices of $\triangle ABC$ (not shown). The area of ABC is 12. Which of the following could be coordinates of vertex C?

(A) $(-4,-4)$ (B) $(-4,4)$ (C) $(2,4)$ (D) $(4,-4)$
(E) all of these

---

19. In the town of Toonerville there are two high schools. In one school, $16\frac{2}{3}\%$ of the 300 seniors are planning to go to college. In the other school, 90% of the 500 seniors are not planning to go to college. What percent of the seniors in both schools are planning to go to college?

(A) 12.5%   (B) 13.3%   (C) 15%   (D) 43.3%   (E) 87.5%

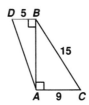

20. In the accompanying figure, $\angle BAC$ and $\angle DBA$ are right angles. $AC = 9$, $BC = 15$, and $DB = 5$. What is the length of AD?

(A) 17   (B) $\sqrt{74}$ (C) $5\sqrt{2}$ (D) 13   (E) 19

21. If $4x = 8y$, then $\frac{x}{y}$ equals

    (A) $\frac{2}{3}$ (B) $\frac{3}{2}$ (C) $\frac{1}{2}$ (D) 2   (E) 3

---

22. The dial of a meter is divided into equal divisions from 0 to 60. When the needle points to 48, the meter registers 80 amperes. What is the maximum number of amperes that the meter will register?

    (A) 33.5   (B) 92   (C) 100   (D) 102   (E) 120

---

23. On a scale drawing A is 5 inches and B is drawn 11 inches. If the actual size of B is 5 meters, then the size (in meters) of A is

    (A) $2\frac{3}{11}$ (B) $4\frac{6}{11}$ (C) 5   (D) 10   (E) 11

---

24. $ab = 50$, $a^2 = 100$, $b^2 = 25$; $(a - b)^2 =$

    (A) 5   (B) $5\sqrt{3}$ (C) 25   (D) 50   (E) 75

---

25. Perfume can be purchased in a 0.6-ounce bottle for $18 or in a 2-ounce bottle for $50. The difference in price per ounce is

    (A) $1.50   (B) $2.50   (C) $5.00   (D) $10.00   (E) $25.00

IF YOU FINISH BEFORE TIME IS CALLED, YOU MAY CHECK YOUR WORK ON THIS SECTION ONLY. DO NOT TURN TO ANY OTHER SECTION IN THE TEST.   **S T O P**

SECTION 3

29 Questions—30 minutes

For each question in this section, select the best answer from among the choices given and fill in the corresponding space on the answer sheet.

Each question below consists of a related pair of words or phrases, followed by five pairs of words or phrases labeled A through E. Select the pair that <u>best</u> expresses a relationship similar to that expressed in the original pair.

Example:

CRUMB : BREAD ::   (A) ounce : unit   (B) splinter : wood
  (C) water : bucket   (D) twine : rope
   (E) cream : butter

Ⓐ ● Ⓒ Ⓓ Ⓔ

30. CLASP : BRACELET ::   (A) snap : hook   (B) buckle : belt
(C) diamond : ring   (D) wrist : watch   (E) cuff : trousers

31. FLEET : SHIPS ::   (A) team : coaches   (B) planet : satellites
(C) shelf : books   (D) committee : meetings   (E) pack : wolves

32. BANK : MONEY ::   (A) cask : wine   (B) ring : diamond
(C) chain : link   (D) body : germ   (E) transfusion : blood

33. FLIMSY : STRENGTH ::   (A) fancy : beauty
(B) hazardous : danger   (C) wary : caution
 (D) slippery : smoothness   (E) clumsy : grace

34. OBSTINATE : MULISH ::   (A) gruff : doglike   (B) clever : dull
(C) inanimate : beastly   (D) coy : kittenish
 (E) domestic : fawning

35. REFUGEE : ASYLUM ::   (A) patient : illness
(B) hermit : solitude   (C) tutor : education
   (D) convict : prison   (E) judge : courtroom

36. INANE : MEANING ::   (A) vacant : space   (B) random : plan
(C) affluent : wealth   (D) certain : direction
   (E) aesthetic : beauty

37. SAP : VITALITY ::   (A) sweeten : temperament
(B) divert : traffic   (C) invest : income   (D) drain : wound
   (E) deplete : resources

38. COUNTESS : NOBILITY ::   (A) judge : jury   (B) celebrity : fans
(C) professor : faculty   (D) miser : parsimony
   (E) nurse : surgery

39. CHAFF : WHEAT ::   (A) mote : dust   (B) gold : lead
(C) dregs : wine   (D) roll : bread   (E) vine : tomato

40. EPHEMERAL : PERMANENCE ::   (A) erratic : predictability
(B) immaculate : cleanliness   (C) commendable : reputation
   (D) spurious : emulation   (E) mandatory : obedience

41. OGLE : OBSERVE ::   (A) haggle : outbid   (B) clamor : dispute
(C) discern : perceive   (D) flaunt : display   (E) glare : glower

---

The passages below are followed by questions on their content; questions following a pair of related passages may also be based on the relationship between the paired passages. Answer the questions on the basis of what is <u>stated</u> or <u>implied</u> in the passages and in any introductory material that may be provided.

Questions 42–52 are based on the following passages.

The following passages deal with the exotic world of subatomic physics. Passage 1, written by a popularizer of contemporary physics, was published in 1985. Passage 2 appeared in a general magazine in 1993.

Passage 1

The classical idea of matter was something with solidity and mass, like wet stone dust pressed in a fist. If matter was composed of atoms, then the atoms too must have solidity
Line and mass. At the beginning of the twentieth century the atom
(5) was imagined as a tiny billiard ball or a granite pebble writ small. Then, in the physics of Niels Bohr, the miniature billiard ball became something akin to a musical instrument, a finely tuned Stradivarius 10 billion times smaller than the real thing. With the advent of quantum mechanics, the musical in-
(10) strument gave way to pure music. On the atomic scale, the solidity and mass of matter dissolved into something light and airy. Suddenly physicists were describing atoms in the vocabulary of the composer—"resonance," "frequency," "harmony," "scale." Atomic electrons sang in choirs like
(15) seraphim, cherubim, thrones, and dominions. Classical distinctions between matter and light became muddled. In the new physics, light bounced about like particles, and matter undulated in waves like light.

In recent decades, physicists have uncovered elegant
(20) subatomic structures in the music of matter. They use a strange new language to describe the subatomic world: *quark, squark, gluon, gauge, technicolor, flavor, strangeness, charm*. There are *up* quarks and *down* quarks, *top* quarks and *bottom* quarks. There are particles with *truth* and *antitruth*,
(25) and there are particles with *naked beauty*. The simplest of the constituents of ordinary matter—the proton, for instance— has taken on the character of a Bach fugue, a four-part counterpoint of matter, energy, space, and time. At matter's

heart there are arpeggios, chromatics, syncopation. On the
(30) lowest rung of the chain of being, Creation dances.

Already, the astronomers and the particle physicists are engaged in a vigorous dialogue. The astronomers are prepared to recognize that the large-scale structure of the universe may have been determined by subtle interactions of
(35) particles in the first moments of the Big Bang. And the particle physicists are hoping to find confirmation of their theories of subatomic structure in the astronomers' observations of deep space and time. The snake has bitten its tail and won't let go.

Passage 2

(40) Imagine an infinitesimal particle that is as heavy as a large atom and less tangible than a shadow. For 15 years, hundreds of physicists have been chasing such an improbable phantom. Their quarry is the top quark, the sole missing member of a family of subatomic particles that form the basic
(45) building blocks of matter. Of six types of quarks that are believed to exist, five have already been discovered. "The top," says Harvard University theorist Sheldon Glashow, "is not just another quark. It's the last blessed one, and the sooner we find it, the better everyone will feel."

(50) Physicists will celebrate because the top is the absent jewel in the crown of the so-called Standard Model, a powerful theoretical synthesis that has reduced a once-bewildering zoo of particles to just a few fundamental constituents, including three whimsically named couplets of quarks. Up and
(55) down quarks combine to create everyday protons and neutrons, while charm and strange quarks make up more esoteric particles, the kind produced by accelerators and high-energy cosmic rays. In 1977 physicists discovered a fifth quark they dubbed bottom, and they have been looking for its
(60) partner, top, ever since. Not finding it would amaze and befuddle particle physicists. Without the top, a large chunk of

the theoretical edifice, like an arch without a keystone, would
come crashing down.

Theorists have already deduced that the top quark is
(65) heavier than any known particle. "A single top quark," exclaims Fermilab physicist Alvin Tollestrup, "probably weighs
at least as much as a whole silver atom does." (With an
atomic weight of 108, a silver atom is made up of hundreds
of up and down quarks.) Exactly how much top quarks weigh
(70) is a question scientists are anxious to answer, but first they
must find some to measure—a task considerably compli-
cated by the fact that in nature these massive but ethereal en-
tities made only a cameo appearance, just after the Big Bang.

Top quarks emerged from the primordial radiation
(75) "around a thousandth of a billionth of a second after the Big
Bang," estimates University of Michigan theorist Gordon
Kane. But as the early universe expanded and cooled, they
vanished. Their fleeting existence left behind a fundamental
puzzle that physicists are struggling to solve: What makes
(80) some particles so massive while others—photons, for example—have no mass at all? Because of its boggling heft, the
top quark should help illuminate what mysterious mecha-
nisms—including perhaps other, still weightier particles—are
responsible for imparting mass, and hence solidity, to the
(85) physical world.

12. Which of the following would be the most appropriate title for the
Passage 1?

(A) Linguistic Implications of Particle Physics
(B) The Influence of Music on Particle Interactions
(C) Matter's Transformation: The Music of Subatomic Physics
(D) Trends in Physics Research: Eliminating the Quark
(E) The Impossible Dream: Obstacles to Proving the Existence of
Matter

43. The author of Passage 1 refers to quarks, squarks, and charms (paragraph 2) primarily in order to

   (A) demonstrate the similarity between these particles and earlier images of the atom
   (B) make a distinction between appropriate and inappropriate terms
   (C) object to suggestions of similar frivolous names
   (D) provide examples of idiosyncratic nomenclature in contemporary physics
   (E) cite preliminary experimental evidence supporting the existence of subatomic matter

44. The author's tone in the second paragraph of Passage 1 can best be described as one of

   (A) scientific detachment
   (B) moderate indignation
   (C) marked derision
   (D) admiring wonder
   (E) qualified skepticism

45. "Matter's heart" mentioned in line 28 is

   (A) outer space
   (B) the subatomic world
   (C) the language of particle physics
   (D) harmonic theory
   (E) flesh and blood

46. In lines 38–39, the image of the snake biting its tail is used to emphasize

   (A) the dangers of circular reasoning
   (B) the vigor inherent in modern scientific dialogue
   (C) the eventual triumph of the classical idea of matter
   (D) the unity underlying the astronomers' and particle physicists' theories
   (E) the ability of contemporary scientific doctrine to swallow earlier theories

47. The author of Passage 2 describes the top quark as "an improbable phantom" because it is

   (A) nonexistent
   (B) discoverable
   (C) lively
   (D) visionary
   (E) elusive

48. Glashow's comment in lines 46–49 reflects his

   (A) apprehension
   (B) impatience
   (C) imagination
   (D) jubilation
   (E) spirituality

49. From the term's use, we can infer that a "cameo appearance" (line 73) is most likely

   (A) noisy
   (B) colorful
   (C) explosive
   (D) brief
   (E) massive

50. The author of Passage 2 does all of the following EXCEPT

   (A) cite an authority
   (B) use a simile
   (C) define a term
   (D) pose a question
   (E) deny a possibility

51. In its assessment of the investigation of the nature of matter, Passage 2 differs from Passage 1 by

   (A) evoking more fully the poetic nature of the search
   (B) addressing more directly the social benefits of the project
   (C) explaining more fully the objectives of the physicists
   (D) giving more emphasis to the difficulties of the investigation
   (E) placing more weight on the inventiveness of scientific
       terminology

52. As Passage 2 suggests, since the time Passage 1 was written, the Standard Model has

   (A) determined even more whimsical names for the subatomic
       particles under discussion
   (B) taken into account the confusion of the particle physicists
   (C) ruled out some of the particles whose existence had been
       previously hypothesized
   (D) refuted significant aspects of the Big Bang theory of the
       formation of the universe
   (E) collapsed for lack of proof of the existence of top quarks

Questions 53–58 are based on the following passage.

The following passage, written in the twentieth century, is taken from a discussion of John Webster's seventeenth-century drama The Duchess of Malfi.

The curtain rises; the Cardinal and Daniel de Bosola enter from the right. In appearance, the Cardinal is something between an El Greco cardinal and a Van Dyke noble lord. He
Line has the tall, spare form—the elongated hands and features—
(5) of the former; the trim pointed beard, the imperial repose, the commanding authority of the latter. But the El Greco features are not really those of asceticism or inner mystic spirituality. They are the index to a cold, refined but ruthless cruelty in a highly civilized controlled form. Neither is the imperial repose
(10) an aloof mood of proud detachment. It is a refined expression of satanic pride of place and talent.

To a degree, the Cardinal's coldness is artificially cultivated. He has defined himself against his younger brother Duke Ferdinand and is the opposite to the overwrought emo-
(15) tionality of the latter. But the Cardinal's aloof mood is not one of bland detachment. It is the deliberate detachment of a methodical man who collects his thoughts and emotions into the most compact and formidable shape—that when he strikes, he may strike with the more efficient and devastating force.
(20) His easy movements are those of the slowly circling eagle just before the swift descent with the exposed talons. Above all else, he is a man who never for a moment doubts his destined authority as a governor. He derisively and sharply rebukes his brother the Duke as easily and readily as he mocks
(25) his mistress Julia. If he has betrayed his hireling Bosola, he uses his brother as the tool to win back his "familiar." His court dress is a long brilliant scarlet cardinal's gown with white cuffs and a white collar turned back over the red, both collar and cuffs being elaborately scalloped and embroidered.
(30) He wears a small cape, reaching only to the elbows. His

cassock is buttoned to the ground, giving a heightened effect
to his already tall presence. Richelieu would have adored his
neatly trimmed beard. A richly jeweled and ornamented cross
lies on his breast, suspended from his neck by a gold chain.

(35)   Bosola, for his part, is the Renaissance "familiar"
dressed conventionally in somber black with a white collar.
He wears a chain about his neck, a suspended ornament, and
a sword. Although a "bravo," he must not be thought of as a
leather-jacketed, heavy-booted tough, squat and swarthy. Still
(40) less is he a sneering, leering, melodramatic villain of the Vic-
torian gaslight tradition. Like his black-and-white clothes, he
is a colorful contradiction, a scholar-assassin, a humanist-
hangman; introverted and introspective, yet ruthless in action; moody and reluctant, yet violent. He is a man of schol-
(45) arly taste and subtle intellectual discrimination doing the
work of a hired ruffian. In general effect, his impersonator
must achieve suppleness and subtlety of nature, a highly
complex, compressed, yet well restrained intensity of temperament. Like Duke Ferdinand, he is inwardly tormented, but
(50) not by undiluted passion. His dominant emotion is an intel-
lectualized one: that of disgust at a world filled with knavery
and folly, but in which he must play a part and that a lowly,
despicable one. He is the kind of rarity that Browning loved to
depict in his Renaissance monologues.

53. The primary purpose of the passage appears to be to

    (A) provide historical background on the Renaissance church
    (B) describe ecclesiastical costuming and pageantry
    (C) analyze the appearances and moral natures of two dramatic
        figures
    (D) explain why modern audiences enjoy *The Duchess of Malfi*
    (E) compare two interpretations of a challenging role

54. The word "spare" in line 4 means

    (A) excessive
    (B) superfluous
    (C) pardonable
    (D) lean
    (E) inadequate

55. In lines 20–21, the author most likely compares the movements of the Cardinal to those of a circling eagle in order to emphasize his

    (A) flightiness
    (B) love of freedom
    (C) eminence
    (D) spirituality
    (E) mercilessness

56. As used in the third paragraph, the word "bravo" most nearly means

    (A) a courageous man
    (B) a national hero
    (C) a clergyman
    (D) a humanist
    (E) a mercenary killer

57. The word "discrimination" in line 45 means

    (A) prejudice
    (B) villainy
    (C) discretion
    (D) favoritism
    (E) discernment

58. The author of the passage assumes that the reader is

    (A) familiar with the paintings of El Greco and Van Dyke
    (B) disgusted with a world filled with cruelty and folly
    (C) ignorant of the history of the Roman Catholic Church
    (D) uninterested in psychological distinctions
    (E) unacquainted with the writing of Browning

IF YOU FINISH BEFORE TIME IS CALLED, YOU MAY CHECK YOUR WORK ON THIS SECTION ONLY. DO NOT TURN TO ANY OTHER SECTION IN THE TEST.

S T O P

SECTION 4

25 Questions—30 minutes

Some formulas you may find useful in solving some questions

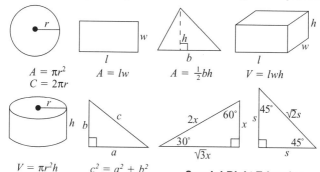

$A = \pi r^2$
$C = 2\pi r$

$A = lw$

$A = \frac{1}{2}bh$

$V = lwh$

$V = \pi r^2 h$

$c^2 = a^2 + b^2$

Special Right Triangles

Triangle: The sum of the measure in degrees of the angles of a triangle is 180.

If $\angle CDA$ is a right angle, then

(1) area of $\triangle ABC = \dfrac{AB \times CD}{2}$

(2) $AC^2 = AD^2 + DC^2$

The number of degrees of arc in a circle is 360.

The measure in degrees of a straight line is 180.

Definitions of symbols:

$\leq$	is less than or equal to	$\geq$	is greater than or equal to
$\parallel$	is parallel to	$\perp$	is perpendicular to
$=$	is equal to	$\neq$	is unequal to
$<$	is less than	$>$	is greater than

<u>Notes:</u> (1) The use of a calculator is permitted. All numbers used are real numbers. (2) Figures that accompany problems in this test are intended to provide information useful in solving the problems. They are drawn as accurately as possible EXCEPT when it is stated in a specific problem that the figure is not drawn to scale. All figures lie in a plane unless otherwise indicated.

This section contains two types of questions. You have 30 minutes to complete both types. You may use any available space for scratchwork.

PART I: QUANTITATIVE COMPARISON QUESTIONS

Questions 26–40 each consist of two quantities in boxes, one in Column A and one in Column B. You are to compare the two quantities and on the answer sheet fill in

A if the quantity in Column A is greater;
B if the quantity in Column B is greater;
C if the two quantities are equal;
D if the relationship cannot be determined from the information given.

Notes: (1) In some questions, information is given about one or both of the quantities to be compared. In such cases, the given information is centered above the two columns and is not boxed. (2) In a given question, a symbol that appears in both columns represents the same thing in Column A as it does in Column B. (3) Letters such as x, n, and k stand for real numbers.

Column A	Column B

26. x^3 x^2

The sum of a, b, and c, three consecutive integers, is 18.

27. abc 210

	Column A	Column B

$x = 1$ and $y = -1$

28. $\dfrac{a(x + y)}{b}$ $\qquad\qquad$ $\dfrac{2a(x + y)}{b}$

$$\frac{x}{-y - z} = \frac{-a}{y + z}$$

29. $\qquad x$ $\qquad\qquad a$

$$3x + 5y = 15 + 5y$$

30. $\qquad \dfrac{x}{5}$ $\qquad\qquad 1$

---

31. The time elapsed from $\qquad$ 2 hours,
8:55 A.M. until 10:15 $\qquad$ 40 minutes
the same morning

Z is 4 miles from Y.
X is 3 miles from Y.

32. The distance from X to Z $\qquad\qquad$ 5 miles

A bag contains 3 red marbles, 4 white marbles, and 5
green marbles. One marble is drawn without looking.
At the same time a coin is tossed two times.

33. Probability of drawing $\qquad$ Probability of tossing
a white marble. $\qquad$ two heads.

<u>Column A</u>   <u>Column B</u>

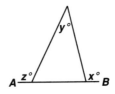

AB is a straight line and *x* = 100, *y* = 40.

34.   *z*   *x* + *y*

---

35. $\dfrac{BC}{AB} \cdot \dfrac{AC}{BC}$ 1

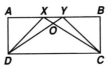

ABCD is a rectangle.

36.   The area of △*XOD*   The area of △*YOC*

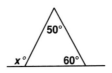

37.   *x*   70

	Column A	Column B
38.	The product of $2\frac{1}{2}$ and its reciprocal	The product of $3\frac{1}{2}$ and its reciprocal

---

39.	$3x$	$(-2)x$

40.	The area of a rectangle with length equal to 8 feet	The area of a square with side equal to 8 feet

---

PART II: STUDENT-PRODUCED RESPONSE QUESTIONS

Each of the remaining 10 questions (41–50) requires you to solve the problem and enter your answer by marking the spaces in the special grid, as shown in the examples below.

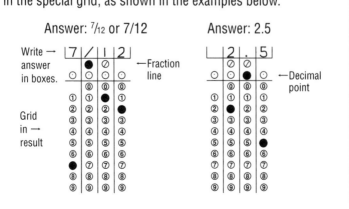

Answer: 201
Either position is correct.

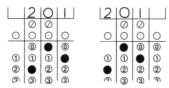

<u>Note</u>: Your may start your answers in any column, space permitting. Columns not needed should be left blank.

- Mark no more than one space in any column.

- Because the answer sheet will be machine-scored, **you will receive credit only if the spaces are filled in correctly**.

- Although not required, it is suggested that you write your answer in the boxes at the top of the columns to help you fill in the spaces correctly.

- Some problems may have more than one correct answer. In such cases, grid only one answer.

- No question has a negative answer.

- **Mixed numbers** such $2\frac{1}{2}$ must be gridded as 2.5 or $\frac{5}{2}$. (If $2\frac{1}{2}$ is gridded, it will be interpreted as $\frac{21}{2}$, not $2\frac{1}{2}$.)

- **Decimal Accuracy:** If you obtain a decimal answer, **enter the most accurate value that the grid will accommodate**. For example, if you obtain an answer such as 0.6666..., you should record the result as .666 or .667. **Less accurate values such as .66 or .67 are not acceptable**.

- Acceptable ways to grid $\frac{2}{3}$ = .6666 . . .

41. How many dimes must I give the postal clerk for thirty 25¢ postage stamps?

_____

42. Twenty minutes after a car enters a turnpike it is 20 miles from the entrance gate. What was the average speed (in miles per hour)?

_____

43. If the diameter of a circle is doubled, what will the area be multiplied by?

_____

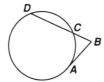

44. ∠B is formed by secant _DCB_ and tangent _AB_. If the measure of ∠B is 70° and $\widehat{CA}$ is 70°, how many degrees are in $\widehat{DC}$?

_____

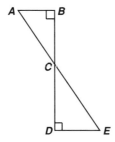

45. In the accompanying figure, _ACE_ and _BCD_ are straight lines and _B_ and _D_ are right angles. What is the length of _AB_ if _BC_ = 12, _CD_ = 16, and _DE_ = 12?

_____

46. What is the sum of $\frac{0.3}{9}$ and $\frac{0.6}{9}$?

___

47. Lori can prepare 9 envelopes for mailing in 12 minutes. This task includes typing the address, assembling and enclosing the contents, and affixing the proper postage. How many envelopes can she prepare in 8 hours?

___

48. If $2^{x+2} = 16$, what does x equal?

___

49. The notation on the map reads "Scale: 1 inch = 150 miles." What is the distance (in miles) from Waban to Madison, which are $3\frac{1}{2}$ inches apart on this map?

___

50. A jar contains four red marbles, seven green marbles, and some blue marbles. If the probability of randomly selecting a marble that is *not* green is $\frac{2}{3}$, how many blue marbles are in the jar?

___

IF YOU FINISH BEFORE TIME IS CALLED, YOU MAY CHECK YOUR WORK ON THIS SECTION ONLY. DO NOT TURN TO ANY OTHER SECTION IN THE TEST.   **S T O P**

Answer Key

Section 1   Verbal

1. **C**	7. **C**	13. **C**	19. **A**	25. **C**
2. **E**	8. **A**	14. **D**	20. **A**	26. **E**
3. **B**	9. **B**	15. **B**	21. **A**	27. **D**
4. **B**	10. **C**	16. **B**	22. **C**	28. **A**
5. **C**	11. **D**	17. **E**	23. **D**	29. **E**
6. **C**	12. **A**	18. **B**	24. **B**	

Section 2   Math

Note: Each correct answer to the mathematics questions is keyed by number to the corresponding math topic. These numerals refer to the topics listed below.

1. Basic Fundamental Operations	9. Averages
2. Algebraic Operations	10. Motion
3. Using Algebra	11. Ratio and Proportion
4. Exponents, Roots, and Radicals	12. Mixtures and Solutions
5. Inequalities	13. Work
6. Fractions	14. Coordinate Geometry
7. Decimals	15. Geometry
8. Percent	16. Quantitative Comparisons
	17. Data Interpretation

1. **C** (2)	8. **C** (1)	15. **B** (15)	22. **C** (11)
2. **D** (1, 6, 7)	9. **D** (2)	16. **C** (15)	23. **A** (11)
3. **B** (4, 6, 7)	10. **B** (6)	17. **E** (15)	24. **C** (2)
4. **E** (3, 14)	11. **E** (3, 8)	18. **E** (14, 15)	25. **C** (1)
5. **E** (4)	12. **A** (6)	19. **A** (8)	
6. **A** (1, 7)	13. **D** (15)	20. **D** (15)	
7. **A** (2)	14. **C** (2)	21. **B** (4)	

Section 3   Verbal

31. **D**	37. **A**	43. **A**	49. **D**	55. **B**
32. **B**	38. **B**	44. **D**	50. **E**	56. **D**
33. **D**	39. **B**	45. **A**	51. **D**	57. **B**
34. **B**	40. **B**	46. **B**	52. **B**	58. **A**
35. **C**	41. **E**	47. **D**	53. **B**	59. **A**
36. **C**	42. **E**	48. **D**	54. **D**	60. **D**

Section 4   Math

26. **D** (4, 16)	30. **C** (2)	34. **B** (15, 16)	38. **C** (6, 16)
27. **C** (1, 16)	31. **B** (1, 8)	35. **C** (15, 16)	39. **D** (2, 16)
28. **C** (2)	32. **D** (15)	36. **C** (15, 16)	40. **D** (15, 16)
29. **C** (2)	33. **A** (1, 4)	37. **A** (15, 16)	

(1)

41 7 5

(10)

42 6 0

Section 4 (continued)

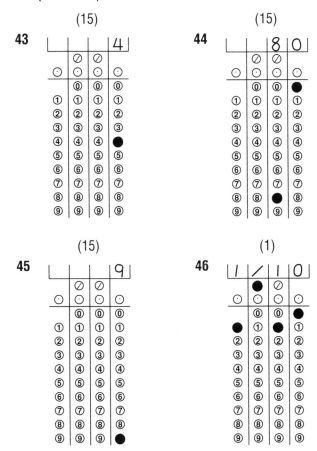

Section 4 (continued)

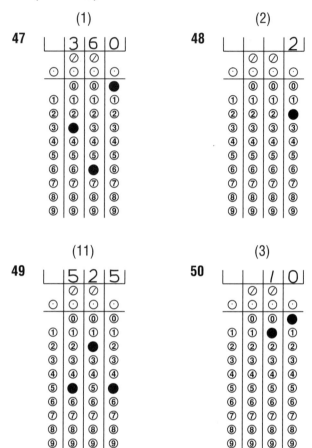

ANSWER EXPLANATIONS

Verbal Reasoning   Section 1

1. **(C)** Someone tired of being chased by reporters would logically seek to escape to *seclusion* (an isolated place of withdrawal).

2. **(E)** Oliver asks for more because his first helping has been too *meager* (skimpy).

3. **(B)** If bilingual education is more than a mere stopgap (a somewhat negative description), it must possess certain positive qualities. Thus it has *advantages over* education in a single tongue. Note the use of *far from* to signal the contrast between the negative and positive views on bilingual education.

4. **(B)** The word "despite" signals a contrast. Despite the advertised *praises*, she had doubts—she remained a *skeptic about* the product. Note also that "singing the praises of" is a cliché, a customary phrase.

5. **(C)** A tyrant or harsh ruler would *browbeat* or bully his subjects, yet if such methods helped players win games, they might be unworried or *untroubled* by them. Note the conjunction *although*, which signals a contrast.

6. **(C)** The police want the assault victim to give them a clear, understandable story; therefore, they're willing to wait until he's completely *lucid* (clearheaded; intelligible).

7. **(C)** *Ornate* means highly decorated. An ornate building would stand out from simple, unadorned neighbors: it would be *conspicuous* for its flamboyance.

8. **(A)** Words like "courage" and "philosophy" are *abstractions* (words representing ideas rather than concrete objects).

9. **(B)** The columnist was *acerbic* (bitingly sarcastic) in writing of those who provoked or *irritated* her. Note the use of *but* to establish the contrast between the two clauses, and the use of *even* to indicate that the missing word is stronger than *bitter*.

10. **(C)** By definition, an *expatriate* is one who lives in a foreign country in preference to living in his or her native land. Stein is a classic example of the expatriate American.

11. (D) Because the tendency to migrate exists in all time periods, you cannot fully explain it on the basis of any single time period. Your explanation, like the phenomenon itself, must be *independent* of any particular period of time. The conjunction *since* is used here as a synonym for *because*; it indicates a cause and effect relationship.

12. (A) People who consider only material goods worth their respect are guilty of *crass* (unrefined, grossly stupid) materialism. Note that the phrase "crass materialism" is a cliché, a commonplace expression.

13. (C) The politicians do not forsake center stage. However, if they did forgo being the center of attention once in a while, the public might like them better for their *self-effacement* (withdrawal from attention).

14. (D) Someone *sanctimonious* makes a show of religious faith; someone truly *pious* or devout does not.

15. (B) If the rare earths are actually present to some degree in essentially all minerals, then they are not rare after all. Thus the term "rare earths" is a *misnomer* (incorrect designation), for the rare earths are actually *ubiquitous* (omnipresent; found everywhere). Watch out for words that signal the unexpected. Note the use of "paradoxically" here.

16. (B) By definition, an excessive or grandiloquent literary work lacks *economy* or conciseness in verbal expression. Note that you are dealing with a secondary meaning of *economy* here.

17. (E) By stating that the public loves a simple explanation and by commenting on how much easier it is for schoolchildren to ignore what happened on the American continent from 1492 to 1620, the historian-author reveals a *superior* attitude toward the public at large, who are content with easy answers.

18. (B) The democracy-rejecting Pilgrims would have been amazed to find themselves held up or *cited* as defenders of democracy.

19. (A) The Pilgrims had been given a royal patent legally empowering them to settle in a certain area. Because they had decided to colonize a different area, some of the group felt that once they were ashore no laws would bind them. The compact bound the signers to obey the laws of the colony. It thus served to *establish legal authority within the colony*.

20. **(A)** In debunking the image of the Mayflower Compact as the cornerstone of American democracy, the author reveals himself to be an *iconoclast*, an attacker of established beliefs.

21. **(A)** According to the passage, the Pilgrims signed the Mayflower Compact in order of rank: first, the gentlemen; next, the "goodmen" or yeoman-farmers; finally, the servants. In doing so they showed their *respect for the social hierarchy*.

22. **(C)** Welty's father used his telescope to observe the moon and the Big Dipper. An eager amateur astronomer, he clearly *made a point of observing* eclipses and other major astronomical phenomena.

23. **(D)** Welty calls her father a "pretty good weather prophet," saying he had "the country boy's accurate knowledge of the weather and its skies." In support of this, she describes his going out on the porch first thing in the morning for a look at the weather and a sniff. This suggests he sniffed the air *to detect signs of changes in the weather*.

24. **(B)** Caring for his children, the father warned them to take *preventative steps* (such as moving away from the windows during electrical storms) to avoid being hit by lightning.

25. **(C)** Exhilarated by the thunderstorm (she "always loved a storm!"), the mother stands apart from the rest of the family, urging them to share her excitement over the *sounds of the storm*.

26. **(E)** Running through thunderstorms unworried by lightning bolts, Welty's mother was clearly *less apt to foresee problems* than Welty's father was; she also was *more apt to enjoy the moment*.

27. **(D)** Welty's father held dear his beliefs in progress and in the future; these were his fondest, *most cherished* beliefs.

28. **(A)** Welty's ambition was to beat the milk in the churn and make butter while her mother read to her; her mother finished reading the story before Welty finished *manufacturing butter* for her.

29. **(E)** Welty calls her autobiography *One Writer's Beginnings*. In this passage she shows how her father and mother, with their different gifts, were preparing her for life, especially for the life of a writer. Her father gave her his love of ingenious devices, his countryboy's knowledge of terrain. Her mother gave her books, a love of reading, a sense of the sound of words. Both parents helped form her "strong meteorological sensibility" that affected her later tales.

Mathematical Reasoning   Section 2

1. **(C)** As x increases in value, the denominator $(x + 1)$ also increases and the value of the fraction $\dfrac{1}{x+1}$ decreases. The values of expressions I and II will both increase as the value of x increases.

2. **(D)** (A) $\frac{1}{5} = 0.2$ (B) $\left(\frac{1}{5}\right)^2 = \frac{1}{25} = 0.04$ (C) 0.3

   (D) $\sqrt{0.16} = 0.4$

   (E) $0.01\pi = 0.01\,(3.14) = 0.0314$

3. **(B)** In both (A) $(0.25)^2 = \left(\frac{1}{4}\right)^2$ and (C) $\left(\frac{1}{4}\right)^4$, raising to a power makes the fraction smaller.

   (B) $\sqrt{\frac{1}{4}} = \frac{1}{2}$ and $\frac{1}{2} > \frac{1}{4}$.   (D) $0.04 = \frac{4}{100}$ and

   (E) $\frac{1}{250}$ are both very small.

4. **(E)** Dividing each term of the second equation by 2 makes it $x + 3y = 9$, and therefore the two equations are equivalent. Any point that lies on one must lie on the other; their graphs are identical. Thus, it is necessary to test each point by substituting in only one of the two equations to see whether it is satisfied. Point $(3,4)$ does not check: $3 + 3(4) \neq 9$.

5. **(E)** If $ab^2c^3 > 0$, then $(ac)(b^2c^2) > 0$. Because b^2c^2 is always positive, the factor (ac) must be positive in order that the product $(ac)(b^2c^2)$ is positive.

6. **(A)** Outside radius = 0.775 inch
   Inside radius = 0.625 inch
   Difference = 0.15

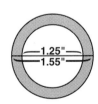

1.25"
1.55"

7. **(A)** $4x = 3y$; subtract $3y$, and then $4x - 3y = 0$.

8. **(C)** \$8 must equal the remaining $\frac{2}{10}$ of the price. Therefore $\frac{1}{10}$ is \$4, and $\frac{10}{10}$, the whole price, is \$40.

9. (D) $x + \frac{1}{2} + x - \frac{1}{2} = 5$

$\qquad\qquad 2x = 5$

10. (B) $\dfrac{\text{molasses}}{\text{molasses} + \text{sugar}} = \dfrac{2}{2 + 3} = \dfrac{2}{5}$

11. (E) 20% of 20 or $\frac{1}{5} \cdot 20 = 4$

$\% = \frac{?}{100}$

$\frac{?}{100} \cdot 2 = 4$

$\frac{(2)(?)}{100} = 4;$ $\quad (2)(?) = 400;$ $\quad ? = 200$

12. (A) Winning candidate got $\frac{3}{5}$ of the votes. One loser received $\frac{1}{4}$ of $\frac{2}{5}$ or $\frac{1}{10}$. Since the other loser received $\frac{3}{4}$ of $\frac{2}{5}$, he must have received more votes than the one who received $\frac{1}{10}$ of the votes.

13. (D) Let $x =$ height of water in tank.
Volume of water in first tank $= (18'')(6'')(8'')$.
This volume is the same for the second tank $= (36'')(18'')(x)$.

$(\overset{3}{\cancel{36}})(\cancel{18})(x) = (\overset{}{\cancel{18''}})(\cancel{6''})(\overset{4}{\cancel{8''}})$
$3x = 4$
$x = 1\frac{1}{3}$ inches

14. (C) $\qquad r = \dfrac{rs}{1 - s}$

$\qquad r - rs = rs$

$\qquad\qquad r = 2rs$

$\qquad\qquad \dfrac{r}{2r} = s$

$\qquad\qquad \frac{1}{2} = s$

Substitute in $s^2 + 2s + 1$:

$\left(\frac{1}{2}\right)^2 + (2)\left(\frac{1}{2}\right) + 1$

$\frac{1}{4} + 1 + 1 = 2\frac{1}{4}$

15. (B) Let x = radius of circle.

$OA = OB$ = radius

$$\frac{(OA)(OB)}{2} = \frac{\text{area of}}{\text{triangle}} = \frac{7}{\pi}$$

$$\frac{(x)(x)}{2} = \frac{7}{\pi}$$

$$\frac{x^2}{2} = \frac{7}{\pi}$$

$\pi x^2 = 14$ [area of circle $(\pi)(\text{radius})^2$]

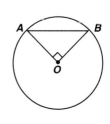

16. (B) Let x = side of square
$x^2 + x^2 = 36$
[Pythagorean Theorem]
$2x^2 = 36$
$x^2 = 18$
(area of square)

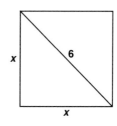

17. (E) $2x + (3x - 10)° + (3x + 30)° = 180°$
$2x + 3x - 10° + 3x + 30° = 180°$
$8x = 160°$
$x = 20°$
Therefore one angle = $2x$ or $40°$
A second angle = $60° - 10°$ or $50°$
The third angle is a right angle, since $60° + 30° = 90°$.

18. (E) The base of $\triangle ABC$ is 6 units. The altitude must be 4 units to attain an area of 12. All choice have altitudes of 4.

19. (A) $16\frac{2}{3}\%$ or $\frac{1}{6}$ of 300 = 50

10% or $\frac{1}{10}$ of 500 = 50

Total number going to college = 100

$\frac{100}{800} = \frac{1}{8} = 12\frac{1}{2}\%$ or 12.5%

20. (D) $\triangle BAC$ is a 3-4-5 right triangle with $AC = 3(3)$ and hypotenuse $BC = 3(5)$; therefore $AB = 3(4)$ or 12.
$\triangle ABD$ is a 5-12-13 right triangle; therefore $AD = 13$.

21. (B) Because $4^x = 8^y$, $(2^2)^x = (2^3)^y$ or $2^{2x} = 2^{3y}$.

Thus, $2x = 3y$ and $\dfrac{x}{y} = \dfrac{3}{2}$.

22. (C) A reading of 48 corresponds to 80 amperes. Let a reading of 60 correspond to x amperes.

$$\frac{48}{80} = \frac{60}{x}$$
$$48x = 4800$$
$$x = 100$$

23. (A) $\dfrac{A}{B} = \dfrac{5"}{11"} = \dfrac{x \text{ meters}}{5 \text{ meters}}$

$11x = 25$

$x = 2\frac{3}{11}$

24. (C) $(a - b)^2 = a^2 - 2ab + b^2$

Substitute: $100 - 2(50) + 25$

$100 - 100 + 25 = 25$

25. (C) If 0.6 ounce costs $18

$\dfrac{0.6}{1.0} = \dfrac{\$18}{x}$; $0.6x = 18$; $6x = 180$; $x = \$30$.

Since 1 ounce costs $30 and the price in the larger bottle is $25 per ounce, the difference per ounce is $5.

Verbal Reasoning   Section 3

30. (B) A *clasp* is the fastening on a *bracelet*. A *buckle* is the fastening on a *belt*. (Function)

31. (E) A *fleet* is a group of *ships*. A *pack* is a group of *wolves*. (Group and Member)

32. (A) One stores *money* in a *bank*. One stores *wine* in a *cask*. (Function)

33. (E) *Flimsy* means weak and lacking in *strength*. *Clumsy* means awkward and lacking in *grace*. (Antonym Variant)

34. (D) A person who is *obstinate* or stubborn may be called *mulish* (like a mule). A person who is *coy* or pretends shyness may be called *kittenish* (like a kitten). (Definition)

35. (B) A *refugee* seeks *asylum* or shelter. A *hermit* seeks *solitude* or isolation. (Defining Characteristic)

36. (B) Something that is *inane* or senseless lacks *meaning*, by definition. Something that is *random* or haphazard by definition lacks a *plan*. (Antonym Variant)

37. (E) To *sap vitality* is to weaken or exhaust liveliness. To *deplete resources* is to reduce supplies. (Defining Characteristic)

38. (C) A *countess* is a member of the *nobility*, the aristocrats. A *professor* is a *member* of the *faculty*, the teaching staff. (Group and Member)

39. (C) Just as the *wheat* is separated from the worthless straw or *chaff*, the *wine* is separated from the worthless sediment or *dregs*. (Part to Whole)

40. (A) Something that is *ephemeral* (fleeting, transient) lacks *permanence*. Something that is *erratic* (unpredictable) lacks *predictability*. (Antonym Variant)

41. (D) To *ogle* is to *observe* or look at someone provocatively (in an attention-getting manner). To *flaunt* is to *display* or show off something provocatively (in an attention-getting manner). (Manner)

42. (C) The opening paragraph discusses changes in the idea of matter, emphasizing the use of musical terminology to describe the concepts of physics. The second paragraph then goes on to develop the theme of the music of matter.
Choice B is incorrect. Music does not directly influence the interactions of particles; physicists merely use musical terms to describe these interactions.

43. (D) The author mentions these terms as examples of what he means by the strange new language or *idiosyncratic nomenclature* of modern particle physics.

44. (D) In his references to the elegance of the newly discovered sub-atomic structures and to the dance of Creation, the author conveys his *admiration* and *wonder*.

45. (B) "Matter's heart," where the physicist can observe the dance of Creation, is *the subatomic world*, the world of quarks and charms.

46. (D) The image of the snake swallowing its tail suggests that the astronomers' and physicists' theories are, at bottom, one and the same. In other words, there is an *underlying unity* connecting them.

47. (E) Like a ghost, the top quark evades its pursuers. It is *elusive*.

48. (B) Glashow is eager for the end of the hunt. His words ("last blessed one," "the sooner…the better") reflect his *impatience*.

49. (D) The fact that top quarks appeared just after the Big Bang and shortly thereafter vanished suggests that a cameo appearance must be *brief*.

50. (E) The author of Passage 2 cites authorities (Glashow, Tollestrup, Kane) and use similes ("like an arch without a keystone"). She defines the top quark as the theoretical sixth member of the group of subatomic particles that make up the basic building blocks of matter. She poses a question about what makes certain particles more massive than others. However, she never *denies a possibility*.

51. (C) While Passage 1 primarily attempts to convey to the reader a sense of the wondrousness of the physicists' discoveries, Passage 2 tries to make sense of just what the physicists' are looking for. Thus, it *explains more fully the objectives* or aims of the physicists.

52. (C) Passage 2 states that the new theoretical model of the subatomic world "has reduced a once-bewildering zoo of particles to just a few fundamental constituents." Passage 1, for its part, lists all sorts of colorful terms—squark, gauge, technicolor, flavor—whose names fail to appear in Passage 2. This suggests that some of these specific particles whose existence had been previously hypothesized have been *ruled out* by the new theoretical synthesis.

53. **(C)** The author provides the reader both with physical details of dress and bearing and with comments about the motives and emotions of the Cardinal and Bosola. Choice A is incorrect. The passage scarcely mentions the church. Choice B is incorrect. The description of ecclesiastical costumes is only one item in the description of the Cardinal. Choice D is incorrect. While audiences today might well enjoy seeing the characters acted as described here, the author does not cite specific reasons why the play might appeal to modern audiences. Choice E is incorrect. The author's purpose is to describe two separate roles, not to compare two interpretations of a single role.

54. **(D)** "Spare" is being used to describe the Cardinal's physical appearance. He is tall and *lean*.

55. **(E)** The eagle is poised to strike "with exposed talons." It, like the Cardinal, gathers itself together to strike with greater force. The imagery suggests the Cardinal's *mercilessness*.
    Choice A is incorrect. The Cardinal is not *flighty* (light-headed and irresponsible); he is cold and calculating. Choice B is incorrect. He loves power, not freedom. Choice C is incorrect. An eagle poised to strike with bare claws suggests violence, not *eminence* (fame and high position). Choice D is incorrect. Nothing in the passage suggests he is spiritual.
    Beware of eye-catchers. "Eminence" is a title of honor applied to cardinals in the Roman Catholic church. Choice C may attract you for this reason.

56. **(E)** Although Bosola is not a "leather-jacketed" hoodlum, he is a hired "assassin," a "hangman" (despite his scholarly taste and humanist disposition).

57. **(E)** The author is contrasting the two sides of Bosola, the scholar and the assassin. As a scholar, he is a man of perceptive intellect, noted for discrimination or *discernment*.

58. **(A)** The casual references to the elongated hands and features of El Greco's work and to the trim beards and commanding stances in the work of Van Dyke imply that the author assumes the reader has seen examples of both painters' art.

Mathematical Reasoning   Section 4

26. (D) The value of x may be zero, positive, or negative.

27. (C) Since the sum of the consecutive integers $a + b + c = 18$, then $a = 5$, $b = 6$, and $c = 7$.
$\therefore (a)(b)(c) = (5)(6)(7) = 210$.

28. (C) $\dfrac{a(x + y)}{b} = \dfrac{a(1 - 1)}{b} = \dfrac{a(0)}{b} = 0$

$\dfrac{2a(x + y)}{b} = \dfrac{2a(1 - 1)}{b} \dfrac{2a(0)}{b} = 0$

29. (C) *Multiply* $\dfrac{-a}{y + z}$ *by* $\dfrac{-1}{-1} = \dfrac{a}{-y - z}$

$\therefore \dfrac{x}{-y - z} = \dfrac{a}{-y - z}$

$\therefore x = a$

30. (C) $3x + 5y = 15 + 5y$

$\qquad 3x = 15$

$\qquad x = 5$

$\qquad \dfrac{x}{5} = 1$

31. (B) 1 hour and 20 minutes or $1\frac{1}{3}$ hours elapse from 8:55 A.M. to 10:15 A.M.

32. (D) Z could be anywhere on circumference of circle with radius $= 4$. X could be anywhere on circumference of circle with radius $= 3$.

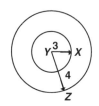

33. (A) There is a total of 12 marbles. Since 4 of these marbles are white, the probability of drawing a white marble is $\frac{4}{12} = \frac{1}{3}$. The probability of obtaining a head is $\frac{1}{2}$. The probability of obtaining two heads on two successive tosses is $\frac{1}{2} \times \frac{1}{2} = \frac{1}{4}$. Since $\frac{1}{3} > \frac{1}{4}$, the probability of drawing white marble is greater than the probability of tossing two heads.

34. (B) Since $x = 100$, $m = 180 - 100$ or 80.
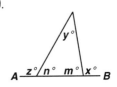
$y + m = 40 + 80$ or 120
$z = y + m$ (exterior angle of $\triangle$)
$z = 40 + 80$
$z = 120$
$x + y = 140$

35. (C) Since the base angles are equal, $AB = AC$.

$$\therefore \frac{\widehat{BC}}{AB} \cdot \frac{AC}{\widehat{BC}} = 1$$

36. (C) $\triangle$s XDC and YDC share the base DC. Since $ABCD$ is a rectangle, XDC and YDC have equal altitudes. Therefore XDC and YDC are equal in area. Subtracting the area of DOC from both XDC and YDC gives YOC equal in area to XOD.

37. (A) $y = 180 - (50 + 60)$ or 70
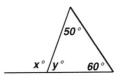
Or, $x = 50 + 60$, since the exterior angle of a triangle equals the sum of both remote interior (nonadjacent) angles.

38. (C) The product of any number and its reciprocal is 1. Both products are therefore 1.

39. (D) If $x = 1$, $3x = 1$ and $(-2)x = -2$
If $x = -1$, $3x = -3$ and $(-2)(x) = +2$

40. (D) Since the width of the rectangle is not given, its area cannot be determined.

41. (75) $(30)(25¢) = 750$ cents or 75 dimes

42. (60) Time = 20 minutes or $\frac{1}{3}$ hour

$$\frac{\text{distance}}{\text{time}} = \text{rate}$$

$$\frac{20}{\frac{1}{3}} = 60 \text{ miles per hour}$$

43. (4) Let diameter $= d$.

Then radius $= \dfrac{d}{2}$

$$Area = \dfrac{\pi d^2}{4}$$

If diameter is doubled, diameter $= 2d$, then

radius $= \dfrac{2d}{2} = d.$

Area $= \pi d^2$, which is four times $\dfrac{\pi d^2}{4}$

44. (80) $\angle B = \frac{1}{2}(\widehat{DA} - \widehat{CA})°$
$70° = \frac{1}{2}(\widehat{DA} - 70°)$
$140° = \widehat{DA} - 70°$
$210° = \widehat{DA}$
$\widehat{DA} + \widehat{CA} + \widehat{DC} = 360°$
$210° + 70° + \widehat{DC} = 360°$
$\widehat{DC} = 360° - 280°$
$\widehat{DC} = 80°$

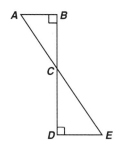

45. (9) $\angle ACB = \angle DCE$ (vertical angles)
The two right triangles are similar.
The corresponding sides are
$$\dfrac{CD}{BC} = \dfrac{DE}{AB}$$
$$\dfrac{16}{12} = \dfrac{12}{x}$$
$$16x = 144$$
$$x = 9$$

46. $\frac{1}{10}$ **or 0.1** $\dfrac{0.3}{9} + \dfrac{0.6}{9} = \dfrac{0.9}{9} = \dfrac{9}{90} = \dfrac{1}{10}$

47. (360) 12 minutes $= \frac{1}{5}$ hour.

Let $x =$ number of envelopes to be prepared in 8 hours.

$$\frac{9 \text{ envelopes}}{\frac{1}{5} \text{ hour}} = \frac{x}{8 \text{ hrs.}}$$

$$\frac{1}{5}x = 72$$

$$x = (72)(5) = 360$$

48. (2) Because $(2)(2)(2)(2) = 16$, then $x + 2 = 4$ and $x = 2$.

49. (525) If 1 inch $= 150$ miles, then $3\frac{1}{2}$ inches $= (3\frac{1}{2})(150)$ or 525 miles.

50. (10) Let $x =$ number of blue marbles.

$$P(\text{not green}) = P(\text{red or blue}) = \frac{4 + x}{4 + 7 + x} = \frac{2}{3}$$

$$3(4 + x) = 2(11 + x)$$

$$3x + 12 = 2x + 22$$

$$x = 10$$

The jar contains 10 blue marbles.

ANSWER SHEET—Test 2

Section 1

1 Ⓐ Ⓑ Ⓒ Ⓓ Ⓔ
2 Ⓐ Ⓑ Ⓒ Ⓓ Ⓔ
3 Ⓐ Ⓑ Ⓒ Ⓓ Ⓔ
4 Ⓐ Ⓑ Ⓒ Ⓓ Ⓔ
5 Ⓐ Ⓑ Ⓒ Ⓓ Ⓔ
6 Ⓐ Ⓑ Ⓒ Ⓓ Ⓔ
7 Ⓐ Ⓑ Ⓒ Ⓓ Ⓔ
8 Ⓐ Ⓑ Ⓒ Ⓓ Ⓔ
9 Ⓐ Ⓑ Ⓒ Ⓓ Ⓔ
10 Ⓐ Ⓑ Ⓒ Ⓓ Ⓔ
11 Ⓐ Ⓑ Ⓒ Ⓓ Ⓔ
12 Ⓐ Ⓑ Ⓒ Ⓓ Ⓔ
13 Ⓐ Ⓑ Ⓒ Ⓓ Ⓔ
14 Ⓐ Ⓑ Ⓒ Ⓓ Ⓔ
15 Ⓐ Ⓑ Ⓒ Ⓓ Ⓔ
16 Ⓐ Ⓑ Ⓒ Ⓓ Ⓔ
17 Ⓐ Ⓑ Ⓒ Ⓓ Ⓔ
18 Ⓐ Ⓑ Ⓒ Ⓓ Ⓔ
19 Ⓐ Ⓑ Ⓒ Ⓓ Ⓔ
20 Ⓐ Ⓑ Ⓒ Ⓓ Ⓔ
21 Ⓐ Ⓑ Ⓒ Ⓓ Ⓔ
22 Ⓐ Ⓑ Ⓒ Ⓓ Ⓔ
23 Ⓐ Ⓑ Ⓒ Ⓓ Ⓔ
24 Ⓐ Ⓑ Ⓒ Ⓓ Ⓔ
25 Ⓐ Ⓑ Ⓒ Ⓓ Ⓔ
26 Ⓐ Ⓑ Ⓒ Ⓓ Ⓔ
27 Ⓐ Ⓑ Ⓒ Ⓓ Ⓔ
28 Ⓐ Ⓑ Ⓒ Ⓓ Ⓔ
29 Ⓐ Ⓑ Ⓒ Ⓓ Ⓔ

Section 2

1 Ⓐ Ⓑ Ⓒ Ⓓ Ⓔ
2 Ⓐ Ⓑ Ⓒ Ⓓ Ⓔ
3 Ⓐ Ⓑ Ⓒ Ⓓ Ⓔ
4 Ⓐ Ⓑ Ⓒ Ⓓ Ⓔ
5 Ⓐ Ⓑ Ⓒ Ⓓ Ⓔ
6 Ⓐ Ⓑ Ⓒ Ⓓ Ⓔ
7 Ⓐ Ⓑ Ⓒ Ⓓ Ⓔ
8 Ⓐ Ⓑ Ⓒ Ⓓ Ⓔ
9 Ⓐ Ⓑ Ⓒ Ⓓ Ⓔ
10 Ⓐ Ⓑ Ⓒ Ⓓ Ⓔ
11 Ⓐ Ⓑ Ⓒ Ⓓ Ⓔ
12 Ⓐ Ⓑ Ⓒ Ⓓ Ⓔ
13 Ⓐ Ⓑ Ⓒ Ⓓ Ⓔ
14 Ⓐ Ⓑ Ⓒ Ⓓ Ⓔ
15 Ⓐ Ⓑ Ⓒ Ⓓ Ⓔ
16 Ⓐ Ⓑ Ⓒ Ⓓ Ⓔ
17 Ⓐ Ⓑ Ⓒ Ⓓ Ⓔ
18 Ⓐ Ⓑ Ⓒ Ⓓ Ⓔ
19 Ⓐ Ⓑ Ⓒ Ⓓ Ⓔ
20 Ⓐ Ⓑ Ⓒ Ⓓ Ⓔ
21 Ⓐ Ⓑ Ⓒ Ⓓ Ⓔ
22 Ⓐ Ⓑ Ⓒ Ⓓ Ⓔ
23 Ⓐ Ⓑ Ⓒ Ⓓ Ⓔ
24 Ⓐ Ⓑ Ⓒ Ⓓ Ⓔ
25 Ⓐ Ⓑ Ⓒ Ⓓ Ⓔ

ANSWER SHEET

Section 3

30	Ⓐ	Ⓑ	Ⓒ	Ⓓ	Ⓔ
31	Ⓐ	Ⓑ	Ⓒ	Ⓓ	Ⓔ
32	Ⓐ	Ⓑ	Ⓒ	Ⓓ	Ⓔ
33	Ⓐ	Ⓑ	Ⓒ	Ⓓ	Ⓔ
34	Ⓐ	Ⓑ	Ⓒ	Ⓓ	Ⓔ
35	Ⓐ	Ⓑ	Ⓒ	Ⓓ	Ⓔ
36	Ⓐ	Ⓑ	Ⓒ	Ⓓ	Ⓔ
37	Ⓐ	Ⓑ	Ⓒ	Ⓓ	Ⓔ
38	Ⓐ	Ⓑ	Ⓒ	Ⓓ	Ⓔ
39	Ⓐ	Ⓑ	Ⓒ	Ⓓ	Ⓔ
40	Ⓐ	Ⓑ	Ⓒ	Ⓓ	Ⓔ
41	Ⓐ	Ⓑ	Ⓒ	Ⓓ	Ⓔ
42	Ⓐ	Ⓑ	Ⓒ	Ⓓ	Ⓔ
43	Ⓐ	Ⓑ	Ⓒ	Ⓓ	Ⓔ
44	Ⓐ	Ⓑ	Ⓒ	Ⓓ	Ⓔ
45	Ⓐ	Ⓑ	Ⓒ	Ⓓ	Ⓔ
46	Ⓐ	Ⓑ	Ⓒ	Ⓓ	Ⓔ
47	Ⓐ	Ⓑ	Ⓒ	Ⓓ	Ⓔ
48	Ⓐ	Ⓑ	Ⓒ	Ⓓ	Ⓔ
49	Ⓐ	Ⓑ	Ⓒ	Ⓓ	Ⓔ
50	Ⓐ	Ⓑ	Ⓒ	Ⓓ	Ⓔ
51	Ⓐ	Ⓑ	Ⓒ	Ⓓ	Ⓔ
52	Ⓐ	Ⓑ	Ⓒ	Ⓓ	Ⓔ
53	Ⓐ	Ⓑ	Ⓒ	Ⓓ	Ⓔ
54	Ⓐ	Ⓑ	Ⓒ	Ⓓ	Ⓔ
55	Ⓐ	Ⓑ	Ⓒ	Ⓓ	Ⓔ
56	Ⓐ	Ⓑ	Ⓒ	Ⓓ	Ⓔ
57	Ⓐ	Ⓑ	Ⓒ	Ⓓ	Ⓔ
58	Ⓐ	Ⓑ	Ⓒ	Ⓓ	Ⓔ

Section 4

26	Ⓐ	Ⓑ	Ⓒ	Ⓓ
27	Ⓐ	Ⓑ	Ⓒ	Ⓓ
28	Ⓐ	Ⓑ	Ⓒ	Ⓓ
29	Ⓐ	Ⓑ	Ⓒ	Ⓓ
30	Ⓐ	Ⓑ	Ⓒ	Ⓓ
31	Ⓐ	Ⓑ	Ⓒ	Ⓓ
32	Ⓐ	Ⓑ	Ⓒ	Ⓓ
33	Ⓐ	Ⓑ	Ⓒ	Ⓓ
34	Ⓐ	Ⓑ	Ⓒ	Ⓓ
35	Ⓐ	Ⓑ	Ⓒ	Ⓓ
36	Ⓐ	Ⓑ	Ⓒ	Ⓓ
37	Ⓐ	Ⓑ	Ⓒ	Ⓓ
38	Ⓐ	Ⓑ	Ⓒ	Ⓓ
39	Ⓐ	Ⓑ	Ⓒ	Ⓓ
40	Ⓐ	Ⓑ	Ⓒ	Ⓓ

ANSWER SHEET

Section 4 (continued)

Only the filled-in spaces in the grids will be scored. Credit will not be given for answers written above the grids.

41 ⬚⬚⬚⬚   42 ⬚⬚⬚⬚   43 ⬚⬚⬚⬚   44 ⬚⬚⬚⬚

45 ⬚⬚⬚⬚   46 ⬚⬚⬚⬚   47 ⬚⬚⬚⬚   48 ⬚⬚⬚⬚

49 ⬚⬚⬚⬚   50 ⬚⬚⬚⬚

PRACTICE PSAT TEST 2
SECTION 1

29 Questions—30 minutes

For each question in this section, choose the best answer from among the choices given and fill in the corresponding space on the answer sheet

---

Each sentence below has one or two blanks, each blank indicating that something has been omitted. Beneath the sentence are five words or sets of words labeled A through E. Choose the word or set of words that, when inserted in the sentence, <u>best</u> fits the meaning of the sentence as a whole.

Example:

Medieval kingdoms did not become constitutional republics overnight; on the contrary, the change was ----.

(A) unpopular   (B) unexpected   (C) advantageous
(D) sufficient   (E) gradual

---

1. Her audacious approach won her an interview when a less ---- method would have been sure to fail.

   (A) daring   (B) ingratiating   (C) conventional
   (D) intelligent   (E) arrogant

2. The plot of the motion picture *Hoosiers* is ----; we have all seen this story, the tale of an underdog team going on to win a championship, in one form or another countless times.

   (A) inept   (B) absorbing   (C) intricate   (D) controversial
   (E) trite

3. Whenever Ginger's brother played a trick on her, she would spend hours thinking up diabolical ways in which to ----.

   (A) retaliate   (B) retrench   (C) prevaricate   (D) sublimate
   (E) reconcile

4. The term *metaphysics* has long had a bad name in scientific circles, and the ---- hasn't quite faded.

   (A) bloom   (B) glory   (C) taint   (D) idiom   (E) appeal

5. Because both male and female egrets display the same plumage during breeding season, ---- the two sexes is extremely difficult.

   (A) evolving from   (B) distinguishing between
   (C) generalizing about   (D) maneuvering around
   (E) accommodating to

6. Although there are still ---- outbreaks of typhoid fever from time to time, no persistent, extended typhoid epidemic has occurred in the past forty years.

   (A) therapeutic   (B) synchronized   (C) devastating
   (D) sedentary   (E) sporadic

7. Knowing that the results of future experiments might well cause her to ---- her hypothesis, she voiced ---- opinion which she insisted was subject to change.

   (A) modify...an unqualified   (B) qualify...a definitive
   (C) abandon...a dogmatic   (D) alter...a blunt
   (E) rethink...a tentative

8. Although he was ---- by nature, he ---- contact with others during the period of his trial.

   (A) gracious...sought   (B) magnanimous...attempted
   (C) altruistic...evaded   (D) gregarious...shunned
   (E) prodigal...avoided

9. Although Maria Montessori gained fame for her innovations in ----, it took years before her teaching techniques were common practice in American schools.

   (A) democracy   (B) sophistry   (C) philanthropy
   (D) technology   (E) pedagogy

10. Language, culture, and personality may be considered independently of each other in thought, but they are ---- in fact.

    (A) autonomous   (B) pervasive   (C) equivocal
     (D) inseparable   (E) immutable

11. Since depression seems to result when certain cells in the brain receive too little of two key chemicals, the neurotransmitters norepinephrine and serotonin, one goal of treatment is to make more of the chemicals ---- the nerve cells that need them.

    (A) analogous to   (B) dependent on   (C) available to
     (D) regardless of   (E) interchangeable with

12. The sudden shift from ---- to ---- in Hugo's novels can startle readers, especially when he abruptly juxtaposes a scene of chaste and holy love with one of coarse and profane licentiousness.

    (A) devotion...frivolity   (B) piety...ribaldry
     (C) vulgarity...adultery   (D) decorum...salubrity
      (E) purity...maturity

13. In the end, the *Normandie* lacked even the dignity of being sunk by the enemy at sea; she burned and went down ---- at her Manhattan pier in 1942, while incompetents were transforming her into a troop ship.

    (A) majestically   (B) ignominiously   (C) militantly
     (D) negligently   (E) auspiciously

14. Hoving ---- refers to the smuggled Greek urn as the "hot pot," not because there were doubts about its authenticity or even great reservations as to its price, but because its ---- was open to question.

    (A) mendaciously...exorbitance
     (B) characteristically...genuineness   (C) colloquially...origin
      (D) repeatedly...fraudulence   (E) cheerfully...function

15. This psychological biography presents a picture of a deeply ---- individual, unable to ---- anyone else's success, whose ruthless pursuit of recognition and fame has been marked by hypocritical gestures of openness and affection.

    (A) altruistic...comprehend   (B) egotistical...tolerate
     (C) modest...admit   (D) apathetic...match   (E) indolent...vilify

16. She conducted the interrogation not only with dispatch but with
----, being a person who is ---- in manner yet subtle in
discrimination.

(A) elan...enthusiastic   (B) equanimity...abrupt
  (C) finesse...expeditious   (D) zeal...doctrinaire
    (E) trepidation...cursory

Each passage below is followed by questions based on its content. Answer the questions following each passage on the basis
of what is <u>stated</u> or <u>implied</u> in that passage and in any introductory material that may be provided.

Questions 17–21 are based on the following passage.

*In the following passage, the celebrated author and chef M. F. K.
Fisher considers the greater implications of a small shipboard
incident.*

The Captain's Dinner was strange. We were off the coast
of Lower California. The water was so calm that we could
hear flying fish slap against it. We ate at a long table out on
Line deck, under an awning between us and the enormous stars.
(5)   The Captain looked well in his white uniform, and smiled
almost warmly at us all, probably thanking God that most of
us would leave him in a few days. The waiters were excited,
the way the Filipino boys used to be at boarding school when
there was a Christmas party, and the table looked like some-
(10) thing from a Renaissance painting.
     There were galantines and aspics down the center, with
ripe grapes brought from Italy and stranger fruits from all the
ports we'd touched, and crowning everything two stuffed
pheasants in their dulled but still dashing feathers. There
(15) were wineglasses on stems, and little printed menus, proof

that this masterpiece of a meal was known about in Rome, long since.

We ate and drank and heard our own suddenly friendly voices over the dark waters. The waiters glided deftly, per-
(20) haps dreaming that they served at Maxim's instead of on this fifth-rate freighter, and we drank Asti Spumanti, undated but delightful.

And finally, while we clapped, the chef stood before us, bowing in the light from the narrow stairs. He wore his high
(25) bonnet and whites, and a long-tailed morning coat, and looked like a drawing by Ludwig Bemelmans, with oblique sadness in his pasty outlines.

There was a silence after our applause. He turned ner-vously toward the light, and breathed not at all. We heard
(30) shufflings and bumps. Then, up through the twisting white closeness of the stairway, borne on the backs and arms of three awestruck kitchen boys, rose something almost too strange to talk about.

The chef stood back, bowing, discreetly wiping the
(35) sweat from his white face. The Captain applauded. We all clapped, and even cheered. The three boys set the thing on a special table.

It was a replica, about as long as a man's coffin, of the cathedral at Milano. It was made in white and pink sugar.
(40) There was a light inside, of course, and it glowed there on the deck of the little ship, trembling in every flying buttress with the Mexican ground swell, pure and ridiculous; and some-thing about it shamed me.

It was a little dusty. It had undoubtedly been mended,
(45) after mighty storms, in the dim galleys of a hundred ships, better but never worse than this. It was like a flag flying for the chef, a bulwark all in spun sugar against the breath of corruption. It was his masterpiece, made years ago in some famous kitchen, and he showed it to us now with dignity.

17. It can be inferred from the passage that the author is most likely

(A) a student at a boarding school
(B) an officer of a vessel at anchor
(C) an enemy of the ship's captain
(D) a passenger near the end of a voyage
(E) a newcomer on board the vessel

18. The author's general attitude toward the freighter in the third and fourth paragraphs is best described as

(A) condescending
(B) suspicious
(C) bitter
(D) apathetic
(E) admiring

19. It can be inferred from the passage that Maxim's (paragraph 4) was most likely which of the following?

I. A renowned restaurant
II. An eminent cargo vessel
III. A desirable place to work

(A) I only
(B) II only
(C) I and III only
(D) II and III only
(E) I, II, and III

20. The evidence in the passage suggests that the chef most likely sweats

(A) from his labors in transporting the replica
(B) from the heat of the kitchen
(C) because he is afflicted with shortness of breath
(D) out of fear for his irreplaceable creation
(E) from his exertions in constructing the cathedral

21. Which of the following statements best expresses the author's impression of the chef?

(A) Reduced to working on cargo vessels, he is ashamed of his loss of professional prestige.

(B) Although he has come down in the world, he retains the memory of his youthful achievements.

(C) He applies himself with diligence to new creations, hoping to gain renown.

(D) He prefers heading his own kitchen to working as an underling in a more famous establishment.

(E) Despite his early promise, he is unable to create an original work of art.

Questions 22–29 are based on the following passage.

The following passage is taken from a book documenting the woman's rights movement in the United States.

During the decade of 1880–1890 it was becoming increasingly evident that the factors which had brought about
the existence of two separate suffrage institutions were
Line steadily diminishing in importance.
(5)   The National Woman Suffrage Association had been
launched by the intellectually irrepressible Elizabeth Cady
Stanton and the ever catholic Susan B. Anthony. Both were
ready to work with anyone, whatever their views on other
matters, as long as they wholeheartedly espoused woman
(10) suffrage. Consequently in its earlier years the National was
both aggressive and unorthodox. It damned both Republi-
cans and Democrats who brushed the suffrage question
aside. It was willing to take up the cudgels for distressed
women whatever their circumstances, be they "fallen
(15) women," divorce cases, or underpaid seamstresses.
The American Woman Suffrage Association, by contrast,
took its tone and outlook from a New England which had
turned its back on those fiery days when abolitionists, men
and women alike, had stood up to angry mobs. Its advocacy

(20) of worthy causes was highly selective. Lucy Stone was not interested in trade unionism and wished to keep the suffrage cause untarnished by concern with divorce or "the social evil." The very epitome of the American's attitude was its most distinguished convert and leader, Julia Ward Howe—

(25) erudite, honored lay preacher, the revered author of "The Battle Hymn of the Republic," who cast a highly desirable aura of prestige and propriety over the women's cause.

It was not that Mrs. Howe in herself made suffrage respectable; she was a symbol of the forces that were

(30) drawing the suffrage movement into the camp of decorum. American society was becoming rapidly polarized. The middle class was learning to identify organized labor with social turmoil. A succession of strikes during the depression of 1873–1878, in textiles, mining, and railroads,

(35) culminated in the Great Railroad Strike of 1877 involving nearly 100,000 workers from the Atlantic coast to the Mississippi valley; they did not help to reassure women taught by press and pulpit to identify any type of militancy with radicalism. Nor was this trend allayed by the

(40) hysteria whipped up over the Molly Maguire trials for secret conspiracy among Pennsylvania coal miners, or the alleged communistic influences at work in such growing organizations as the Knights of Labor and the A. F. of L. The existence of a small number of socialists was used to

(45) smear all organized labor with the taint of "anarchism." The crowning touch took place during the widespread agitation for an eight-hour day in 1886 when a bomb, thrown by a hand unknown to this day into a radical meeting in Chicago's Haymarket Square, touched off a

(50) nation-wide wave of panic.

The steady trend of the suffrage movement toward the conservative and the conventional during the last twenty years of the nineteenth century must be viewed in this setting, in order to avoid the misconception that a few conserva-

(55) tive women took it over, through their own superior ability

and the passivity of the former militants. Even the latter were changing their views, judging by their actions. It was one thing to challenge the proprieties at the Centennial of 1876; ten years later it would have been inconceivable even to the
(60) women who took part in the demonstration. Susan Anthony herself would have thought twice about flouting Federal election laws and going to jail in an era which witnessed the Haymarket hysteria.

Moreover the social makeup of the suffrage leadership
(65) was changing perceptibly. There were fewer housewives or women who did the greater part of their own work, and more professionals, writers, and women of substantial means. Those who had begun the struggle in want and penury—living, like Lucy Stone and Abby Kelley, on whatever pittance
(70) they could wring out of their lecturing—had by now achieved some measure of comfort and ease. Even the spartan Susan Anthony, who dipped continually into her meager finances for the sake of the cause, had comfortably situated friends in most cities, who cared for her on her endless lecture and
(75) campaign trips; whenever she was in Washington she stayed at the Riggs Hotel, whose owners put a suite at her disposal, sometimes for months at a time.

Along with increased means (always more evident in the lives of the individual women than in the suffrage organiza-
(80) tions' finances, which continued on a deplorable hand-to-mouth basis) came greater influence and prestige. Twenty years had seen a profound change of public attitude. Woman suffrage was not yet generally accepted, but it was no longer considered the province of eccentrics and crackpots. It
(85) boasted influential friends in Congress, and the annual conventions of the National Association in Washington were the occasion, not only of hearings before Congressional committees and lobbying "on the hill," but of White House teas and receptions.

22. The author's primary purpose in the passage is to

(A) contrast Susan B. Anthony with Julia Ward Howe
(B) recount the advances in the suffrage movement from 1880 to 1890
(C) account for the changes occurring in the suffrage movement from 1880 to 1890
(D) explain the growing divisions within the women's movement
(E) point out aspects of the suffrage movement that exist in contemporary feminism

23. The word "espoused" in line 9 means

(A) married
(B) championed
(C) reconciled
(D) despised
(E) endowed

24. Which of the following statements is most compatible with the early principles of the National as described in the passage?

(A) Advocates of suffrage should maintain their distance from socially embarrassing "allies."
(B) Marital and economic issues are inappropriate concerns for the suffrage movement.
(C) Propriety of behavior should characterize representatives of the women's cause.
(D) A nominal espousal of woman suffrage is worthy of suffragist support.
(E) The concerns of all afflicted women are the concerns of the suffrage movement.

25. The passage singles out Julia Ward Howe as an example of

(A) a venerated figurehead
(B) an overzealous advocate
(C) a heterodox thinker
(D) an ordained cleric
(E) a militant activist

26. The word "touch" in line 46 means

(A) physical contact
(B) slight amount
(C) close personal communication
(D) request for additional funds
(E) detail completing an effect

27. The author's attitude toward the public reaction to the Molly Maguire trials is that the reaction was

   (A) appropriate
   (B) disorganized
   (C) overwrought
   (D) necessary
   (E) understated

28. The author stresses the growing antiradical bias of the American middle class during the decade 1880–1890 in order to

   (A) question a trend that proved destructive to the suffrage movement
   (B) explain the unexpected emergence of an able body of radical leaders
   (C) refute the contention that Anthony was unchanged by her experiences
   (D) correct a misapprehension about changes in the suffrage movement
   (E) excuse the growing lack of militancy on the part of the National

29. The passage suggests that, by 1890, attempts to effect woman suffrage by violating the proprieties and defying Federal laws would probably have been viewed even by movement members with

   (A) indifference
   (B) defiance
   (C) disapprobation
   (D) respect
   (E) optimism

IF YOU FINISH BEFORE TIME IS CALLED, YOU MAY CHECK YOUR WORK ON THIS **S T O P** SECTION ONLY. DO NOT TURN TO ANY OTHER SECTION IN THE TEST.

SECTION 2

25 Questions–30 minutes

Some formulas you may find useful in solving some questions

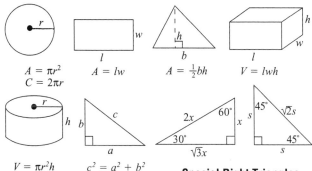

$A = \pi r^2$
$C = 2\pi r$

$A = lw$

$A = \frac{1}{2}bh$

$V = lwh$

$V = \pi r^2 h$

$c^2 = a^2 + b^2$

Special Right Triangles

Triangle: The sum of the measure in degrees of the angles of a triangle is 180.

If $\angle CDA$ is a right angle, then

(1) area of $\triangle ABC = \dfrac{AB \times CD}{2}$

(2) $AC^2 = AD^2 + DC^2$

The number of degrees of arc in a circle is 360.

The measure in degrees of a straight line is 180.

Definitions of symbols:

$\leq$	is less than or equal to	$\geq$	is greater than or equal to
$\parallel$	is parallel to	$\perp$	is perpendicular to
$=$	is equal to	$\neq$	is unequal to
$<$	is less than	$>$	is greater than

Notes: (1) The use of a calculator is permitted. All numbers used are real numbers. (2) Figures that accompany problems in this test are intended to provide information useful in solving the problems. They are drawn as accurately as possible EXCEPT when it is stated in a specific problem that the figure is not drawn to scale. All figures lie in a plane unless otherwise indicated.

In this section solve each problem, using any available space on the page for scratchwork. Then decide which is the best of the choices given and fill in the corresponding space on the answer sheet.

---

1. $(146 \times 117) + (173 \times 146) + (146 \times 210)$ equals

(A) 69,000   (B) 70,000   (C) 71,000   (D) 72,000
(E) 73,000

---

2. A certain grade of eggs has a weight of 24 to 26 ounces per dozen. What is the minimum weight (in ounces) of 69 such eggs?

(A) 138   (B) 143   (C) 149   (D) 1656   (E) 1716

---

3. A boy has 85 cents in 12 coins consisting of nickels and dimes. How many coins are nickels?

(A) 5   (B) 6   (C) 7   (D) 8   (E) 9

---

4. L is east of M and west of N, J is southeast of N, M is southeast of F. Which is the farthest west?

(A) F (B) G (C) J (D) M (E) N

5. If $a - 1$ is an even integer, which of the following must be odd?

  I. $3(a - 3)$
  II. $2a + 1$
  III. $a(a - 1)$

  (A) I only   (B) II only   (C) III only   (D) I and III only
  (E) I, II and III

---

6. If n is a positive integer, which of the following could be a possible value of $\dfrac{-1^n}{(-1^n)}$?

  I. 1
  II. −1
  III. $\dfrac{1}{n}$

  (A) I only   (B) II only   (C) III only   (D) I and III only
  (E) I, II and III

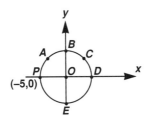

7. In this figure the lettered points are on the circumference of the circle with center O. Which letter represents the point with coordinates (5, 0)?

  (A) A (B) B (C) C (D) D (E) E

8. For what values of n and d is $\dfrac{n}{d} > 1$?

(A) $n = 5, d = 6$ (B) $n = 3, d = 2$ (C) $n = 1, d = 2$
(D) $n = 1, d = 1$ (E) $n = 0, d = 1$

9. The cost of sending a telegram to a certain city is 85¢ for the first 15 words and $3\frac{1}{2}$¢ for each additional word, exclusive of tax. How many words did my telegram contain if I paid $1.97, which included a tax of 70¢?

(A) 12   (B) 27   (C) 36   (D) 47   (E) 147

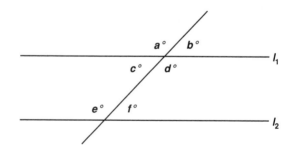

10. If $l_1 \parallel l_2$, then all of the following are true EXCEPT
(A) $d = a$ (B) $c = f$ (C) $e = a$ (D) $f = b$ (E) $c = d$

11. $\dfrac{2m}{3} = \dfrac{b}{a}, \dfrac{2m}{b} =$

(A) $\dfrac{a}{b}$ (B) $\dfrac{3}{a}$ (C) $\dfrac{a}{3}$ (D) a (E) b

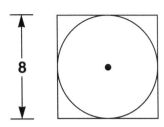

12. A dart is thrown so that it lands inside the square in the accompanying diagram. If there is an equally likely chance that the dart will land at any point in the interior of the square, what is the probability that the dart lands inside the circle?

(A) $\dfrac{\pi}{8}$ (B) $\dfrac{\pi}{6}$ (C) $\dfrac{\pi}{4}$ (D) $\dfrac{\pi}{3}$ (E) $\dfrac{\pi}{2}$

---

13. What is the value of $\dfrac{3y^2 - x^2}{\frac{1}{2}a^3}$ when $x = -2$, $y = 3$, and $a = -1$?

(A) $2\dfrac{7}{8}$ (B) -46 (C) 46 (D) -64 (E) 64

---

14. By selling a television set for $260 a dealer finds he is making a profit of 30% of cost. At what price must he sell it to make a profit of 40% of cost?

(A) $196.00   (B) $254.80   (C) $280.00   (D) $282.00
(E) $322.00

---

15. What percent of a foot is a yard?

(A) 3%   (B) $\dfrac{1}{3}$%   (C) $33\dfrac{1}{3}$%   (D) $333\dfrac{1}{3}$%

16. How long is the shadow of a 35-foot tree, if a 98-foot tree casts a 42-foot shadow at the same time?

(A) 14 ft.   (B) 15 ft.   (C) 16 ft.   (D) 17 ft. (E) 18 ft.

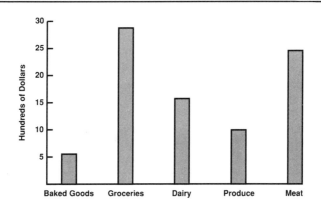

17. This graph shows the sales (in millions) for Fine Supermarket Chain in 1992. By how many millions of dollars did the sales in the meat department exceed the sales in the dairy department?

(A) 1   (B) 10   (C) 15   (D) 18   (E) 100

18. During a storewide sale many articles were reduced by 25%. To restore these articles to their original prices they must now increase their price by

(A) 25%   (B) 27.5%   (C) $33\frac{1}{3}$ %   (D) 40%   (E) 50%

19. Of Peru's 22 million people, about 60% are mestizos (people of mixed Spanish and Indian heritage), 30% are Andean Indians, and 10% are white. Which of the following expresses the number (in millions) in each of the 3 groups?

(A) 13.2 mestizos, 6.6 Andean Indians, and 2.2 whites.
(B) 2.2 mestizos, 13.2 Andean Indians, and 6.6 whites.
(C) 6.6 mestizos, 2.2 Andean Indians, and 13.2 whites.
(D) 2.2 mestizos, 13.0 Andean Indians, and 6 whites.
(E) 13.2 mestizos, 2.2 Andean Indians, and 6.6 whites.

---

20. Strawberries that formerly sold for $1.20 per pint are now packaged in two-pint boxes that sell for $3.00. The ratio of the old price to the new price is

(A) 1:5   (B) 2:5   (C) 3:5   (D) 4:5   (E) 5:4

---

21. In right $\triangle ABC$, leg AB = leg BC. The area of the triangle is 12.5. Hypotenuse AC equals

(A) $\sqrt{5}$ (B) $5\sqrt{2}$ (C) 5   (D) $4\sqrt{5}$ (E) 25

---

22. A point, X, is 25 feet from the center of a circle. If the diameter of the circle is 14 feet, what is the length (in feet) of a tangent from point X to the circle?

(A) $\sqrt{29}$ (B) 18   (C) $15\sqrt{2}$ (D) 24   (E) $\sqrt{673}$

---

23. Linda did 24 problems out of 25 correctly. In the next test she did twice as many examples correctly but received a mark only half as good. How many problems were there in the second test?

(A) 25   (B) 48   (C) 50   (D) 75   (E) 100

---

24. If a garage can wash 5 cars in 25 minutes, how long would it take to wash 25 cars?

(A) 2 hrs.   (B) 2 hrs. 5 min.   (C) 5 hrs.   (D) 25 hrs.
(E) none of these

25. A secondhand car dealer sold a car for Mr. Dee and, after deducting 5% commission, remitted $4750 to Mr. Dee. What was the selling price of the car?

(A) $2375   (B) $4773   (C) $5000   (D) $5500
(E) $50,000

IF YOU FINISH BEFORE TIME IS CALLED,
YOU MAY CHECK YOUR WORK ON THIS   **S T O P**
SECTION ONLY. DO NOT TURN TO ANY
OTHER SECTION IN THE TEST.

SECTION 3

29 Questions—30 minutes

For each question in this section, choose the best answer from among the choices given and fill in the corresponding space on the answer sheet.

Each question below consists of a related pair of words or phrases, followed by five pairs of words or phrases labeled A through E. Select the pair that best expresses a relationship similar to that expressed in the original pair.

Example:

CRUMB : BREAD ::   (A) ounce : unit   (B) splinter : wood
  (C) water : bucket   (D) twine : rope
   (E) cream : butter

Ⓐ ● Ⓒ Ⓓ Ⓔ

30. PRY : CROWBAR ::   (A) peek : curtain   (B) skate : rink
(C) leap : frog   (D) perch : rooster   (E) dig : shovel

31. SIDEWALK : PEDESTRIAN ::   (A) hangar : plane
(B) sidecar : motorcycle   (C) highway : robber
(D) boardwalk : shore   (E) waterway : boat

32. STUDIO : SCULPTOR ::   (A) gallery : painting
(B) smithy : blacksmith   (C) gymnasium : spectator
(D) park : monument   (E) apartment : renter

33. INTIMIDATE : FEAR ::   (A) mitigate : pain
(B) commiserate : sorrow   (C) exasperate : irritation
(D) exonerate : guilt   (E) remunerate : poverty

34. INSIPID : FOOD ::   (A) savory : potions   (B) musky : aroma
(C) vapid : remarks   (D) horrendous : noise
(E) spectacular : views

35. CONFINE : PRISONER ::   (A) impeach : governor
    (B) trace : fugitive   (C) detain : suspect   (D) testify : witness
    (E) ambush : sentry

36. ARIA : DIVA ::   (A) opera : librettist   (B) soliloquy : actor
    (C) compound : chemist   (D) air : melody
    (E) duet : conductor

37. OPHTHALMOLOGIST : EYES ::   (A) entomologist : ears
    (B) apologist : tongue   (C) dermatologist : skin
    (D) philatelist : coins   (E) geologist : genes

38. IRKSOME : CHAFE ::   (A) awesome : distress
    (B) tiresome : endure   (C) fulsome : praise   (D) lurid : shock
    (E) pallid : allure

39. SKIRMISH : BATTLE ::   (A) quiz : examination   (B) injury : scar
    (C) detour : road   (D) ambush : retreat   (E) recital : concert

40. MALINGERER : WORK ::   (A) recluse : company
    (B) thief : plunder   (C) arbitrator : negotiation
    (D) benefactor : philanthropy   (E) counselor : client

41. OGLE : FLIRTATIOUSNESS ::   (A) observe : nonchalance
    (B) mute : intensity   (C) gape : astonishment
    (D) squint : diffidence   (E) peer : effrontery

The passages below are followed by questions on their content; questions following a pair of related passages may also be based on the relationship between the paired passages. Answer the questions on the basis of what is <u>stated</u> or <u>implied</u> in the passages and in any introductory material that may be provided.

Questions 42–47 are based on the following passage.

The following passage on the formation of oil is excerpted from a novel about oil exploration written by Alistair MacLean.

Five main weather elements act upon rock. Frost and ice fracture rock. It can be gradually eroded by airborne dust. The action of the seas, whether through the constant move-
Line ment of tides or the pounding of heavy storm waves, re-
(5) morselessly wears away the coastlines. Rivers are immensely powerful destructive agencies—one has but to look at the Grand Canyon to appreciate their enormous power. And such rocks as escape all these influences are worn away over the eons by the effect of rain.

(10) Whatever the cause of erosion, the net result is the same. The rock is reduced to its tiniest possible con-stituents—rock particles or, simply, dust. Rain and melting snow carry this dust down to the tiniest rivulets and the mightiest rivers, which, in turn, transport it to lakes, inland
(15) seas and the coastal regions of the oceans. Dust, however fine and powdery, is still heavier than water, and whenever the water becomes sufficiently still, it will gradually sink to the bottom, not only in lakes and seas but also in the slug-gish lower reaches of rivers and where flood conditions exist,
(20) in the form of silt.

And so, over unimaginably long reaches of time, whole mountain ranges are carried down to the seas, and in the process, through the effects of gravity, new rock is born as layer after layer of dust accumulates on the bottom, building
(25) up to a depth of ten, a hundred, perhaps even a thousand feet, the lowermost layers being gradually compacted by the immense and steadily increasing pressures from above, until the particles fuse together and reform as a new rock.

It is in the intermediate and final processes of the new
(30) rock formation that oil comes into being. Those lakes and seas of hundreds of millions of years ago were almost choked by water plants and the most primitive forms of aquatic life. On dying, they sank to the bottom of the lakes and seas along with the settling dust particles and were grad-
(35) ually buried deep under the endless layers of more dust and more aquatic and plant life that slowly accumulated above

them. The passing of millions of years and the steadily increasing pressures from above gradually changed the decayed vegetation and dead aquatic life into oil.

(40)   Described this simply and quickly, the process sounds reasonable enough. But this is where the gray and disputatious area arises. The conditions necessary for the formation of oil are known; the cause of the metamorphosis is not. It seems probable that some form of chemical catalyst is in-

(45) volved, but this catalyst has not been isolated. The first purely synthetic oil, as distinct from secondary synthetic oils such as those derived from coal, has yet to be produced. We just have to accept that oil is oil, that it is there, bound up in rock strata in fairly well-defined areas throughout the world

(50) but always on the sites of ancient seas and lakes, some of which are now continental land, some buried deep under the encroachment of new oceans.

42. According to the author, which of the following statements is (are) true?
  I. The action of the seas is the most important factor in erosion of the earth's surface.
  II. Scientists have not been able to produce a purely synthetic oil in the laboratory.
  III. Gravity plays an important role in the formation of new rock.

  (A) I only
  (B) II only
  (C) III only
  (D) I and III only
  (E) II and III only

43. The Grand Canyon is mentioned in the first paragraph to illustrate

  (A) the urgent need for dams
  (B) the devastating impact of rivers
  (C) the effect of rain
  (D) a site where oil may be found
  (E) the magnificence of nature

44. According to the author, our understanding of the process by which oil is created is

(A) biased
(B) systematic
(C) erroneous
(D) deficient
(E) adequate

45. We can infer that prospectors should search for oil deposits

(A) wherever former seas existed
(B) in mountain streambeds
(C) where coal deposits are found
(D) in the Grand Canyon
(E) in new rock formations

46. The author does all of the following EXCEPT

(A) describe a process
(B) state a possibility
(C) cite an example
(D) propose a solution
(E) mention a limitation

47. The word "reaches" in line 21 means

(A) grasps
(B) unbroken stretches
(C) range of knowledge
(D) promontories
(E) juxtapositions

Questions 48–58 are based on the following passages.

In Passage 1, the author discusses British attitudes toward Americanisms. In Passage 2, the author deals with the same topic, but in a somewhat different manner. The authors of both passages are American.

Passage 1

Twenty years before the Revolution, Samuel Johnson was already denouncing a book by an American as "a tract of corruption, to which every language widely diffused must al-
Line ways be exposed." Johnson's own experience and common
(5) sense certainly told him that linguistic change was inevitable,

but his intense conservatism also told him that any change
was likely to be for the worse—especially if it was the work
of ignorant provincials, remote from the civilizing influence of
London. Johnson considered even the Scots semibarbarous;
(10) it would have been surprising had he viewed the Americans
any less sourly.

Johnson's view of American English remained typical of
English literary opinion for well over a century. Thus in 1808,
an English magazine denounced the "torrent of barbarous
(15) phraseology" that threatened to "destroy the purity of the
English language." Another critic found American writing
loaded with "a great multitude of words which are…as utterly
foreign as if they had been adopted from Chinese or Hebrew."
The first criticism was obviously fatuous: how can one talk of
(20) the "purity" of a language that had been borrowing from foreign tongues, with both hands, for centuries? The second
was simply ignorant: the much-deplored "Americanisms" of
the early nineteenth century were, in their great majority,
English, not borrowed. Some were English words that had
(25) fallen out of cultivated use in the old country; thus Americans
said "fall" where educated Englishmen said "autumn." Indeed, of the two, "fall" was the more authentically "English"—if the term means anything—being directly derived
from Old English, while "autumn" was a French import. Like-
(30) wise, the phrase "I guess" meaning "I suppose," used by
English writers until well into this century as a virtual trade-
mark of eccentric American speech, goes back to Chaucer (*Of
twenty yeer of age he was, I gesse.*) Others, as we've seen,
were old English words with new meanings, while still others
(35) were new compounds—but compounded out of English elements, according to the rules of English syntax. "Belittle,"
target of several critics, was modeled on such respectable
English verbs as "befoul," used since the fourteenth century,
while "lengthy," another supposed barbarism, was equally
(40) analogous to "weighty," used since around 1500.

American commentators, then and later, repeatedly made these points—with an occasional assist from colleagues across the Atlantic—but it made no difference to most English travelers and critics, who continued to berate
(45) American English, along with American manners and morals, in terms that were at best unreasonable and at worst viciously dishonest. Frances Trollope, mother of the novelist, reported in 1832 that during her entire stay in America she had seldom "heard a sentence elegantly turned and correctly
(50) pronounced." A few years later, Dickens, after his fabulously successful American tour, wrote that outside New York and Boston, grammar was "more than doubtful" and that "the oddest vulgarisms" were acceptable. Perhaps the lowest blow came in 1863, from Henry Alford, Dean of Canterbury.
(55) Though he had never visited America, he bewailed "the process of deterioration which our Queen's English has undergone at the hands of the Americans," and finished by denouncing them for conducting "the most cruel and unprincipled war in the history of the world." Since earlier writers had
(60) denounced America for tolerating the slavery which that unprincipled war would abolish, it was clear that for a certain type of Englishman, *anything* America did, in language or politics, was wrong.

Though nobody has conducted a poll on the subject, my
(65) own feeling is that most British writers today take a less jaundiced view of American English. They may or may not use Americanisms themselves, but see no reason why Americans should not use them. Many, perhaps the majority, would agree with the view put forward by the American critic Bran-
(70) der Matthews nearly a century ago: "A Briticism is none the worse because it is known only to the inhabitants of the British Isles, and an Americanism is not to be despised because it is current only in America. The question is not where it was born, but whether it is worthy to live."

Passage 2

(75)   In the field of language an Americanism is generally regarded by the English as ipso facto obnoxious, and when a
new one of any pungency begins to force its way into British
usage the guardians of the national linguistic chastity belabor
it with great vehemence and predict calamitous conse-
(80) quences if it is not put down. If it makes progress despite
these alarms, they often switch to the doctrine that it is really
old English and search the Oxford Dictionary for examples of
its use in Chaucer's time; but while it is coming in they give it
no quarter. Here the unparalleled English talent for discover-
(85) ing moral obliquity comes into play, and what begins as an
uproar over a word sometimes ends as a holy war to keep the
knavish Yankee from undermining and ruining the English
Kulture and overthrowing the British Empire.

48. The corruption to which Johnson refers (line 3) is

(A) philosophical
(B) moral
(C) physical
(D) linguistic
(E) financial

49. The author of Passage 1 is unsurprised by Johnson's sour view of
Americans because

(A) Americans are descended from the Scots, whom Johnson also
despised
(B) given America's even greater distance from London than
Scotland's, Johnson was sure to find anything American
barbarous
(C) as a British writer, Johnson despised Americans for stealing
many of their common phrases from his fellow authors
(D) Johnson was still smarting from the American colonies'
rebellion against the British crown
(E) in sharp contrast to Johnson, Americans are determined
proponents of change

50. By the phrase "with both hands," the author most likely intends to suggest that the borrowing has been

(A) evenhanded
(B) immoderate
(C) foolish
(D) enervating
(E) ambidextrous

51. Passage 1's author states in defense of Americanisms that many of the new compound words coined by Americans

(A) are patterned on traditional English usage
(B) possess a liveliness unmatched by comparable English words
(C) have fallen out of cultivated use in America
(D) are actually Latinate in derivation
(E) are less barbarous than Chaucerian spelling

52. The word "turned" in line 49 means

(A) revolved
(B) transformed
(C) shifted
(D) phrased
(E) diagrammed

53. The author of Passage 1 quotes Brander Matthews (lines 70–74) in order to

(A) cite a contemporary viewpoint
(B) present a measured judgment
(C) provide a happy ending
(D) propose a hypothesis
(E) expose a logical fallacy

54. According to Passage 2, if an Americanism finds acceptance in British usage, the English

(A) refuse to allow the word to be included in the dictionaries
(B) deny that it really is an Americanism
(C) feel that their cultural level is lowered
(D) will not admit that it is accepted
(E) claim that it is not American slang but good American usage

55. With which one of the following statements about British English would the author of Passage 2 be most likely to agree?

(A) British English contains less slang than American English.
(B) British English is lacking in humor.
(C) British English is no longer a growing language.
(D) The alertness of literary critics has preserved the purity of British English.
(E) The absorption of Americanisms into British English is inevitable.

56. The author of Passage 2 regards the British assumption of American linguistic inferiority with

(A) wholehearted approval
(B) grudging acceptance
(C) bitter resentment
(D) sardonic humor
(E) watchful concern

57. The phrase "put down" in line 80 is best taken to mean that Americanisms should be

(A) written down
(B) set in an appropriate context
(C) ranked below foreign phrases
(D) thoroughly suppressed
(E) badly expressed

58. The author of Passage 2 would most likely react to the opinion voiced in lines 64–66 that most British writers today take a less jaundiced view of American English with

(A) marked relief
(B) grudging approval
(C) deceptive caution
(D) wholehearted regret
(E) outright incredulity

IF YOU FINISH BEFORE TIME IS CALLED,
YOU MAY CHECK YOUR WORK ON THIS   **S T O P**
SECTION ONLY. DO NOT TURN TO ANY
OTHER SECTION IN THE TEST.

SECTION 4

25 Questions—30 minutes

Some formulas you may find useful in solving some questions

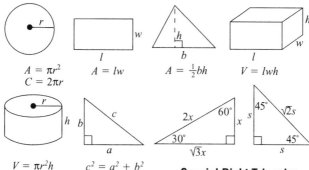

$A = \pi r^2$
$C = 2\pi r$

$A = lw$

$A = \frac{1}{2}bh$

$V = lwh$

$V = \pi r^2 h$

$c^2 = a^2 + b^2$

Special Right Triangles

Triangle: The sum of the measure in degrees of the angles of a triangle is 180.

If ∠ *CDA* is a right angle, then

(1) area of △*ABC* = $\dfrac{AB \times CD}{2}$

(2) $AC^2 = AD^2 + DC^2$

The number of degrees of arc in a circle is 360.

The measure in degrees of a straight line is 180.

Definitions of symbols:

≤ is less than or equal to

‖ is parallel to

= is equal to

< is less than

≥ is greater than or equal to

⊥ is perpendicular to

≠ is unequal to

> is greater than

Notes: (1) The use of a calculator is permitted. All numbers used are real numbers. (2) Figures that accompany problems in this test are intended to provide information useful in solving the problems. They are drawn as accurately as possible EXCEPT when it is stated in a specific problem that the figure is not drawn to scale. All figures lie in a plane unless otherwise indicated.

This section contains two types of questions. You have 30 minutes to complete both types. You may use any available space for scratchwork.

PART I: QUANTITATIVE COMPARISON QUESTIONS

Questions 26–40 each consist of two quantities in boxes, one in Column A and one in Column B. You are to compare the two quantities and on the answer sheet fill in

A if the quantity in Column A is greater;
B if the quantity in Column B is greater;
C if the two quantities are equal;
D if the relationship cannot be determined from the information given.

Notes: (1) In some questions, information is given about one or both of the quantities to be compared. In such cases, the given information is centered above the two columns and is not boxed.
(2) In a given question, a symbol that appears in both columns represents the same thing in Column A as it does in Column B.
(3) Letters such as x, n, and k stand for real numbers.

Column A	Column B
$\dfrac{6 + 6 + 6}{6 - 6 - 6}$	$\dfrac{3 + 3 + 3}{3 - 3 - 3}$

26.

	Column A	Column B

$$x = 0.000001$$

27. $\sqrt{x}$ $100x$

---

28. $\sqrt[3]{(\sqrt{64})}$ $\sqrt{(\sqrt[3]{64})}$

$$x^2 = 25$$

29. x 5

$$0 < p < q$$

30. $\dfrac{1}{q}$ $\dfrac{1}{p}$

$$a = 2, b = 1, \text{ and } c = 0$$

31. $4a + 2b + 3c^3$ 10

---

32.   105% of 500   50% of 1000

Column A	Column B

$$2x + y = 16$$

33. x y

---

34.   The average of the measure of the angles of quadrilateral *ABCD*   The measures of the angle of square *KLMN*

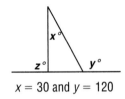

$x = 30$ and $y = 120$

35. z 90

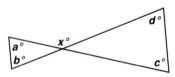

36. $a + b + c + d$ x

Column A   Column B

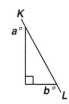

KL is a straight line.

37. $a + b$ 270

$$2^{n+2} = 8$$

38. n 3

$$x > 1$$
$$y > 1$$

39. $xy + 5$ $x(y + 5)$

AC is the hypotenuse of $\triangle ABC$.

40.   Measure of $\angle B$ Sum of the measures
                                                of $\angle A$ and $\angle C$

PART II: STUDENT-PRODUCED RESPONSE QUESTIONS

Each of the remaining 10 questions (41–50) requires you to solve the problem and enter your answer by marking the spaces in the special grid, as shown in the examples below.

Answer: $^{7}/_{12}$ or 7/12   Answer: 2.5

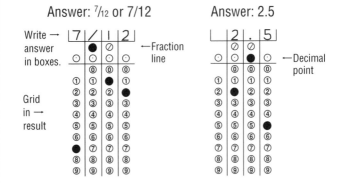

Answer: 201
Either position is correct.

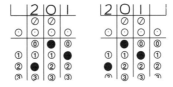

<u>Note</u>: Your may start your answers in any column, space permitting. Columns not needed should be left blank.

- Mark no more than one space in any column.

- Because the answer sheet will be machine-scored, **you will receive credit only if the spaces are filled in correctly**.

- Although not required, it is suggested that you write your answer in the boxes at the top of the columns to help you fill in the spaces correctly.

- Some problems may have more than one correct answer. In such cases, grid only one answer.

- No question has a negative answer.

- **Mixed numbers** such 2½ must be gridded as 2.5 or ⁵/₂. (If 2½ is gridded, it will be interpreted as ²¹/₂, not 2½.)
- **Decimal Accuracy:** If you obtain a decimal answer, **enter the most accurate value that the grid will accommodate**. For example, if you obtain an answer such as 0.6666..., you should record the result at .666 or .667. **Less accurate values such as .66 or .67 are not acceptable**.
- Acceptable ways to grid ²/₃ = .6666 . . .

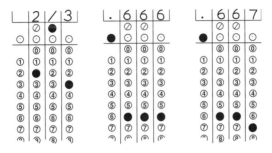

41. A disease killed $\frac{2}{3}$ of the chickens on a farm. The owner then inoculated $\frac{1}{2}$ of the remaining chickens to prevent infection. If 100 were inoculated, how many chickens were lost before the treatment?

42. If 4% of motorists on the turnpike leave at a certain exit and 5% of these go to one particular motel for lodging, out of every 10,000 motorists how many motorists may be expected to go to this motel?

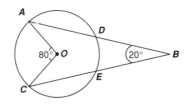

43. *ADB* and *CEB* are secants of circle *O*. If $\angle AOC \cong 80$ and $\angle B \cong 20$, how many degrees are in $\widehat{DE}$?

_____

44. A rectangular field 50 meters in width and 120 meters in length is divided into two fields by a diagonal line. What is the length of fence (in meters) required to enclose one of these fields?

_____

45. If there are 5 to 8 eggs in a pound, what is the maximum number of eggs in 40 pounds?

_____

46. How many four-cent baseball cards can I purchase without receiving change for one dollar after buying 20 three-cent cards?

_____

47. How many ounces are there in a cup of shredded coconut if 6 cups weigh one pound?

_____

48. A man who owned $\frac{1}{4}$ share of a business sold $\frac{1}{3}$ of his control last year and sold $\frac{5}{12}$ of his remaining share this year. What part of the business does he now own?

_____

49. If a score of 17 is added to a set of 10 data scores the mean (average) of the set becomes 14. What is the mean (average) of the original set of scores?

50. If $AB = 12$ and $BC = 6$, what is the length of a segment joining the midpoints of AB and BC? (Diagram is not to scale.)

IF YOU FINISH BEFORE TIME IS CALLED, YOU MAY CHECK YOUR WORK ON THIS SECTION ONLY. DO NOT TURN TO ANY OTHER SECTION IN THE TEST.

S T O P

Answer Key

Section 1   Verbal

1. **A**	7. **E**	13. **B**	19. **C**	25. **A**
2. **E**	8. **D**	14. **C**	20. **D**	26. **E**
3. **A**	9. **E**	15. **B**	21. **B**	27. **C**
4. **C**	10. **D**	16. **C**	22. **C**	28. **D**
5. **B**	11. **C**	17. **D**	23. **B**	29. **C**
6. **E**	12. **B**	18. **A**	24. **E**	

Section 2   Math

Note: Each correct answer to the mathematics questions is keyed by number to the corresponding math topic. These numerals refer to the topics listed below.

1. Basic Fundamental Operations	9. Averages
2. Algebraic Operations	10. Motion
3. Using Algebra	11. Ratio and Proportion
4. Exponents, Roots, and Radicals	12. Mixtures and Solutions
5. Inequalities	13. Work
6. Fractions	14. Coordinate Geometry
7. Decimals	15. Geometry
8. Percent	16. Quantitative Comparisons
	17. Data Interpretation

1. **E** (1)	8. **B** (2)	15. **D** (8)	22. **D** (15)
2. **A** (1)	9. **B** (1)	16. **B** (11)	23. **E** (1)
3. **C** (3)	10. **E** (15)	17. **B** (1, 17)	24. **C** (3)
4. **A** (15)	11. **B** (2)	18. **C** (8)	25. **C** (8)
5. **B** (1)	12. **C** (1)	19. **A** (8)	
6. **D** (4)	13. **B** (6)	20. **D** (11)	
7. **D** (14)	14. **C** (8)	21. **B** (15)	

Section 3   Verbal

30. **E**	36. **B**	42. **E**	48. **D**	54. **B**
31. **E**	37. **C**	43. **B**	49. **B**	55. **E**
32. **B**	38. **D**	44. **D**	50. **B**	56. **D**
33. **C**	39. **A**	45. **A**	51. **A**	57. **D**
34. **C**	40. **A**	46. **D**	52. **D**	58. **E**
35. **C**	41. **C**	47. **B**	53. **B**	

Section 4   Math

26. **C** (6, 16)	30. **B** (6, 16)	34. **C** (15, 16)	38. **B** (4, 16)
27. **A** (4)	31. **C** (2, 16)	35. **C** (15, 16)	39. **B** (2, 16)
28. **C** (4)	32. **A** (8, 16)	36. **A** (15, 16)	40. **C** (15, 16)
29. **D** (2, 16)	33. **D** (2, 16)	37. **C** (15, 16)	

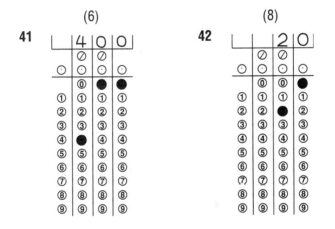

(6)   (8)

41   42

Section 4 (continued)

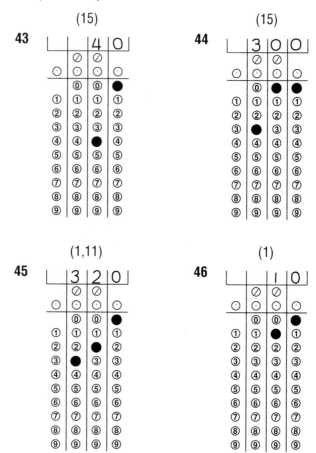

(15)

43 | | | 4 | 0 |

(15)

44 | | 3 | 0 | 0 |

(1,11)

45 | | 3 | 2 | 0 |

(1)

46 | | | 1 | 0 |

Section 4 (continued)

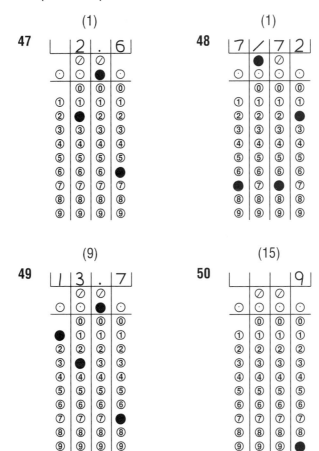

ANSWER EXPLANATIONS

Verbal Reasoning   Section 1

1. (**A**) An audacious or *daring* approach succeeded; a less daring approach would have failed.

2. (**E**) A plot that people have seen over and over again is by definition *trite* (stale; overdone). Note that the second clause gives you the information you need to fill in the word missing in the first clause.

3. (**A**) Ginger spent hours thinking up wicked ways to pay her brother back for his trick. In other words, she tried to *retaliate*.

4. (**C**) A bad name stains or *taints* one's reputation.

5. (**B**) Plumes are feathers. If the male and female birds have the same plumage, they must look alike. Therefore, *distinguishing between* the males and females, telling them apart, must be difficult.

6. (**E**) *Although* signals a contrast. You are looking for a word that is an antonym or near-antonym for *persistent* and *extended*. That word is *sporadic* (occasional; intermittent).

7. (**E**) The scientist is aware that future data may cause her to change her opinion. Therefore, she is willing to express only a *tentative* (temporary; provisional) opinion.

8. (**D**) A *gregarious* or sociable person normally seeks the company of others. However, because of his legal problems, this usually sociable individual is *shunning* or avoiding others.
Note how the signal word *although* sets up a contrast.

9. (**E**) The innovations for which Maria Montessori became famous were creative teaching techniques; they transformed the field of *pedagogy* (teaching; art of education).

10. (**D**) The statement asserts that the three are not in fact independent or separate but are instead *inseparable*. Again, the signal word (in this case, *but*) sets up a contrast that lets you know you are looking for an antonym or near-antonym of *independent*.

11. (C) If depression occurs when nerve cells get too little of certain chemicals, it makes sense to have these cells get more of the chemicals. This can be done by making more of the chemicals *available* to the cells.

12. (B) The contrast in Hugo is between *piety* or devotion ("a scene of chaste and holy love") and *ribaldry* or indecency (a scene of "coarse and profane licentiousness").
Note that the sentence's parallelism demands that the two missing words be antonyms or near-antonyms.

13. (B) To sink *ignominiously* is to do so shamefully or disgracefully. Such an end lacks dignity or honor. Note again how the clue to the missing word in one clause can be found in the clause without the blank. In this case, the key phrase is "lacked…the dignity of being sunk."

14. (C) In calling the smuggled urn a "hot pot," Hoving is speaking informally or *colloquially*. (*Hot* here is a slang term meaning stolen or illegally obtained.) Because the urn had been smuggled in to the country, there clearly were unresolved questions about its *origin*.

15. (B) An *egotistical* or self-centered and conceited person would find it difficult to *tolerate* or bear someone else's success.

16. (C) That the interrogator is subtle in discrimination or judgment shows she can conduct matters with *finesse* (tact; delicacy); that she is *expeditious* (efficient and prompt) in manner shows she can conduct matters with dispatch or speed.
Note the use of parallel structure in this sentence.

17. (D) The author is a passenger who has been aboard while the boat has touched at several ports (lines 12–13).

18. (A) The author is *condescending* in commenting on dulled feathers and fifth-rate freighters.

19. (C) Since the waiters are said to be dreaming they served at Maxim's, it is most likely that Maxim's is both a famous restaurant and a desirable place to work.

20. (D) The chef sweats because he is nervous while his delicate sugar cathedral is being carried up the stairs.

21. (B) The chef originally made the sugar cathedral in a famous kitchen. He has come down in the world, but retains his self-esteem.

22. (C) The passage points out that in this period the differences between the two branches of the suffrage movement were diminishing in importance. Thus, it is *accounting for changes* occurring in the movement. Choice A is incorrect. Both are mentioned (along with other suffragist leaders) in the context of the movements they led, but, while the movements are directly contrasted, Anthony and Howe are not directly contrasted. Choice B is incorrect. The movement did not advance in this period. Choice D is incorrect. The divisions were becoming less important, not more so, as the two branches became increasingly alike in nature. Choice E is incorrect. It is unsupported by the passage.

23. (B) Fighting to win women the right to vote, Stanton and Anthony were willing to work with anyone who espoused or *championed* their cause.

24. (E) The National took up the cudgels and fought for *all* women in distress, whatever their social or economic standing.

25. (A) The revered Mrs. Howe stood for the forces of propriety that were engulfing the suffragist movement. The embodiment of decorum, she was a *venerated figurehead* to be admired and respected, not a revolutionary firebrand to be followed into the battle. Choice B is incorrect. Nothing in the passage suggests Mrs. Howe was overzealous. Choice C is incorrect. Mrs. Howe was orthodox in her thinking, not heterodox. Choice D is incorrect. A lay preacher is by definition not a member of the clergy. Therefore, Mrs. Howe was not an ordained cleric. Choice E is incorrect. Mrs. Howe was characterized by a lack of militancy.

26. (E) The author describes the Haymarket incident as the crowning touch in the anti-labor smear campaign because the bombing was the final *detail completing* the image of organized labor as a hotbed of terrorists and radicals.

27. (C) The author refers to the public's reaction to the Molly Maguire trials as "hysteria" that was "whipped up" or deliberately incited. Clearly, her attitude towards it is that it was *overwrought* or overexcited. Note how the use of words that convey emotion ("hysteria") help you to determine the author's attitude to the subject.

28. (D) The first sentence of the fourth paragraph indicates that the author's concern is to avoid a misconception or *correct a misapprehension* about what caused the trend towards conservatism in the suffrage movement.

29. (C) If even the radical Susan B. Anthony would have had second thoughts about flouting or disregarding Federal election laws, we may logically infer that the ordinary, not quite so militant movement member would have viewed such actions with disapproval or *disapprobation*.

Mathematical Reasoning   Section 2

1. (E) Factor: $146(117 + 173 + 210)$
$146(500) = 73,000$

2. (A) Minimum weight of 1 dozen eggs $= 24$ ounces
Minimum weight of 1 egg $= 2$ ounces
Minimum weight of 69 eggs $= 138$ ounces

3. (C) Let $x =$ number of nickels.
$12 - x =$ number of dimes.
$5x =$ value (in cents) of nickels
$10(12 - x)$ or $120 - 10x =$ value (in cents) of dimes
$5x + 120 - 10x = 85$
$-5x = -35$
$x = 7$

4. (A) F   (see diagram)

5. (B) Because $a - 1$ is even, a must be an odd integer. I is not correct: $a - 3$ and $3(a - 3)$ result in even integers. II is correct: $2a$ is even and $2a + 1$ results in an odd integer. III is not correct: $(a - 1)$ is even and $a(a - 1)$ results in an even integer.

6. (D) The numerator, -1^n, has the value -1 for any positive integral value of n. The denominator, $(-1)^n$, equals 1 for any positive integral value of n that is even, but it equals -1 for any positive integral value of n that is odd. Thus, $-1 \div 1 = -1$, but $-1 \div (-1) = 1$.

7. (D) Since *PO* is a radius and $PO = 5$, *OD* is also a radius and therefore $OD = 5$. Since *D* is on the *x*-axis, *OD* is (5,0).

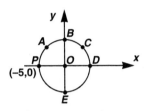

8. (B) For $\dfrac{n}{d}$ to be greater than 1, we must have $n > d$.

This is true only in choice **B**.

9. (B) Cost $-$ tax $= \$1.97 - .70 = \$1.27$
Cost of first 15 words $= 85¢$
Cost of additional words $= 42¢$
At $3\frac{1}{2}$ per word, 12 additional words were sent.
Total number of words $= 15 + 12 = 27$

10. (E) Since the lines are parallel, $c = f$ (alternate interior angles) (B); $e = a$ (corresponding angles) (C); and for the same reason $f = b$ (D). For (A), $d = a$ because they are vertical angles. In (E) the angles are supplementary.

11. (B) $\dfrac{2m}{3} = \dfrac{b}{a}$ and $\dfrac{2m}{b} = \dfrac{3}{a}$ (exchange terms of the means)
In either case product of means $=$ product of extremes.

12. (C) Because the diameter of the inscribed circle equals the length of the side of the square, radius of the circle is $\frac{1}{2}(8) = 4$.
P (lands inside circle) $=$

$$= \frac{\text{Area of Circle}}{\text{Area of Square}}$$

$$= \frac{\pi(4)^2}{8^2}$$

$$= \frac{16\,\pi}{64}$$

$$= \frac{\pi}{4}$$

13. (B) Substitute: $\dfrac{3(3)^2 - (-2)^2}{\frac{1}{2}(-1)^3}$

$\dfrac{3(9) - (4)}{(\frac{1}{2})(-1)} = \dfrac{27 - 4}{-\frac{1}{2}} = \dfrac{23}{-\frac{1}{2}} = 23 \div -\frac{1}{2}$

$= (23)(-2) = -46$

14. (C) \$260 = 130% of the cost = 1.3 of the cost. Let x = cost.
$1.3x = \$260$
$13x = \$2600$
$x = \$200$ (cost)
40% of 200 = \$80; new selling price = \$200 + 80 = \$280

15. (D) $\dfrac{1 \text{ yard}}{1 \text{ foot}} \times 100 = \%; \dfrac{3 \text{ feet}}{1 \text{ foot}} \times 10 = 300\%$

16. (B) Let x = size of shadow of 35-foot tree.
$\dfrac{\text{size of tree}}{\text{size of shadow}} = \dfrac{98'}{42'} = \dfrac{35'}{x}$
$98x = (42)(35)$
$98x = 1470$
$x = 15$ ft.

17. (B) Hint: Draw lines on the graph for the 2 departments involved. Meat = \$25 million, Dairy = \$15 million. The difference is \$10 million.

10. (C) Price during sale is 75% of normal price.
$\dfrac{25\%}{75\%} = \dfrac{1}{3} = 33\dfrac{1}{3}\%$

19. (A) Hint: Do the calculations and match the choices.
mestizos: $(22)(0.6) = 13.2$
Andean Indian: $(22)(0.3) = 6.6$
whites: $(22)(0.1) = 2.2$. Choose (A).

20. (D) Old price for 2 pints was \$2.40; present price is \$3.00.
Ratio = $\dfrac{\$2.40}{\$3.00} = \dfrac{240}{300} = \dfrac{24}{30} = \dfrac{4}{5} = 4{:}5$

21.(B) Let x = leg AB or leg BC.

$$\text{Area} = \frac{1}{2}(x)(x)$$

$$\text{Area} = \frac{x^2}{2}$$

$$\text{Area} = \frac{x^2}{2} = 12.5 \text{ [given]}$$

$$x^2 = 25$$

$$x = 5 \text{ (each leg)}$$

From the 45°-45°-90° triangle, $a = 5$, so $a\sqrt{2} = 5\sqrt{2}$.

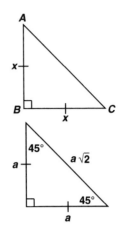

22. (D) Since the diameter is 14, a radius OP is 7. Since radius $OP \perp$ to tangent PX, OPX is a right $\triangle$.

$\therefore (PX)^2 + 7^2 = 25^2$

$(PX)^2 = 576$ and $PX = 24$ feet

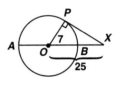

23. (E) First test: $\frac{24}{25} = 96\%$. Second test: 48% and 48 correct.

Let x = number of problems in the second test.

$$\frac{48}{x} = 48\%; \ \frac{48}{x} = \frac{48}{100}; x = 100$$

24. (B) It will take 5 times as much time.
5×25 minutes = 125 minutes = 2 hours 5 minutes

25. (C) The dealer remitted 95% of selling price.
Let x = the selling price. 95% (or .95) of x = \$4750
$.95x = 4750$; $95x = 475000$ and $x = \$5000$

Verbal Reasoning   Section 3

30. (E) A *crowbar* is a tool used for *prying*; a *shovel* is a tool used for *digging*.   (Definition)

31. (E) A *pedestrian* travels along a *sidewalk*; a *boat* travels along a *waterway*.   (Function)

32. (B) A *sculptor* works in a *studio*; a *blacksmith* works in a *smithy.*
(Worker and Workplace)

33. (C) To *intimidate* someone is to cause that person *fear*; to *exasperate* someone is to cause that person *irritation.* (Cause and Effect)

34. (C) By definition, *food* that is *insipid* (dull; tasteless) lacks flavor; *remarks* that are *vapid* (inane; empty) lack sense.
(Defining Characteristic)

35. (C) One *confines* a *prisoner* to keep him in prison. One *detains* a *suspect* to keep him in custody. (Purpose)

36. (B) A *diva* (singer) performs an *aria*; an *actor* performs a *soliloquy.*
(Defining Characteristic)

37. (C) An *ophthalmologist* is a physician who specializes in treating disorders of the *eyes*; a *dermatologist* is a physician who specializes in treating disorders of the *skin.* (Defining Characteristic)

38. (D) Something *irksome* (annoying; vexing) by definition *chafes*; something *lurid* (revolting; horrifying) by definition *shocks.*
(Definition)

39. (A) A *skirmish* (minor military engagement) is less important than a *battle.* A *quiz* is less important than an *examination.*
(Degree of Intensity)

40. (A) A *malingerer* (someone who goofs off) shuns *work*; a *recluse* (hermit) shuns *company.* (Defining Characteristic)

41. (C) To *ogle* (look at someone coquettishly) indicates *flirtatiousness*; to *gape* (stare at in wonder) indicates *astonishment.*
(Action and Its Significance)

42. (E) You can arrive at the correct answer by the process of elimination. Statement I is false. While sea action plays a part in erosion, the author does not say it is the most important factor in erosion. Therefore, you can eliminate Choices A and D. Statement II is true. The first purely synthetic oil "has yet to be produced." Therefore, you can eliminate Choice C. Statement III is true. New rock is born or created "through the effects of gravity." Therefore, you can eliminate Choice B. Choice E, the correct answer, is left.

43. (B) The Grand Canyon is mentioned in the context of rivers as "immensely powerful destructive agencies." The dramatic canyon illustrates the *devastating impact* a river can have.

44. (D) In the last paragraph the author states that "the cause of the metamorphosis" of decayed vegetation and dead aquatic life into oil is not known. We lack full understanding of the process by which oil is created; therefore, our understanding is *deficient*. Choice C is incorrect. Our knowledge is not *erroneous* or false; it is simply incomplete.

45. (A) The last sentence states that oil is always found "on the sites of ancient seas and lakes."

46. (D) The author describes several processes (erosion, rock formation, oil formation). He states the possibility that a chemical catalyst is involved in oil formation. He cites the Grand Canyon as an example of what a river can do to the land. He mentions the limitation of our ability to produce oil synthetically. However, he never proposes a solution to any problem.

47. (B) The term *reaches* here refers to the vast, *unbroken stretches* of time it takes for the mountains to erode and, out of their dust, for new rock to be formed at the bottom of the sea.

48. (D) Johnson is writing of exposing languages to corruption. The corruption to which he refers is therefore *linguistic*.

49. (B) The author judges Johnson's view of Americans on the basis of Johnson's well-known views of the Scots. Because the Scots lived relatively far from London ("civilization" to Johnson), he considered them less than civilized. *Given America's even greater distance from London*, to Johnson anything American would inevitably have seemed wholly barbarous.

50. (B) Think of a child using both hands to grab as many toys as possible. The author is suggesting that the English language has borrowed many, many words from foreign languages. In other words, the borrowing has been unrestrained or *immoderate*.

51. (A) Even the new terms, according to the author, are "compounded out of English elements, according to the rules of English syntax." In other words, *patterned on traditional English usage*.

52. (D) To turn a sentence is to fashion or *phrase* it, giving it shape.

53. (B) The author takes Matthews' view to represent the majority view-point held by responsible, "less jaundiced" authorities. Thus, he quotes Matthews to *present a measured judgment*.

54. (B) Sentence 2 indicates that those Americanisms that make progress with the British public (that is, find acceptance and are popularly used) are co-opted by the British, who say such terms are really old English and therefore not really Americanisms at all.

55. (E) Since the British, according to this passage, justify their adoption of Americanisms by maintaining they are actually British terms whose use dates back to ancient days ("Chaucer's time"), it is clear that these terms are being incorporated into British English and that this *absorption of Americanisms is inevitable*.

56. (D) Obviously, the author does not take the British attitude of superiority seriously. He exaggerates their position, talking about holy wars, and poking fun at them with such terms as "guardians of the national linguistic chastity." He looks on their assumption of American linguistic inferiority with *humor*, but there is an edge to his amusement: he is *sardonic* (mocking) in ridiculing them.

57. (D) The author uses "put down" here in much the same way one would use it in the phrase "putting down a riot." He believes the British authorities want all Americanisms *thoroughly suppressed*.

58. (E) Given the extreme stand he takes about the British "guardians of the national linguistic chastity" engaging in a holy war against those who violate the noble English language, the author of Passage 2 seems very unlikely to believe that any such moderate view of American English could prevail. His most likely reaction, therefore, would be one of *outright incredulity* or disbelief.

Mathematical Reasoning   Section 4

26. (C) Note that multiplying both numerator and denominator of fraction B by 2 results in fraction A, and thus does not change the fraction's value.

27. (A) Because $0.000001 = 10^{-6}$ $\sqrt{x}, = \sqrt{10^{-6}} = 10^{-3} = 0.001$.
Also, $100x = 100 (0.000001) = 0.0001$. Because $0.001 > 0.0001$, $\sqrt{x}$ is greater than $100x$.

28. (C) Because $\sqrt[3]{(\sqrt{64})} = \sqrt[3]{8} = 2$ and $\sqrt{(\sqrt[3]{64})} = \sqrt{4} = 2$, the two radical expressions are equal.

29. (D) $x^2 = 25$ and $x = +5$ and -5

30. (B) The denominator in $\dfrac{1}{q}$ is larger than the denominator in $\dfrac{1}{p}$.

31. (C) $4a + 2b - 3c^3 = (4)(2) + (2)(1) - 3(0) = 8 + 2 = 10$

32. (A) 105% of 500 = 525 and 50% of 1000 = 500

33. (D) Two different equations are required to find two unknowns.

34. (C) The sum of the angles of any quadrilateral is 360°.
$360° \div 4 = 90°$
A square is a quadrilateral with sides equal and each angle $\triangleq 90°$.

35. (C) Since $y = 120$, $a = 60$. Since the exterior angle of a triangle equals the sum of both remote interior angles, $z = x + a$. Since $x = 30$ [given], $z = 30 + 60$ or 90.

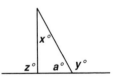

36. (A) $x = a + b$ (see answer 35)
$x < a + b + c + d$ or, $a + b + c + d > x$

37. (C) $a + x = 180$
$b + y = 180$
$a + x + b + y = 360$
Since $x + y = 90$, $a + b = 270$.

38. (B) Since $2^3 = 8$ and $2^{n+2} = 8$, then $n + 2 = 3$ and $n = 1$.

39. (B) $x(y + 5) = xy + 5x$
Column A = $xy + 5$
Column B = $xy + 5x$
$5x > 5$ since $x > 1$

40. (C) (In a right triangle the right angle is opposite the hypotenuse)

$\angle B \cong 90$

$\angle A + \angle C \cong 90$

41. (400)   100 chickens $= \frac{1}{2}$ of $\frac{1}{3}$

100 chickens $= \frac{1}{6}$

$600 = \frac{6}{6}$

$600 =$ number before disease struck

$\frac{2}{3}$ of $600 = 400$ (number of chickens lost before treatment)

42. (20)   5% of 4% $= (.05)(.04) = .0020 = .2\%$ or $\frac{.2}{100}$

$\frac{.2}{100} = \frac{20}{10,000}$

43. (40) $\widehat{AC} = 80°$ since central $\angle \cong 80$.

Let $x =$ number of degrees in $\widehat{DE}$.

$\angle B = \frac{1}{2}(\widehat{AC} - \widehat{DE})°$

$20° = \frac{1}{2}(80° - x)$

$40° = 80° - x$

$-40° = -x$

$x = 40°$

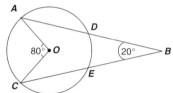

44. (300)   Draw AC.

Observe right $\triangle ABC$.

Observe ratio of 5:12.

$\triangle ABD$ is a 5:12:13 $\triangle$ with each dimension multiplied by 10.

$AC = 130$ meters

Perimeter $= 50 + 120 + 130 = 300$ meters

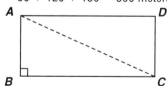

45. (320)   Maximum number of eggs in one pound $= 8$

Maximum number of eggs in 40 pounds $= 320$

46. (10)   Cost of twenty three-cent cards = 60¢
For 40¢, one can buy 10 four-cent cards.

47. (1.6)   Let x = number of ounces in one cup.
$$\frac{6 \text{ cups}}{16 \text{ ounces}} = \frac{1 \text{ cup}}{x \text{ ounces}}$$
$6x = 16$
$x = 2.6+$
Therefore the best answer is 2.6.

48. $\frac{7}{72}$ Since he sold $\frac{1}{3}$ of $\frac{1}{4}$, he still held $\frac{2}{3}$ of $\frac{1}{4}$ or $\frac{1}{6}$. This year he sold $\frac{5}{12}$ of his remaining share, so he held $\frac{7}{12}$ of $\frac{1}{6}$ or he still holds $\frac{7}{72}$ of the business.

49. (13.7)   Let S = sum of original set of scores.
x = mean of original set of scores.
$$\frac{S + 17}{11} = 14 \text{ or } S + 17 = 154 \text{ so } S = 137.$$

Therefore, mean of original set of 10 scores = $\frac{137}{10}$ = 13.7

50. (9)   Let X be the midpoint of AB and Y be the midpoint of BC.
XB = 6 and BY = 3. XY = 9.